Vietnam War Refugees in Guam

Also by Nghia M. Vo and from McFarland

The ARVN and the Fight for South Vietnam (2021)
Legends of Vietnam: An Analysis and Retelling of 88 Tales (2012)
Saigon: A History (2011)
The Vietnamese Boat People, 1954 and 1975–1992 (2006)
The Bamboo Gulag: Political Imprisonment in Communist Vietnam (2004)

Edited by Nghia M. Vo

The Viet Kieu in America: Personal Accounts of Postwar Immigrants from Vietnam (2009)

Vietnam War Refugees in Guam

A History of Operation New Life

NGHIA M. VO

McFarland & Company, Inc., Publishers
Jefferson, North Carolina

ISBN (print) 978-1-4766-8699-8
ISBN (ebook) 978-1-4766-4417-2

LIBRARY OF CONGRESS AND BRITISH LIBRARY
CATALOGUING DATA ARE AVAILABLE

Library of Congress Control Number 2022011874

© 2022 Nghia M. Vo. All rights reserved

No part of this book may be reproduced or transmitted in any form or by any means, electronic or mechanical, including photocopying or recording, or by any information storage and retrieval system, without permission in writing from the publisher.

On the cover: first wave refugees dressed in their ao-dai (courtesy Operation New Life After Action Report, published by the US Government); a refugee doctor holds sick call for his countrymen (courtesy Operation New Life After Action Report, published by the US Government); *background* Guam © 2021 YCPMKK Gallery/Shutterstock

Printed in the United States of America

*McFarland & Company, Inc., Publishers
Box 611, Jefferson, North Carolina 28640
www.mcfarlandpub.com*

To the Guamanians and Americans
who opened their arms
to welcome the Vietnamese
to the U.S. and the world.

Acknowledgments

It took me ten years to complete this book. Among the many people who supported and sustained this effort, I would like to mention Mrs. Gwen Wyttenbach, wife of then Navy Captain Wyttenback (Ret.), who was on active duty on Guam when this story took place. Wyttenbach later bought two paintings from one of the evacuees during a painting exhibition on Guam Island. They also sponsored Navy Captain Nguyễn Văn Thông and his two daughters out of the camp. It was more than three decades later that I had the chance to meet Gwen and her two children though the introduction of Captain Wyttenbach at one of the conferences organized by SACEI (Saigon Arts, Culture, and Education Institute) in Fairfax, Virginia, in 2009. She showed me her album of photos and pictures detailing her volunteering effort during the Operation New Life and gave me the idea of writing a book about Guam and the operation. The concept, however, languished for many long years before I finally completed it. It was a tragic and momentous period in the lives of the South Vietnamese and of their young nation, South Vietnam. I would also like to thank Ms. Thuy Bui and her friends who supported the concept of "Saigon Arts," a non-profit organization dedicated to promoting Vietnamese-American culture.[1]

Contents

Acknowledgments vi
Introduction 1

1. The Last Days of Saigon 7
2. The Vietnamese Navy and the *Trường Xuân* 23
3. Task Force 76 and USS *Kirk* 35
4. Guam's Preparations 50
5. Operation New Life 71
6. Life in the Guam Camps 82
7. First, Second, and Third Wave Arrivals 96
8. Repatriates and the *Thương Tín I* Odyssey 110
9. Auxiliary Team and Sponsors 130
10. The Other Camps 138
11. Follow Up and Untold Stories 148
12. The Two Vietnams 159

Abbreviations 171
Appendix I: Chronology of Important Events (1975) 173
Appendix II: Motion 177
Appendix III: By the Numbers 179
Chapter Notes 181
Bibliography 189
Index 193

Introduction

Guam, 1975. This territory of the United States in the middle of the vast Pacific Ocean is so small, so far away and so isolated that it was unknown to a lot of people. About 5,800 miles west of San Francisco and 1,200 miles east of the Philippines, that tiny speck in the middle of the Pacific Ocean in 1975 is largely unknown even to Americans. When the South Vietnamese arrived on this island, some Americans, friends or potential sponsors, tried to reach them by postal mail. Many placed Guam in the Indian Ocean, the Philippines, or in South America. A letter was addressed to a faculty member of the university: "University of Guam, Agana, Guam, British West Indies, 96910." The zip code was correct and saved the day.[1]

As for the Vietnamese, they surely could be forgiven for their lack of geographical knowledge, for no one was allowed to travel abroad during the war, except students and military personnel. However, some had heard a few times about these great metallic birds—the B-52 strategic bombers—coming from Guam to unload their deadly bombs on war zones in Vietnam. But they had never thought of trying to locate that island.

This book details the story of how the displaced and distraught South Vietnamese landed on Guam on their way to the mainland U.S.; it is also a tribute and an expression of gratitude toward the good-hearted Guamanians and U.S. military personnel who pulled out all the stops to welcome them on the island. Without their heart-warming welcome, it is possible that many evacuees would either have died somewhere in the Pacific Ocean or suffered from severe psychological problems following the fall of Saigon. The operation, code-named New Life, was one of the most important and most successful U.S. military operations in the last five decades: it brought comfort and saved 130,000 lives.

Guam became the shining light at the end of the tunnel for these evacuees who in 1975 lost everything, including their homeland. When they decided to leave South Vietnam to get out of the reach of the communists, they did not know where to go. All they thought about was to jump on a boat, or whatever was floating—a barge, a military landing craft, an old fishing boat, a navy ship—to get out of the country and to avoid persecution from the invaders. They were frightened, distraught, and desperate. Most did not have the time to take anything with them but just ran away with whatever they had at hand. A few exceptions were well prepared and well connected: they arrived on Guam a week or two before the rest of the people landed. The majority, however, did not know where to go. They just looked for a spot on a boat and hoped for the best: a new place to live, a safe one, somewhere where they could find more freedom than under a communist system. The rest would come after.

And this was the response of Washington. With vigor and speed, it acted to resettle more than 130,000 evacuees[2] from Southeast Asia, most of them South Vietnamese. On 18 April 1975, President Ford created the Interagency Task Force (IATF), which allowed evacuees to come to the U.S. under the parole authority of the attorney general. This was funded by a $405 million congressional appropriation under Public Law 94-23.

Operation New Life turned out to be one of the greatest humanitarian efforts accomplished by the U.S. government, the U.S. military forces, and the people of Guam. It took place over an intensive three-month period of collective work. Without their help, there would have been no place for the Indochinese—there were also Cambodians and Laotians, besides the Vietnamese—to settle and to live. This is in dramatic contrast to the late 1970s and 1980s, when without any third country receiving them, refugees from these countries would be left lingering without any future in the squalid Southeast Asian camps in Thailand, Malaysia, Indonesia, Hong Kong and the Philippines.

The process of getting the evacuees out of Vietnam involved two phases. The first, Operation Frequent Wind, dealt with the evacuation of the Americans, third country nationals, and Vietnamese out of Saigon. The second phase, called Operation New Life, received the evacuees and delivered them to continental U.S. (CONUS) camps. Operation New Life, as its name indicates, settled the evacuees into a new life in a new country.

Although many books have been written about the Vietnamese coming to the U.S., there are none that deals with that special moment of their arrival on Guam Island. Although more than 130,000 people landed in Guam, most of them left the island after a short stay of a few weeks, without leaving any major footprint during that period.

Introduction 3

Many books have been written about the "boat people,"[3] the reeducation camps,[4] and the Vietnamese-Americans[5]; and even the military has issued a few after-the-fact books[6] about their dealings with the evacuees. But that period of their landing and stay in Guam remains a big unknown in the American and Vietnamese literature. The present book tries to fill that huge social and historical void. Younger generations, historians, no doubt will be interested in knowing more about what happened during that postwar period, how that massive influx of people was managed, transferred, and absorbed into the U.S. society, and how they are doing now. This is an important topic and a unique experience that certainly would interest many people.

Chapter 1, "The Last Days of Saigon," details the events in Saigon, the former capital of South Vietnam, and on the battlefield (Xuân Lộc), which forced the Americans to scramble to get out of the country. Saigon was shelled and bombed while the government changed hands and anxious citizens looked for ways to get out. U.S. Ambassador Martin in the final last days of Saigon and South Vietnam activated Operation Frequent Wind level IV, which called for the complete evacuation of Americans, third country nationals, and Vietnamese who were closely associated with the Americans.

Chapter 2, "The Vietnamese Navy and the *Trường Xuân*," describes how Captain Kiêm Đỗ and Rick Armitage plotted to commandeer the Vietnamese navy fleet, a total of 31 navy ships out of the Saigon naval port, along with 30,000 evacuees right under the eyes of the incoming communists. Their harrowing trip ended in Subic Bay, the Philippines.

Chapter 3 describes Task Force 76, the USS *Kirk*, the *Pioneer Contender*, an armada of Seventh U.S. Navy ships that were anchored in the South China Sea waiting to pick the evacuees up. They were able to rescue 40,000 evacuees and 100 South Vietnamese aircraft and deliver them safely to Guam.

Chapter 4 details the Guam preparations, beginning with a short history of Guam. It then relates how preparations were made on Guam to receive the evacuees at a time when the total number of the evacuees was still unknown. This involves a delicate discussion between Washington, D.C., navy officials, and the local Guam government.

Chapter 5, "Operation New Life," describes the reception and outbound shipment of the evacuees to mainland U.S. It involves the resettlement problems in Guam, local camps and problems, and processing difficulties.

Chapter 6, "Life in the Guam Camps," details the three largest camps in Guam: the tent city at Orote Point, Asan Camp, and the Tin

City. Three interesting evacuees and their work in Guam are described: Tony Lâm, the Asan Camp manager who ran the camp for three months; Nguyễn Tài Ngọc; and an entrepreneurial artist, Nguyễn Văn Mộc.

Chapter 7, "First, Second, and Third Wave Arrivals," discusses the differences between these three groups on Guam in 1975 as well as the reactions by Americans to these new evacuees. While the first and second waves were closely connected to the Americans through their positions, the third wave reflected a broad cross section of the South Vietnamese society of the time. This section does not discuss the arrivals of the boat people, in 1978 and subsequent years.

Chapter 8, "Repatriates and the *Thương Tín I* Odyssey," describes the various and at times violent protests conducted on Guam by some 2,000-plus anxious repatriates who wanted to secure their return to Vietnam. The painful consequences of the repatriation are described by the captain of the returning ship *Thương Tín I*, Trần Đình Trụ, who 16 years later applied for immigration to the U.S.

Chapter 9 describes the work of the auxiliary teams and sponsors. The auxiliaries did their best to soothe the pain and anguish of the evacuees, who not only lost their land in Vietnam but also were lost in the new land. The sponsors did a great job of looking for jobs and helping the evacuees get integrated into the new society.

Chapter 10, about the other camps, details Wake Island and the mainland camps. A total of 15,000 evacuees were flown to and processed on Wake Island, which served as an overflow camp. The mainland camps included Camp Pendleton, Fort Chaffee, Eglin AFB, and Fort Indiantown Gap.

A 40-year follow-up of a few evacuees and their American counterparts is described in Chapter 11: "Follow Up and Untold Stories." The cost of the Operation New Life is also listed.

Chapter 12, "The Two Vietnams," covers the South Vietnamese, who fell in a deep despair: they had lost the war and their country. Moneyless and nationless, they fought for their survival and future. How would they react to the disaster?

The evacuees did not know they were going to Guam. But the landing and short stay in Guam were, for most South Vietnamese, defining times in their lives for various reasons. They were in a bind when Saigon fell in 1975. They had no choice: they had to either surrender to the communists or go somewhere to escape. After an intense, bloody and ferocious 21-year war, animosity between the North and South Vietnamese camps was high. There were a lot of killings on both sides. It was estimated that the South Vietnamese lost 400,000 KIA and the North

Vietnamese close to one million, plus more than one million civilian deaths. The numbers will be discussed in detail later.

They had to go somewhere to escape from the communists' wrath. Who in their right mind would want to drop everything—jobs, possessions, friends, relatives, and country of birth—to migrate to another country after spending decades building up their life in one place? By escaping from communist Vietnam, by making the solemn, grave, and major decision of leaving their country, they had refused to remain subservient to communist control, they had cut off their umbilical cord to their country, and they became jobless and nationless and had to find a way to survive. Although they may have had the illusion that they would someday return to their native homeland (they had no problem with their country, they love Vietnam; it was the communist government that they did not like) the majority so far have not returned despite being abroad for more than four decades. They have remained staunchly anti-communist.

This book recounts a small but important part of the first mass migration of the South Vietnamese to the free countries of the world, including the United States, a story that is evolving and becoming a Vietnamese-American story.

1

The Last Days of Saigon

For a long time, South Vietnamese President Nguyễn Văn Thiệu had been screaming at the top of his lungs that the communists had violated the 1973 Paris Accords, in which they had pledged not to conquer South Vietnam by force. When Phước Long was taken in early 1975 in full violation of the Paris Accords, Washington did not lift a finger. This American weakness emboldened the communists to capture more targets.

The Paris Accords introduced an illusory peace in South Vietnam and allowed the U.S. to get out of Vietnam and the North Vietnamese troops to remain in South Vietnam.[1] The communists used the cease-fire to rebuild their infrastructure and to expand their area of control while eliciting no response from the United States. Nixon had secretly promised Thiệu to use U.S. airpower to support the government of South Vietnam if necessary, to get Thiệu to sign on the peace agreements. If Thiệu refused to sign the draft accord, the U.S. "would cut off all assistance to South Vietnam and would sign a separate agreement with the North Vietnamese."[2]

However, Nixon was driven out of office in 1974 due to the Watergate scandal, and the U.S. Congress refused to appropriate additional military assistance to South Vietnam, citing strong opposition to American involvement in the war by Americans. Military appropriations for South Vietnam for fiscal year 1975 were set at $1 billion in August 1974, but in September the House and Senate appropriated only $700 million. This was to cover shipping costs and operational costs, and it left the South Vietnamese army with less than $450 million.[3]

Economically, South Vietnam was totally dependent on the U.S., since most males had been conscripted: 1.2 million men in a country of 16 million people, or 7.5 percent of the population. Prices had increased 65 percent. Unemployment had skyrocketed with the departure of the last GIs. Worldwide inflation drove up the prices of fertilizers and petroleum. The Arab oil embargo soon quadrupled oil prices. President Thiệu was forced to "wage a poor man's war."[4]

The formidable military machinery that the U.S. had built for the South Vietnamese over decades began to have hiccups. It was no longer held together by the firm American hands. The spare parts, bullets, ammunitions, and fuel stopped flowing to Saigon because of Washington's steep financial aid cuts. The whole machinery began to shudder and break apart. Even to the untrained eyes of civilians, the reality became apparent. When the communists fired 100 mortars and shells at an ARVN (Army of the Republic of Vietnam) target, which could only afford to fire back ten mortars; when critically injured ARVN soldiers could no longer be evacuated on time because of lack air transport; when two or three ambulances transporting wounded soldiers had to be towed by a two-ton truck to save fuel, the writing was on the wall.

By January 1975, Tom Glenn had been working for the U.S. intelligence service in Vietnam for thirteen years. Heading an intelligence office, his role was to advise U.S. Ambassador Graham Martin on intelligence matters and to assist the government of South Vietnam in intelligence gathering and exploitation.[5]

On 9 March 1975, he witnessed the II Corps intelligence chief trying to convince the II Corps commander, General Phạm Văn Phú, that the next attack would target the city of Ban Mê Thuột. The old warrior Phú, relying on his instincts rather than intelligence data, remained unconvinced and beefed up the defense of Pleiku, the II Corps headquarters, instead of Ban Mê Thuột. The CIA was not helpful either.[6]

When the attack came, the poorly defended Ban Mê Thuột fell rapidly, like a ripe fruit, leading to disarray in the highlands. The North Vietnamese had moved three crack divisions (25,000 men) against Ban Mê Thuột, which was defended by only two ARVN battalions, fewer than 1,200 men inside the city, and two more battalions north of town backed by part of a regiment and a few rangers and militia units.

Having lost Phước Long and Ban Mê Thuột back to back in two months, and sensing his grip on South Vietnam becoming less secure, President Thiệu made a risky gamble, which if carried out in a well-organized, unhurried, and methodical way, might work. His plan was to bring his remaining troops from the highlands down to the coastal plain, where he could reorganize the defense of the country. The plan was risky because in the past only a few withdrawals had been completely successful. Withdrawing signals to the enemy that one's army is not strong enough to carry out its task. This could only embolden the enemy. In the French invasion of Russia in 1812, Napoleon brought a huge army of 500,000 soldiers. Facing the Russians' scorched-earth tactics and relentless harassment by Cossacks, he withdrew his army from Russia. The frigid Russian weather did not help either. When Napoleon's army crossed the Berezina River,[7] it had lost 380,000 soldiers and 100,000 others were held prisoner by the Russians. Only 27,000 fit soldiers crossed the river. Napoleon's reputation was deeply shaken.[8]

After Ban Mê Thuột fell on 11 March, Thiệu and his staff met with Phú, the II Corps commander in Cam Ranh Bay, on 14 March. Phú told Thiệu he could hold the highlands for one month if he could get additional reinforcements, air support, and ammunitions. Thiệu almost wept on hearing these words and told Phú he had no troops or equipment left. There was no way to defend Kontum and Pleiku. The army was stretched thin and stockpiles were low. He instead ordered General Phú to withdraw from the highlands as soon as he could, the timing being left to his discretion. Phú was surprised but did not show any reaction.

General Viên, the Chief of Staff, interrupted and suggested using Route 7B, an old logger's road that cut across the region and led to the sea. Although that road had not been used and was not usable for a long time, it was free of enemy forces. Phú just nodded, a slow nod of a tired and worn-out warrior. The casual exchange of questions and opinions certainly did not improve the chance of success of this difficult operation. Moving two divisions on the run over a hilly, unprepared, and difficult road would prove to be more than challenging.[9]

After the fateful meeting, the dispirited Phú flew back to Pleiku, met with his staff, and assigned the job of directing the evacuation to his ranger commander, Brigadier General Phạm Duy Tất. He then flew with his staff to his coastal headquarters in Nha Trang.

In their rush, Tất and his staff failed to order a survey of the road. Chaos was bound to happen, especially when the road turned into a trail that crossed mountainous rivers. New bridges had to be built to accommodate the load of tanks and trucks. Without preparation and using a route that had been rendered unusable some time ago, the convoy became an easy target for enemy snipers, who not only shot at the convoy but indiscriminately shelled soldiers and civilians, causing mayhem. The ARVN retreat turned into a debacle. When stragglers reached the coastal area, an estimated 18,000 soldiers and more than 100,000 civilians had been killed or made prisoners; the II Corps army had been rendered combat ineffective.

In MR 1 (Military Region I), General Ngô Quang Trưởng, the hero who reconquered Quảng Trị City in 1972, had work to do. Thiệu told him to return the Airborne Division to MR 3, which left him four divisions to defend a huge terrain south of the demilitarized area. His choice was to fight back or resign. Bitter and disgruntled, as a good soldier he relented and decided to play by the rules. The center of gravity having changed, on 17 March he had to reposition his troops—the second time in two weeks—first from Quảng Trị to Huế, then from Huế to Đà Nẵng. The area was rugged and mountainous, and with the pulling back of the Airborne Division, he no longer was able to fully protect Huế, only Đà Nẵng south of the Hải Văn Pass.

A day later, the civilians followed suit. No longer feeling protected by MR 1 troops, 150,000 citizens from Quảng Trị and its surrounding areas uprooted themselves and poured onto Highway 1 rushing toward Huế, which soon was overflowing with frightened refugees. They did the same thing in 1972 when the communists broke through the demilitarized zone and invaded the MR 1, and therefore were used to the routine. They returned to their homes by the end of 1972 and by 1975 had to uproot themselves again. However, the enemy was nowhere to be seen yet. The people in Huế in turn became anxious and weary and joined the monstrous wave of honking cars, motorbikes, and overloaded buses rolling south toward Đà Nẵng. The surging masses of people disrupted troop movements and supply lifts. Panic itself became infectious and caught up with the soldiers, who disbanded to help their families. In MR 1, civilians were military dependents: wives and children lived close to their husbands' bases to support them. Only the Marines and the Airborne soldiers stayed in place, because their dependents lived in Saigon.

Then Thiệu changed his mind once more. Although Huế has minimal value militarily, it has a strong spiritual value. Up to the 1880s, it was the capital and cultural center of Vietnam. It had to be defended at all costs. There would be nothing more spectacular than a gallant defense of the old imperial capital. Thiệu, however, did not know how to explain the reversal of his thoughts to his subordinates.

When Trưởng met with Thiệu in Saigon, he thought it was for a routine situation report. Thiệu, who had earlier mentioned that Huế had minimal value from the military point of view, then told him that Huế had to be defended till the last man. Trưởng this time blew up because he could no longer stand it. He could not wage a war by fits and starts, he thundered. Troops had been dispirited by the previous moves and the big guns had been shipped out. The morale of the soldiers would go down further and dispirited troops would lose their will to fight, Trưởng explained to Thiệu. He must have been very upset on his way back to Đà Nẵng, as he was consumed by many conflicting thoughts. Thiệu was wrong to have asked him to fly back and forth from Đà Nẵng to Saigon for consultation; they could have done it over the phone. Thiệu should have left him alone and given him time to think about the upcoming battle. The battle would be a critical one, for it would determine the future of the nation.

The North Vietnamese struck early on 23 March by cutting National

Highway 1 south of Huế, the highway that connected the MR 1 to Saigon. The First ARVN Division was stuck in Huế with no direct land escape route to Đà Nẵng. The masses of refugees moved eastward toward the port of Tân Mỹ, the alternate egress route for the First Division. Roads leading to the port were clogged with troops, materiel, and civilians, who soon were at the mercy of North Vietnamese artillery. The naval ships that were sent by Saigon to evacuate the First Division were forced to remove distraught civilians and soldiers, leaving materiel behind. It only needed a few shells here and there to cause pandemonium within the captive crowd. And the North Vietnamese were experts in raining shells onto any crowd, especially civilian ones. The famed First ARVN Division, which for years had withstood the invasion of the North Vietnamese, disintegrated without a fight. The city of Huế fell two days later.

The North Vietnamese moved in quickly on Đà Nẵng, the second largest city in South Vietnam. They started shelling it on 25 March, causing panic among the refugees who had arrived earlier from Huế. Trưởng had only the Third ARVN Division, the worst under this command, to fight against two communist divisions. On 28 March, the Third Division caught the "fear virus" and disintegrated under the stress of "family syndrome" and the pounding of enemy artillery fire. The general and hero of the 1972 Quảng Tri Campaign could not rally his troops as discipline broke down and the I Corps fell to the communists. The next day, he had to paddle out to a waiting Vietnamese patrol boat like a simple commoner. The general being a poor swimmer, an aide had to assist him all the way. For the next two days, he remained on shipboard, watching his once proud army disintegrate within the burning city. "Some of his military colleagues would later criticize him for not having stayed ashore to die with his command."[10] It was not totally his fault, though, for he had been ready to fight to the end—until Thiệu pulled the Airborne Division out from under him and gave him conflicting and changing orders.

On 8 April, a South Vietnamese pilot who had defected to the communists bombed Independence Palace, following which Saigon instituted a 24-hour curfew. Americans were calling for an evacuation, but instead of the 6,000 or 7,000 the embassy had planned on for evacuation, the number had doubled or tripled. President Ford then ordered all "non-essential" Americans out of Saigon. By 17 April, the evacuation moved into full open mode, and Martin was not even consulted on most points. This drawdown would involve only Americans, eligible diplomats, and others. Security teams might be available if needed.

There would be a total of 13 designated assembly areas where Americans would be picked up. Evacuation would be set up in four phases, where phase one is "a drawdown" and phase four the final "hard pull." A code message would be issued on American Radio Service advising that the Saigon temperature is "105 degrees and rising" followed by approximately the first 30 seconds of "I'm Dreaming of a White Christmas." The message would be broadcast every 15 minutes for two hours. The plan, although ideal, would not work in a besieged city with nervous citizens wanting to get out of the country. Americans carrying suitcases and waiting at the designated areas would be immediately detected by local people, who would gather around them in an attempt to get a free evacuation ride. Civilian buses without army protection would be easily mobbed by the crowd.

While Americans in Saigon were not panicking and felt no reason to panic, thinking that Ford and Martin would get them out in time, the Vietnamese sensed that they were abandoned. There was fear of a blood bath among Vietnamese who were associated with Americans, e.g., secretaries, staff, ARVN officers, businessmen and their families. Huge lines formed in front of the U.S. Consulate as Vietnamese clutching their American-issued identification cards begged for a way out of the country.

For rich Vietnamese, knowing an American became the way out of the country. A crewman of the MSC Green Wave bragged about receiving twelve thousand dollars from the daughter of a rich Chinese family to get her out as a dependent. A Saigon merchant was approached by three different U.S. citizens offering to take him out as a dependent for six to ten thousand dollars.[11]

From 9 to 21 April, the war continued at Xuân Lộc, 37 miles northeast of Saigon. The village controlled Dầu Giây, the junction of Routes 1 and 20 linking Saigon to the eastern part of the country. To have access to the city meant to fight for the control of Xuân Lộc, where one of the fiercest battles of the war would be located. There stood General Lê Minh Đảo and his valiant 18th ARVN division.

The North Vietnamese massed three divisions, the Seventh, Eighth, and 341st, to overrun the 18th ARVN Division. They launched daily infantry and armor attacks on 9, 10, and 11 April after intense artillery fire. These attacks were repulsed, although the town lay in ruins.

At his temporary headquarters in Lộc Ninh, 75 miles north of Saigon, North Vietnamese General Văn Tiến Dũng, facing the tough resistance at Xuân Lộc, discussed the situation with his staff. He felt he was in a winning position. Xuân Lộc was a rock in his path to the gates of Saigon. Unable to take Xuân Lộc, he ordered his units to bypass the town and attack Dầu Giây. On 15 April on Horseshoe Hill, the ARVN fought against wave after wave of enemy assaults until the base of the hill was "covered with enemy bodies and the jungle vegetation ha[d] been completely destroyed ... the green peak of the hill became barren, devoid of vegetation."[12]

The enemy threw in the 95B Division, and the four NVA divisions attacked Dầu Giây, Xuân Lộc, and the Biên Hòa airport, which provided air support to the area. Dầu Giây was overrun on 18 April, and the 18th ARVN Division was encircled. On 20 April, General Nguyễn Văn Toàn, commander of the III Corps, told Lê Minh Đảo to retreat and protect Saigon.

Đảo had two hopes for relief forces, but the superior enemy forces had cut off these hopes. The paratroop brigade had been fighting for its own life in the rubber plantation and could not reach Xuân Lộc. His 18th Division reserve force was bogged down along Highway 1 with no hope of punching through the siege. His troops were fighting well, but he did not have enough manpower to resist the enemy. After a night of heavy shelling, the heaviest in a long time, the two PAVN divisions were coming.

One outpost fell after another. By midmorning of 21 April, it was clear the fight was hopeless. Where the much-honored Airborne, Marines, and First Division had cut and run, the 18th was fighting on. Reluctantly, Đảo gave the order to pull out. Four of the six battalions completed the retreat. Colonel Hiếu stayed on with the remaining two battalions to cover the pullout: 600 men against 10,000 North Vietnamese.[13]

On 17 April, Phnom Penh, the capital of Cambodia, fell to the Khmer communists. Grisly pictures of beheaded officials followed. The slaughter in Cambodia had begun; 2 million people would eventually be exterminated.

For security reasons, Glenn moved from a downtown villa to his office at the DAO, where he slept on a cot beside his desk. He had 43 American civilians working for him and 22 dependents. When Glenn asked for permission to send them back to the States, Ambassador Martin vehemently denied the request. He believed that evacuating the Americans would cause another stampede of Vietnamese; besides, he did not think that the communists could take over Saigon. Besides Americans, he had 2,700 South Vietnamese military personnel who had worked for the U.S. for many years. He was determined to get them out.

On Monday 21 April, Xuân Lộc, 37 miles northeast of Saigon, fell; the last valiant resistance of the 18th ARVN Division had ended. Saigon was encircled by 12 communist divisions.

South Vietnamese president Thiệu resigned. Vice President Trần Văn Hương took over as president. Hương, a former schoolteacher, was mayor of Saigon twice and prime minister from November 1964 to January 1965 and from May to August 1969. He was a clean and well-regarded politician.

On Tuesday 22 April, the U.S. Defense Attaché Office (DAO) suggested that Saigon would not last more than a week. But since Martin was working for the State and not the Defense Department, he could ignore them and had the power to keep everyone in Vietnam. While Martin did not allow evacuation, outgoing commercial airlines and military air transports were full of passengers, Vietnamese and Americans. The embassy explained that it was a reduction in force to free up resources to help the South Vietnamese government.

Glenn let his driver use his U.S. pass to drive the driver's family to the airport in a black Ford sedan with diplomatic plates and to escape whenever they could. He then retrieved the car to drive one of his house servants and the man's family to the airport. As the Vietnamese guards at the gates would not allow anyone without official identification to pass, he hid the family members in the trunk of the car and was waved through. The servant and his family were able to board a C-130 aircraft to Guam. On the other hand, many South Vietnamese officers who were working for him did not want to leave the country because they cared about their troops. One of them, however, told Glenn that he would kill his three children, his wife and himself if he were stuck inside Vietnam. He simply could not live with the communists.[14]

The airlift of Americans and high-risk Vietnamese using C-141 transport aircraft had expanded into a twenty-four-hour affair the day before. A total of over 10,000 people had left Saigon since the beginning of the month. The Senate Judiciary Committee approved a plan waiving entry restrictions for over 130,000 "aliens from Indochina."

Thursday 24 April 1975

Through the wire, Glenn heard that a day earlier, President Ford had announced to a group of students at Tulane University, "The [Vietnam] war is finished."[15] Although evacuation of Vietnamese officials had progressed for a week, there was no permission from Washington to allow evacuees into the U.S. The country was in recession with 8 percent unemployment. The Vietnam War had not been popular in the States, to say the least.

Friday 25 April 1975

The attorney general formally approved the 130,000-alien ceiling negotiated two days earlier. The categories of Vietnamese at risk were virtually endless. They were in sensitive positions, defense attachés, military people. The labor attaché took care of the labor people.[16]

There were more tears than laughs in the evacuation group. The Vietnamese knew this might be the last time they would see Vietnam. They faced uncertain futures abroad. They were leaving behind friends and families, properties, lands, belongings, and country. The leaving was voluntary but heartbreaking. They were leaving the security of having a place to come back to.

American airlifts continued. There were 24 evacuation flights, mostly C141 jets carrying 250 persons each on 24 April, 26 planes on 25 April, and 31 on 26 April. They were, however, many people left behind for one reason or another. Some Central Intelligence Agency people left their local agents in Vietnam and shipped out bar girls. The U.S. Information Agency abandoned much of its staff, despite promises of evacuation. The embassy left many people ticketed for evacuation. By 25 April, Martin reported that 21,000 Vietnamese had departed on U.S. military planes and said, "99 percent of this movement was illegal in accordance with Vietnamese law." His role in the evacuation was kept secret.

Saturday 26 April

On Saturday morning, at the National Assembly House on Tự Do Street right in downtown Saigon, President Trần Văn Hương rose to speak to the 125 members of the South Vietnamese National Assembly. The legislators suspected that Hương had called this special session of the assembly to announce his resignation.

In the night of 26 April, communist sappers penetrated the ammunition depot in Biên Hòa and blew it up. People from nearby areas were awakened by the blast and many were shaken up. The event drove the commotion one notch higher.

Sunday 27 April

Early on Sunday, the communists fired Soviet-built 122-mm rockets into densely populated areas of Saigon, the first time in more than five years. There were five rockets in all, two in the center of town and the rest in the Chinese suburb of Cholon. The blasts killed ten people, injured more than 300 others, and caused a raging fire that left more than 5,000 people homeless, sowing unnecessary fear, pain, and commotion among the already distressed Saigonese. While NVA troops advanced toward Saigon, ARVN ranger and airborne units mounted a defense that was all the more courageous and inexplicable given that many of their senior officers had fled.[17]

Vietnamese civilians continued to surround the compound trying to find a way to get out. They were the disadvantaged ones, those without direct connection to the U.S. or the South Vietnamese government.

The communists continued to tighten their noose around Saigon. They had brought in 15 divisions, with more on the way, against Saigon's five divisions. They blocked Route 1 between Saigon and Tây Ninh and isolated the 25th ARVN Division at Củ Chi. The 304th and 325th NVA divisions overran Long Thành on the east after one of the fiercest tank battles of the war. In the southeast, the Third NVA Division drove the ARVN Third Division out of Bà Rịa. The road to Vũng Tàu was cut off, preventing Ambassador Martin from sending Vietnamese evacuees out of the country from Vũng Tàu.

That day, 7,578 people left Tân Sơn Nhứt Airport on fixed wing aircrafts, the largest single day exodus since the airlift began.

General Dương Văn Minh, or "Big Minh," the president-designate, met with French ambassador Jean Marie Merillon on Sunday. Over and over, he asked the ambassador, "What should I do? What would you do in my situation?" And over and over, Merillon said no one could make decisions for Big Minh. He must make them himself.

After a full day's discussion, members of the National Assembly remained deadlocked on their choice for the next president. They finally asked interim president Trần Văn Hương to nominate his successor. Hương called the Senate leader Trần Văn Lắm to let him know his choice would be General Minh. At 18:45 hours, the assembly reconvened and after further discussion voted to elevate Dương Văn Minh as the next South Vietnamese president. The inauguration was scheduled for the following morning.

Monday 28 April

Then at 04:00 hours, the communists began shelling Tân Sơn Nhứt Airport, hitting the DAO compound and killing two Marines. The impact of the 122-mm shells was so great that the whole DAO building rocked. Then came 138-mm shells that caused further damage. One AC-119 went up in flames, as well as one spotter plane. Both were shot down by heat-seeking missiles within sight of the city of Saigon. Body parts were recovered; a boot with a foot in it; a piece of a rifle.[18]

Minh spent the day interviewing candidates and filling cabinet posts. Only Vũ Văn Mẫu, his long-time associate and leader of the

1. The Last Days of Saigon

Buddhist National Reconciliation Force, and Nguyễn Văn Huyền, a liberal democrat, would immediately join his government as prime minister and vice-president, respectively.[19] Minh sent a delegation composed of Vũ Văn Mẫu, Nguyễn Văn Huyền, and Brigadier General Nguyễn Hữu Hạnh—a protégé of Dương Văn Minh since 1955 who rallied to the Việt Cộng in 1970s and became a communist mole within the ARVN—to meet with the communist delegation at Tân Sơn Nhứt Airport.

By mid-morning General Cao Văn Viên, chairman of the JGS, strode into the U.S. Embassy, was escorted up the rooftop and heli-lifted to DAO. There he changed his uniform to civilian clothes and was heli-lifted out of the DAO tennis court and ferried to the task force offshore. Pending the regime change later in the day, General Khuyên, chief of staff at JGS, doubled as the acting chairman.[20]

By 28 April, according to U.S. Air Force records, 43,439 had left Tân Sơn Nhứt on chartered aircraft or U.S. Air Force planes. About 5,000 had been Americans.

Ten minutes after Minh's speech, air controllers at Tân Sơn Nhứt spotted on their radar screens five A-37 aircraft approaching the airfield at low altitude. Asked to identify themselves, the pilots gave no answers. Instead, they dived down and released bombs over a row of Vietnamese Air Force planes parked on the runway, damaging three AC-119 gunships and several C-47s. After pulling out of their runs, they flew northwards toward the captured Phan Rang airfield. The bombing was followed by soldiers firing in the darkening sky. Gunfire brought traffic to a standstill, while people scurried for shelter. The throngs of refugees who surrounded the U.S. entrance to the airport dispersed. Several South Vietnamese F-5s scrambled into the air trying to intercept the A-37s. But it was too late: the attackers had safely landed at the Phan Rang airfield.

From 22:00 hours, the communists sporadically shelled the airport until the next morning, first with rockets and then after 0430 a.m. the following morning, with artillery.

A spokesman from the Provisional Revolutionary government (PRG) called in to advise that the choice of Big Minh was unacceptable and that his declarations did not meet their demands. All the CIA maneuvering was for naught. The communists were bent on total victory and did not accept one single compromise.

Tuesday 29 April

Rockets hit the airport early on the 29th. At 04:00 hours, a rocket exploded under the wing of a taxiing C-130, causing it to burst into flames minutes later. Three other rockets hit close to the DAO, killing two Marines: Judge and McMahon. These were the last two American casualties of the war.

Following the rocket fire, 130-mm shells were fired at the airport from communist guns with deadly accuracy, ripping the runways and flight line. Frightened Vietnamese soldiers and airmen swarmed into the runway trying to get onto any airplane that was about to take off. Later, South Vietnamese air force pilots fired up their A-37s and F-5s and took off for U Tapao Air Base in Thailand. The premature exodus of South Vietnamese air force had been encouraged by the deputy assistant secretary of state, Von Marbod, who had been sent to Saigon to coordinate the removal of American military equipment.

By 10:51 hours Saigon time, Frequent Wind Option IV was confirmed. In hot and steamy Saigon, operators at the American radio station began playing "White Christmas," signaling that the American pull-out had begun.[21]

Back at the embassy, suffering from pneumonia and under the stress of the previous two weeks of work and an imminent evacuation, Martin took time off to pick up his wife at their home, four blocks from the embassy. His bodyguards objected, arguing that they could pick her up for him. Unable to use his limousine because the crowd had blocked off the entrance gate, he slipped through the recreation compound and walked home, accompanied by his bodyguards. His wife was packed and ready. He looked at his villa one last time, and they all walked back to the embassy. She was later put aboard an Air America chopper and flown to the USS *Denver*, one of the evacuation ships.

Tom Glenn boarded an Air America helicopter at Tân Sơn Nhứt Airport sometime on the afternoon of 29 April, satisfied that his last two men had safely left Saigon. All over the city, fires were burning. Once the helicopter was over the water, it suddenly dropped down to sea water level to avoid surface-to-air missiles. It finally landed on the deck of the USS *Oklahoma City*, flagship of the Seventh Fleet. Someone immediately took his revolver and led him to safety. Others tipped the Huey and dumped it over the water to make way for another plane to land.[22]

The streets of Saigon were filled with all kinds of cars and scooters. The latter carried hopeless and helpless adults and children trying to find ways to escape the besieged town.

Looking out the window of the United Press International (UPI) office in downtown Saigon, Dutch journalist Hubert (Hugh) Van Es saw a helicopter landing on an elevator shaft that rose from the roof of the 22 Gia Long Street building. He quickly grabbed his camera and shot a photograph that became iconic of the Vietnam War. The blue and white

1. The Last Days of Saigon

Bell Huey 205 belonged to Air America, one of the CIA's proprietary airlines. The man in the white shirt was O.B. Harnage, the U.S. Embassy's deputy air operations officer, trying to help a group of South Vietnamese who were climbing a staircase to reach the rooftop. Among those he pulled up was Dr. Thiệt Tấn Nguyễn, a young military doctor who would become an anesthesiologist in Southern California. Next he grabbed Dr. Tống Huỳnh, who would practice family medicine in a suburb of Atlanta.[23]

At noon, olive-colored buses began picking up people at designated areas to bring them to DAO. But when evacuees began gathering at these areas, crowds of Vietnamese mingled in, hoping to be taken along. In the end, there were more people than seats, and even though drivers crammed people in, many had to be left behind. Seventy CIA translators and their families waited in vain at their compound to be picked up by the Americans. So did many others.

It was 15:00 hours when the first 12 helicopters in four V-shaped formations arrived at the airport. During the next hours, 36 helicopters arrived and boarded more than 50 passengers each. By 17:00 hours, there remained 1,300 evacuees and an 800-man security force. As night came, the pilots wanted to stop the flights. The embassy said no, and evacuation at the DAO continued until the night.

In the morning, Saigon streets were quiet because of the 24-hour, government-imposed curfew, but they became busy in the afternoon as people looked for ways to get out of town. People simply disregarded the curfew, because there were no police to enforce it. Angry mobs roamed the streets overturning abandoned cars and setting fires to buildings. Looters joined the fray, carrying out furniture, TV sets or anything that could have value from former residences of Americans. To bring a known person into the embassy enclosure, the Marines would reach down, grab him by the collar and the hair, and yank him up and over the wall. To the Marines, it was just like moving meat. One Marine was handed a paper bag filled with uncut gems. He handed it back. It belonged to a wealthy Chinese businessman who wanted to get his family out of the country.[24]

The evacuation planners had expected at most 2,000 to 3,000 evacuees inside the embassy. However, the number turned out to be larger due to the fact that buses that could not get into DAO had been diverted to the embassy. The two landing zones were located in the courtyard and on the roof. Evacuees were divided into 50-person groups, one on one side, the other on the other side. When a big CH-53 bird came, both groups went in. When a small CH-46 bird arrived, then half of the people went.

Flying conditions were hazardous due to darkness and the gusty winds that came along with the rain. Helicopter pilots had to come in, hover, and drop down 70 feet to get into the embassy grounds. There was not much room to maneuver. The movement was tricky: it was like dropping into a deep hole. Takeoff was just as bad. Normally, they would do a translational maneuver: they would get off the ground, then move forward before pulling straight up. In this case, they had to pull up straight for 70 feet. One helicopter could not take off because of its load. It dropped down and had some people removed but could not get off the ground again. It took some more people off before pulling up without a problem.[25]

In Washington, Secretary Kissinger reported to the president that the DAO evacuation yielded 6,000 people extracted by 81 helicopters flying more than 100 sorties after a six-hour airlift. Due to poor weather, diminishing visibility, and pilots' fatigue, Ford thought about discontinuing the evacuation and resuming early in the morning. However, Ambassador Martin argued that he needed 30 more CH-53 sorties to complete Frequent Wind IV before the communists arrived in town. Washington agreed at 21:00 hours Saigon time.[26]

Flights were sporadic at the embassy at 20:00 hours. No one knew why. Contact made with DAO revealed that the evacuation was completed at DAO before midnight and priority of the birds would be switched to the embassy. But at midnight all flights just stopped, and people in the embassy grounds worried about being left out.

Wednesday 30 April

When the helicopters arrived, they were not the promised CH-53s but the smaller CH-46s, which could carry only 20 people. Kissinger called at 01:30 hours, confirming that the evacuation should be discontinued at 03:45 hours and Martin should board the next to last helicopter.

At 03:20 hours, Polgar wrote the last classified message to Washington, D.C.:

> The severity of the defeat and the circumstances of it, however, would seem to call for a reassessment of the policies of niggardly half measures which have characterized much of our participation here despite the commitment of manpower and resources which were certainly generous. Those who fail to learn from history are forced to repeat it. Let us hope we will not have another Vietnam experience and that we have learned our lesson. Saigon signing off.

It would take another 20 minutes to destroy the equipment.

Flights continued to come until 04:20 hours to ferry out evacuees. The skies then fell silent. Admiral Gayler, convinced that the embassy was a "bottomless pit of refugees," decided to shut down the operation. Then word came at 04:47 that a CH-46 was ready to pick up Ambassador Martin. Kean told the Marine to hold the bird while he spoke to General Carey. The latter told him that the U.S. president had directed that the ambassador should leave now.

Kean relayed the message to Ambassador Martin and Colonel Madison, a member of the Joint Military Team set up under the Paris Accords. Madison argued that he would not leave unless the 420 Vietnamese were evacuated. Kean told him he had the orders. Madison threw his hands in the air, turned around and left.[27]

He went and told Herrington about the order. Herrington, who had been working on the grounds directing the evacuation, was surprised by the order and did not know how to deal with the Vietnamese. He sneaked out the back, telling them he needed to go to the bathroom. He got into the embassy and found all the rooms deserted. He went straight to the roof, where one CH-46 was waiting for him. On the plane out of Saigon were only four Marines. Herrington was disgusted. He thought he could have picked up 45 more people. The helicopter took off.

Among those left behind were South Korean embassy officials, a German priest, embassy firemen who had volunteered to stay on duty until the end, and various U.S. Embassy employees and their families. Among the South Koreans was General Rhee Dai Yong, who once commanded 50,000 Korean troops in Vietnam and would later be imprisoned by the communists. He spent five years in communist reeducation camps.

Luckily, every Marine got safely inside the embassy and the mahogany door was bolted. They climbed the stairs to the rooftop and 20 Marines were sent out each time until the group was down to the last 11. The last chopper took off at 05:24, but a handful of Marines were left behind.

Although daylight came, no aircraft was seen on the horizon until 8:00 hours local time—they had been waiting for more than two hours—when a single unescorted CH-46 dropped down to pick up the last American troops in Vietnam.[28]

The rescue force of 70 choppers and 865 Marines flew over 630 sorties during the last eighteen hours and evacuated a total of 7,053 people including 1,373 Americans, 5,595 Vietnamese, and 85 third-country nationals. Of these, nearly 2,100, including 978 Americans, were helilifted out of the embassy courtyard alone.

The U.S. State Department estimated that the total number of past and present Vietnamese employed by the embassy and their families was 90,000. Of these, Martin, in his testimony to Congress, stated that 22,294 had been evacuated as of 30 April 1975, or about one quarter of the group. The rest were left behind or were obliged to escape on their own.

The Beginning of the Terror State

At 18:00 hours, a heartbreaking situation occurred at the front gate of the Cộng Hòa Military General Hospital, from which emerged a procession of patients in small groups, one leading the other. One hour earlier, a group of communist soldiers had taken over the hospital and ordered everyone to evacuate the hospital without taking anything else, including cars, carts, and medications, except for their clothing. This included physicians, nurses, workers, and patients no matter their medical conditions, whether they had been operated on or not and whether their wounds had healed or not. This was an abominable order, for they had to walk out with their fresh wounds, not knowing where to go. Their homes or units could be hundreds of miles away from this tertiary hospital where they had been evacuated for care. "Seriously wounded soldiers whose limbs were torn and bleeding, some with stomachs cut open and intestines exposed were pulled out to the terrace in front of the hospital gate. Many died in a short time. I had never imagined that such barbarism would happen," wrote Nguyễn Công Luận.[29]

To help these patients, local people called cabs, cars, cyclos, and motorcycles to transport the sickest ones to private and community hospitals for care. They took some of them home to recover before giving them travel money to go back home.

The Vietnamese-Americans called 30 April a day of shame.

In 1977, *National Review* reported that some 30,000 South Vietnamese had been systematically killed using a list of CIA informants left behind by the U.S. Embassy.[30]

> According to Frank Snepp, a CIA analyst who served in Saigon, the American Embassy wasn't able to destroy its top-secret files during the frantic evacuation, and among the information that fell into Communist hands was a list of 30,000 Vietnamese who had worked in the Phoenix Program, a U.S.-sponsored operation responsible for the elimination of thousands of Communist agents. A full report on the massacre of those 30,000 Phoenix cadres is said to have reached the desk of the French ambassador to Saigon by late 1975; he communicated it to Washington, but nothing was done with it.

2

The Vietnamese Navy and the *Trường Xuân*

Below are the stories of people who escaped by sea either on the Vietnamese Navy (VNN) ships or the *Trường Xuân*, a Vietnamese merchant ship. Although a few other ships also participated in this escape, stories about these two ships are well documented.

The Vietnamese Navy Ships

On 25 April 1975, Captain Kiêm Đỗ, the deputy chief of operations staff received a phone call from Rich Armitage regarding an evacuation plan. With Saigon close to falling into the hands of the communists, Rich was assigned by the Department of Defense to remove and destroy as much sensitive material and technology as possible to prevent it from falling into the hands of the North Vietnamese. Additionally, he was urged to bring out as many VNN ships as he could, along with family members of the crew and other civilians.

Rich, a former U.S. Naval Intelligence officer, was well-known to the Vietnamese; he not only spoke Vietnamese but also got along well with his Vietnamese counterparts. Graduating from the Naval Academy in 1967, he was first deployed as a damage control assistant on board the destroyer USS *Buck* (DD-761), which was stationed off the Vietnamese coast and provided gunfire support to forces ashore. On returning to the U.S., he trained and became a counterinsurgency instructor at the naval school in Coronado, California. Lacking challenges, he volunteered for shore duty as an advisor to the VNN on his second tour in 1971. He completed a third tour a year later. In the Mekong delta, he lived with his Vietnamese counterparts and taught them ambush techniques. He ate their food, donned their black pajamas, slept on the ground, and shared their hardships. He was so well liked by the Vietnamese navy personnel that they nicknamed him Trần Phú, with Phú being the Vietnamese translation for Rich and Trần the family name of a Vietnamese hero, Trần Hưng Đạo, who defeated the Chinese at the battle of Bạch Đằng in the thirteenth century CE. Trần Hưng Đạo later had been designated the godfather or protector of the VNN.

Following the signing of the 1973 Paris Accords, he resigned from the navy, feeling that by signing the accords, the U.S. had decided to abandon South Vietnam. But because of his knowledge of the Vietnamese people and armed forces, the DAO in Saigon asked Rich to become the naval, marine, and airborne operations adviser working out of this city. He then went to work at the Pentagon before retiring in the fall of 1974. In April 1975, the Pentagon sent him to Saigon for a last-minute mission: to retrieve as many navy ships as possible. Since he had worked in the past with Captain Kiêm, he decided to contact him once he landed in Saigon.[1]

Kiêm was glad to meet Armitage at this vital juncture. They discussed the overall military situation, which was critical to say the least. The question at that time was whether to evacuate the navy ships or surrender. If they surrendered, tens of thousands of people, civilians and military, would be stuck in Saigon. Their future looked grim. If the navy ships got out and the Saigon government decided to stand and fight, they could always come back to join the fight. But if the navy missed that only chance to get out, it would all be over. The only possible plan was to get out of Saigon with as many people as possible; otherwise those who were left behind might try to hinder the ships' departure. This was also the opinion of the U.S. government, which did not want the ships to fall into the hands of the communists.

For Kiêm, plotting to take the navy out of the country raised troubling issues. First, on the legal and military issue, it was an act of treason against the existing government as well as against the new government, should the communists take over the country. Second, he could not do it by himself; he had to get the approval from the new chief of Naval Operations (CNO), who was Admiral Chung Tấn Cang. What would they do if the CNO turned down their plan? Third, the plan, although creative and helpful for many people, would be dangerous if it were leaked out by anyone down the line. Therefore, Kiêm refused to write it down on paper. If caught, he could always pretend the plan had never existed. Fourth, he needed the cooperation of all the ship captains because without them the ships would never leave the naval base. Also, since the situation was grave, every sailor, officer, and captain knew that the only way to have freedom was to get out of the country.

For many days, Kiêm and Rich wrestled with the logistics of the

2. The Vietnamese Navy and the Trường Xuân

E-plan: timing the departure, getting the ships ready for the operation, and getting the ship captains to cooperate. Notifying and getting fleet commanders involved was extremely important. If agreeable, they could get their ships ready for the voyage, including crew, families, and other passengers. The big problem was the timing of departure. Misjudging the date and time meant that everyone would get stuck in town. However, pulling the ships out too early could set off a mass panic and could backfire. The best way was to call all naval personnel to return to their bases for "security reasons" so they could contact their families, because the ships' crew would not budge without their families left behind.

Of the navy's ninety-seven ships, at least thirty of the forty-five big ships in the Saigon area had a chance of getting out. The rest were either in the repair shop or too disabled to make the trip. On the second day of planning, two anxious skippers had to be disciplined because they had moved their families aboard two well-stocked, well-fueled ships. The CNO had no choice but to discipline them so that the rest of the navy would believe that they had acted on their own.[2]

Decision was taken to activate the E-plan at 18:00 hours on 29 April, with four hours to load up the ships. The date was picked in advance because they did not know when the communists would make their move. It turned out they were correct in their assessment, for had they chosen one day later, the whole fleet would have been stuck in Saigon.

The plan was for all the ships to sail to a rendezvous at Côn Sơn Island, which was 115 miles southeast of Vũng Tàu. Some of the ships had to be dispatched to Vũng Tàu, Nam Căng and Phú Quốc to evacuate the III, IV, and V coastal zones, respectively. It was only on E-day that the ship captains were finally told about the plan and about getting their crew in place. Those who did not want to go, for some reason or another, were told to assist the others as much as possible. Kiêm then sneaked out to inform his family about where and when to meet him and about a secondary route in case the first one failed.

On the evening of 29 April, mutiny almost broke out at the pier where three ships, which had been loading since afternoon, were still lined up abreast. The middle and inner ships were crammed with people, while the outer ship was strangely empty and prevented the inner ships from leaving. Kiêm climbed on the middle ship and told the outer one to cut its ropes to free the other ships. The sailor on the outer ship refused. There was despair from the crowd on the ship. Kiêm then devised a smart stratagem: he collected money from the passengers, who gladly pitched in because they were anxious to get out, and gave it to the sailor of the outer ship. The bribe worked and the ropes were cut.

Although the plan was for the fleet to leave by 18:00 hours, at midnight the last ships were still loading. At that time, a jeep arrived at the pier and a navy person jumped out and barked through a portable loudspeaker.

"This is Captain Bình, the new chief of staff, operations. All ships are to return to Saigon immediately. Repeat: all ships to report back to Saigon."

"This is Captain Kiêm," retorted Kiêm through the ship's transmitter. "I'm the deputy chief of staff, operations. Shut up Bình, you impostor. All ships are to go."

A message then came out through the Command Information Center: "This is Captain Tân, the new CNO. All ships at pier are to remain where they are. All units are to report back to their stations."

"This is Captain Kiêm. Shut up all you phonies. All ships are to go."

Then a distinctive northern voice from the radio lectured everyone about the need to stay back and serve the new government. Kiêm told his men to dismiss the communist propaganda. Then the sound of a flute came up as if to call everyone to return and serve the fatherland. When the silvery notes died away, reaching the transmitter, Kiêm told the skippers to cast off all the lines and start their engines.

The ships began to move, followed by other civilian ships. At that time, they heard the rumbles of tanks that had just arrived at the pier.[3] Luckily no shot was fired by either side.

When the ships approached Côn Sơn Island, they knew they had escaped the communists. Kiêm felt like he was nobody again, as he had completed his job of bringing the navy ships out of Saigon. For the second part of the trip from Côn Sơn Island to the Philippines, the fleet would be under the command of the CNO Chung Tấn Cang and Rick Armitage.

The following is the list of ships ready for departure to the Philippines, from Côn Sơn Island. The *Kirk* crew ship riders were assigned to the VNN ships later during this portion of the trip, which will be described in chapter 3.

Hull#, Ship Name, *Kirk* crew passengers

HQ-01, *Trần Hưng Đạo*, FTG3 W.S. Johnson and BTFA G.W. Malone

HQ-03, *Trần Nhật Duật*, Mr. Richard L. Armitage

HQ-06, *Trần Quốc Toản*, RMC L. Gassaway, ST1 T.A. Sievert, and ST1 D.R. Lucero

HQ-07, *Đống Đa*, II GMT1 T.J. Dixon and HT3 S.N. Hanenkrat

HQ-11, *Chi Linh*, LT (jg) John S. Pine and BTFN R.J. Lalonde

2. The Vietnamese Navy and the Trường Xuân

HQ-12, *Ngọc Hoi*, LT (jg) Scott J. Olin and SN G.E. Harrison
HQ-14, *Vạn Kiếp*, II LT (jg) Donald A. Swain and SA C. Richardson
HQ-16, *Lý Thường Kiệt*, LT Frederick R. Sautter and ADJ2 R.G. Fisher
HQ-228, *Đoàn Ngọc Tảng*, GMGC H.M. Dilulo and TN3 F.L. Soderburg
HQ-229, *Lu Phu Tho*, ADJC G.C. Bingham and STG3 E.W. Kirk
HQ-231, *Nguyễn Đức Bông*, SM1 H.W. Kenway and GMG3 J.R. Sanders
HQ-401, *Han Giang*, LT (jg) Scott L. Steele and BTFN J.D. Scarrow
HQ-402, *Lam Giang* (sunk)
HQ-404, *Hương Giang*, ENS Bruce B. Davidson and OS2 T.D. Schultz
HQ-470, (unknown), IC2 T.A. Powell and EW2 P.E. Lawless
HQ-502, *Thị Nại*, LT (jg) A.E. Porter and SA D.R. Carney
HQ-505, (unknown), LT L.E. Arcuri and ETR2 A.P. Gozdan
HQ-800, *Huỳnh Văn Củ*, ENS Robert A. Pennell and OS3 P.J. Burinskas
PGG-18, (unknown), EWC J.F. Willoughby and STG2 J.R. Wimbrow
Fishing Trawler #1, BTC J.D. Gornto and SA R. Bankston
Fishing Trawler #2, OSC D.T. Burlison and GMG3 G.N. Sanvig

Late on 30 April, Vinh Phạm rode his motor scooter to the naval yard with his wife and child in the back seat. He was lucky. All the ships were gone except for one, still held to the pier by electrical lines and filled with an estimated five thousand men, women, and children. Lâm Giang (HQ-402), a former World War II U.S. Navy "landing ship medium" (LSM), had been in the yard for a major overhaul and repair: its doors refused to close completely, causing water to pour in when underway. Men were actively severing the electric lines with a fire axe in an attempt to free the disabled ship.

Once free of the pier, the vessel swung around stern first, out of control. The steering wheel did not work. Volunteers fought to control it against an uncooperative current, but to no avail. When the vessel approached the bank near Tự Do Street, a North Vietnamese Army (NVA) tank was waiting. Someone hoisted a white shirt as if to offer surrender. The tank did not fire any shots, and the vessel kept going. At dusk, fishing boats and rafts approached the Lâm Giang, bringing in more evacuees. At one river bend, volunteers were finally able to turn the vessel around, and it finally cruised to the sea bow-first. Lâm Giang's pumps did their job pumping out water. At Vũng Tàu, the evacuees breathed sighs of relief as the vessel headed straight to Côn Sơn. There was no food or water on board, and the passengers shared among themselves what they had brought on board. The toilets stopped working, and passengers had to relieve themselves in containers.

By daybreak, they arrived in view of Côn Sơn and found the South Vietnamese fleet. *Kirk* realized the problem with Lâm Giang and radioed the Vietnamese flagship *Trần Nhật Duật* for help (HQ-3). The latter turned around to look for the disabled vessel. On makeshift wooden planks, Lâm Giang passengers were transferred to the *Trần Nhật Duật*. After the passengers reached safety on board the HQ-3, it pulled away and the beaten-up Lâm Giang sank beneath the South China Sea.[4]

Captain Nguyễn Quốc Định was assigned to a small patrol boat with a crew of six. Known as a PCF—Patrol Craft Fast—or Swift Boat, it was designed to patrol the coast lines of central Vietnam to look for contraband and for communists trying to bring supplies into South Vietnam. The 50-foot (16.3-meter) shallow-draft vessels were later used in the interior waterways of the Mekong delta to interdict Việt Cộng movement of arms and munitions and transport Vietnamese forces.

In the spring of 1975, Captain Nguyễn Quốc Định was in Qui Nhơn picking up soldiers and civilians on the coast following the abandonment of the central highlands. He then moved to Cam Ranh Bay to pick up some more people to take them to Saigon. He was on Phú Quốc Island for the relocation of the refugees and then returned to Saigon.

On 29 April, his boat was hauled in for repair. At noon, his commanding officer—a leader of twenty PCFs—told him to go to Côn Sơn Island. Since he did not want to leave his family behind, he assigned three soldiers to watch the boat and walked home, a mile from the Saigon pier. He found his family in distress, not knowing what to do. He explained to them that they should leave town. Using his motorcycle, he dropped his two sons at the pier. By making a few trips, he had his family members gathered on his boat. People offered him money to take them with him, but he told them he had to take care of his family first. He picked up a total of forty people, family members and strangers and left the pier around 11:00 hours on 30 April.

They went down the river, accompanied by two other boats. He was scared because at Rừng Sát, the Saigon River was very narrow and Việt Cộng could fire rockets at them at any time. He then saw a larger civilian boat named *Vong Hong Ni* that carried about three hundred people. The boat captain agreed to take all the PCF passengers.

At Vũng Tàu, they looked for the Seventh Fleet, which had moved somewhere else. Seeing a Vietnamese navy ship passing by, they followed it and went on a seven-day trip all the way to Subic Bay in the Philippines.⁵

Elsewhere, Trần Minh Lợi was looking for ways to get out of Saigon. On 30 April, he went down the river and saw people around a civilian boat having its engines worked on. Once one of the engines was repaired, the skipper allowed him to board. As the boat passed by the Majestic Hotel, a T-54 tank was pulling by it facing the river. People surrounded the tank and climbed on it, keeping it from shoot at the boat.

When the boat arrived at the South China Sea, it flashed an SOS that was picked up by an American navy ship. The Americans boarded the ship and tried to fix the engine, but failed. The refugees were evacuated to the navy ship, which then fired its big guns, trying to sink the disabled boat. They missed several times but finally hit it, causing it to catch fire. The boat slowly drifted toward mainland.⁶

Nguyễn Tài Ngọc says that as he was escaping aboard a ship on the Saigon River,

> the Communists [] were firing artillery into the sea of Vũng Tầu and Cần Giờ to try to kill us. I saw with my own eyes ocean water exploding in the air from bomb shells, forcing hundreds of boats to disperse from gathering around my barge. Our own ship had to increase speed in order to get away, after pulling up the ladder which had been lowered to the barge earlier for the refugees to climb up to the ship. Later on in the U.S., I found out the writer Chu Tử was killed on the ship *Việt Nam Thương Tín* near Cần Giờ. It is ironic that the North Vietnamese Communists, who share the same Vietnamese blood with me, were determined to kill their own people.⁷

Nguyễn Ngọc Bích, a professor at one of the private Saigon universities, left the Saigon wharf with his family at midnight on 29 April without incident. When they passed Vũng Tầu, they were picked up by the *American Challenger*. With a capacity of about 1,000 passengers, the ship picked up 7,500 people. Life aboard the ship was absolute hell as it traveled from Vũng Tầu all the way to Wake Island.

On the night of 30 April, many more boats loaded with people arrived at the ship, asking to be picked up. Once the passengers had been transferred, the Vietnamese boats were set on fire and pushed away. All over the sea, there were eerie fires of boats burning and drifting away. They lit up the water, and it looked like the South China Sea was about to burn.

One Catholic priest wanted to bring on board a Honda motorcycle, but they would not let him. A dentist also wanted to bring his dentist's chair on board. He commented, "This is the only way I could make a living." His request was also denied.⁸

The Last Voyage of the Trường Xuân

At 14:30 hours on 2 May 1975, in the South China Sea, the *Trường Xuân* captain handed a note to his communication officer to be dispatched worldwide. It said,

> The *Trường Xuân* ship carrying more than 3,000 Vietnamese fled Saigon after the Communist invasion. The engine room is submerged in water. The ship will likely sink. We were lucky to be rescued by the *Clara Maersk* of Denmark. On behalf of all the refugees on board, I hereby appeal to all the countries of the free world to accept and save my fellow refugees.
> Signed: Captain Phạm Ngọc Lũy

The communiqué was never sent because the generator room, being submerged in water, was no longer working. The captain and his crew were slowly transferred to the *Clara Maersk* before the *Trường Xuân* sank to the bottom of the sea.[9] That episode marked the end of the *Trường Xuân*, a commercial Vietnamese cargo ship that in her last days was able to bring more than 3,000 evacuees out of besieged Saigon.

The 93-meter-long and 12-meter-wide *Trường Xuân* was powered by 1,500 horsepower and had a loading capacity of 3,000 tons. Built by the Japanese in the 1950s, it had outlasted its capacities. The problem was a non-working pump that allowed water to flow in at a rate of 100 tons per hour, rapidly submerging the engine room and paralyzing the generator.

Trường Xuân had been in pretty bad shape to begin with; it limped out of the Saigon port and had to be towed during the 40-mile trip on the Saigon River to the open sea before finally breaking down at high sea two days after her departure. That was, however, enough to save the lives of almost 4,000 people.

The captain had been working nonstop for the previous three days trying to control the crowd, providing assurance and security, as well as directing the skeletonized crew that tried its best to keep the engine and the pump working. There were no provisions or water on board because the ship was not prepared for a long voyage. The crew consisted of the second mate Trần Văn Chất, telecommunications officer Nguyễn Ngọc Thanh, chief engineer Lê Hồng Phi, mechanic Tôn Hoa, cook Chung A Can and Phạm Ngọc Lũy, the captain. They were six civilians versus a crowd of 3,628 people, many of them ARVN soldiers, still stunned by the sudden order to drop arms against the enemy but well-armed with guns and grenades. This did not include a few Việt Cộng infiltrators, who did everything they could to disrupt the last voyage of the *Trường Xuân*.

A small spark could light up the hidden frustration, powerlessness, and humiliation that had been building up for the last three months in this gathering of strangers. Except for 200 friends and family members, the rest of the crowd were strangers who rushed into the ship at the last minute, trying to escape the horrors of the war.

Tired by three sleepless nights, weakened physically by the lack of food and water, and worn out by the events, the captain ordered the remaining crew to leave the ship immediately. All the passengers had been safely transferred to the *Clara Maersk* earlier. His country had fallen to the communists and his ship was sinking. This was a double blow for a man who did not expect to suffer twice in forty-eight hours. The *Trường Xuân* was like a friend who had accompanied him in all his trips to foreign lands, through calm waters as well as through stormy weather. Now that she was sinking, his heart felt like sinking with her.

Among the passengers were members of parliament, doctors, dentists and judges. There were also members of the navy, air force and army, with ranks from colonel to private, two Catholic priests and two nuns, one Buddhist monk, and students from all of South Vietnam's universities. There were both military and civilian journalists, public servants and private office workers of all fields. The ship brought along singers and song writers. Elvis Phuong was among the group. This was a very broad section of the South Vietnamese society; it was different from the group of people who were rushed away by the Americans. This was a representative section of South Vietnam, the one that was not closely related to the Americans. They all tried to flee. They had done their share and certainly had nothing to share with the communists they had fought against for the last two decades.

Why did they flee?

> They were helpless and hopeless. Before them, "there was just a white infinity, overcast by the foggy mist." Behind them, hatred was burning the country and stopping them from staying. People were fleeing at any cost, by any means, flowing out of Việt Nam like tides of rising and falling water. They were not even afraid of deep oceans. They departed to warn humanity about the dangers of Communism. They left with the hope that one day they could return to a free and peaceful land.[10]

On 17 April, Captain Phạm Ngọc Lũy returned to Vietnam and arrived at pier 5 of the civilian Khánh Hội port. On 20 April, the skipper talked to and bargained with Mr. Trần Đình Trường, the owner of Vishipcolines shipping company, to allow him to use the ship to carry out potential refugees. The owner had other ideas. The skipper's solution was to use the *Trường Xuân*, which had been loading scrap metal for its next voyage, to get people out. The loading was completed on 26 April.

People crowded the American Embassy and the airport because these were the only official places to get out of the country. Those who could get into these places had either power, connections, or money. The rest—those with no connections—had to look for an escape by sea. They were running around like mad people in confused circles. They were frightened and desperate. Anxiety and fear pushed them to do strange things. Rockets and missiles were exploding. The road from Phú Lâm to Hậu Giang and the IV Corps, the countryside where escape could be possible, was blocked by the communists. Those who worked for the Defense Attaché Service, First National City Bank, and Free World Radio were able to escape by air. Others remained calm and refused to leave the country, especially not with the Americans.

The *Tân Nam Việt* was docked next to the *Trường Xuân*, which left early on the 30th without a ship captain. On the 28th, the owner did not make any decision about the *Trường Xuân*. The ship was totally deserted. The crew had left. The chief engineer had not been hired yet. There was no word from the owner about what to do next. The skipper left the ship heartbroken; he did not see any chance of getting out with the *Trường Xuân*.

The neighborhood was desolate. Houses were closed and streets littered with garbage. People in the streets were aimless, but in a hurry. American offices had been ransacked of furniture and equipment. Lawlessness reigned in the city.

Watchful waiting was stressful. The captain did not know what to do. He could not even get the boat ready. He could not think about leaving from another route. To kill time, he went out to see his relatives and friends. His wife and children would be picked up by his wife's sister. They would go out with PM Nguyễn Cao Kỳ. They were stopped at the airport, where heavy congestion was occurring as everyone wanted to get in. Even soldiers dropped their guns at the airport and rushed into it. Where did they expect to go?

The plane was supposed to depart at 02:00 on 29 April. Two hours later, they were still waiting. At 04:00 hours, the airport was hit by incoming missiles fired by the communists. For two hours, bombs and missiles exploded. Houses were hit by rockets and burned. Areas around the airport, the suburbs of Chí Lăng and Phú Nhuận, were also shelled. People died. Many people returned home, as there was no way of flying out. One helicopter was hit near Ngã Bảy (Sen-Corners) District.[11]

Around 16:00 on 29 April, the owner, Trần Đình Trường, finally gave the skipper permission to sail the *Trường Xuân* to Phú Quốc Island with Lê Hồng Phi as chief engineer. Although Saigon was under curfew and still being shelled by rockets, people ignored it, although traffic was less than usual. The skipper went to the pier to check on his ship. The engine room was locked, but no one was on the pier. The second mate showed up and stated that the engineer was picking up his family and would show up.

No one slept that night. Contacts were sent to family members and extended families as well as friends. Special Forces lieutenant Colonel Nguyễn Văn Nghé offered two GMC trucks to transport the 200 evacuees. They were stopped at the pier gate by the guard, who refused to let them in, arguing about the size of the family. A small bribe convinced him to immediately swing the gate open. Hundreds of people rushed in and stood in front of the *Trường Xuân*, while others stormed on the ship through the gangway. Outside the gate, people shoved each other trying to get in. The police fired shots in the air to calm them down.

When Dương Văn Minh announced the surrender at 10:25 on 30 April, hundreds of boats, big and small, left the port, creating huge waves. People suddenly headed toward the *Trường Xuân*. They came from everywhere—from the river, through the riverbank, around the stern, and in front. The poet Bảo Vân was hoisted from a riverboat. There were civilians as well as soldiers, policemen in uniforms led by Lieutenant Colonel Lưu Bình Hảo; Paratrooper Đỗ Duy Nghĩa, Air Force major Đinh Quốc Hưng and his family. A committee was immediately formed to take care of security.

The order to start the boiler had been given a long time ago. The order was given to turn the ship around and start heading to the sea. The steering system was not working. When the steering components were removed, water was found in the oil tube. The ship had been sabotaged. A decision was made to change the oil. The thirty-minute wait was excruciating, as the communists were coming into town. Finally the emergency steering system seemed to be in order. All the moorings were dropped. People continued to try to board while the ship was trying to make a U-turn. The tide slowly helped turn the ship around.

At 13:25, three hours after the surrender, the bell finally sounded the signal for departure. The wind pushed the ship away from the pier and it moved forward on its own. The generator then failed, causing the ship to get stuck against the riverbank. Luckily, the tugboat *Sông An* was able to pull it out. By 07:00 on 1 May, the ship reached the sea: it moved sluggishly in front of the *Bãi Trước* of Vũng Tàu. The beach looked deserted.

Two people shot themselves to death. Brains and blood spurted out at 16:00 and 16:15 on 1 May. These were desperate souls who somehow at the last minute could not think of leaving their country and families for good. At 17:30, a man fell overboard. The captain had the boat turn around.

An S.O.S signal was sent on 2 May. There was a meeting at noon. The *Trường Xuân* finally docked against the *Clara Maersk* at 18:00 hours on 4 May.

Ương's eldest brother rode his moped, carrying his pregnant wife and two children. Another brother rode on a second motorcycle. Ương rode on the back seat of his brother's bike to Nhà Bè, a small fishing village 10 miles from Saigon.[12]

The streets were crowded with people carrying luggage and family members. When they arrived at Nhà Bè, they sat there not knowing what to do. They decided to pool their money together and charter a boat to try to catch a big ship that had passed the pier just before their arrival. They came upon abandoned boats and switched boat four times before landing on a military landing craft with a total of 58 other people. Ten days later, they were picked up by a Singaporean ship that dropped them in Taiwan. They were flown to Guam.

Vietnamese navy ships—the *Trường Xuân*, the *Việt Nam Thương Tín*, and others—did their part in bringing out of Vietnam the huge mass of civilians and military (about 40,000) who were not rich and had no close connections with the Americans. They would arrive through the third wave of the 1975 exodus after one or even two weeks of maritime voyage to Guam. They were the least privileged among those who departed in 1975; but of course, they were more privileged than those who were left behind in Saigon. They accomplished the first part of their trip by themselves: going to the Saigon naval pier and getting on one of these ships that took the long way out of Vietnam to Guam.

At Subic Bay in the Philippines, evacuees from the VNN ships would be transferred to MSC (Military Sealift Command) ships. The latter, along with private Vietnamese ships, would sail for Guam, where they arrived in the second week of May 1975.

3

Task Force 76 and USS *Kirk*

As the fall of Saigon became imminent, between 18 and 24 April 1975, on the order of Washington, the Seventh Fleet set up Task Force 76, which was designed to assist potential refugees to get out of South Vietnam. This chapter documents the role played by Task Force 76 and the Military Sealift Command (MSC) ships in saving the lives of Vietnamese and other Asian evacuees.

Task Force 76 Ships

Never in the history of the Vietnam War had the U.S. Navy deployed its force in such a massive scale as in April 1975 off the South Vietnamese coast. This time, it was not for an aggressive purpose, but for a more pacific role: to pick up and transport Vietnamese and other Asian evacuees. How many would they be? No one really knew at that time, although it was estimated to be up to 10,000 people. The South China Sea was filled with ships. In the end, it was more than 100,000, a sealift of gargantuan proportions, until then unheard of in the history of the Vietnam War.

The sheer number of evacuees was magnified by the suddenness of the outpouring of this mass of people. Although the task force was prepared to pick up evacuees, it was not prepared for the suddenness and the size of the evacuation process: almost overnight, they had to care for, feed, and transport more than 100,000 unknown strangers at sea. There was no place to hold them, screen them, care for them, or feed them in the middle of the ocean. There were no 100,000 lunch boxes, knives, forks, spoons, plates, no 100,000 water bottles stored anywhere, and that was only for one lunch session.

About twenty miles offshore from the South Vietnamese port of Vũng Tàu, Task Force 76 had assembled seventeen amphibious ships, two aircraft carriers, fourteen escorts—mostly destroyers and destroyer escorts like *Kirk*—and eleven replenishment ships. The task force consisted of three subdivisions, organized as follows:

> *Blue Ridge* (LCC 19) (command ship)
> Task Group 76.4 (Movement Transport Group Alpha):
> *Okinawa (LPH 3)*
> *Vancouver (LPD 2)*
> *Thomaston (LSD 28)*
> *Peoria (LST 1183)*
> Task Group 76.5 (Movement Transport Group Bravo):
> *Dubuque (LPD 8)*
> *Durham (LKA 114)*
> *Frederick (LST 1184)*
> Task Group 76.9 (Movement Transport Group Charlie):
> *Anchorage (LSD 36)*
> *Denver (LPD 9)*
> *Duluth (LPD 6)*
> *Mobile (LKA 115)*

The task force was joined by additional ships:

> *Hancock* and *Midway*, carrying Navy, Marine, and Air Force helicopters
> Seventh Fleet flagship *Oklahoma City* (CLG 5)
> Amphibious ships
> *Mount Vernon* (LSD 39)
> *Barbour County* (LST 1195)
> *Tuscaloosa* (LST 1187)
> Eight destroyer types for naval gunfire, escort and area defense.

Rear Adm. Donald Whitmire was the amphibious force commander and was in charge of the evacuation. His flagship was USS *Blue Ridge* (LCC 19). His entire force numbered seventy-three ships.[1]

Far out to sea was another group of seventy-three ships, under the command of Rear Adm. Robert Coogan. His flagship was the USS *Enterprise*. The *Enterprise* and *Coral Sea* carrier attack groups of Task Force 77 in the South China Sea provided air cover, while Task Force 73 ensured logistic support. This was one of the largest fleets ever gathered by the U.S. Navy during the Vietnam War.

The Marine evacuation contingent, the Ninth Marine Amphibious Brigade (Task Group 79.1), consisted of three battalion landing teams, support units, and the deployed security detachments.

Besides this navy force there was the Military Sealift Command (MSC), which had the responsibility for providing sealift and ocean transportation for all U.S. military services as well as other government agencies. The MSC ships were either owned or on long- or short-term charter by the U.S. Navy. MSC ships used during this operation included the following:

SS *American Racer*
SS *Green Forest*
SS *Green Port*
SS *Green Wave*
SS *Pioneer Commander*
SS *Pioneer Contender*
SS *Trans-Colorado*
USNS *Greenville Victory*
USNS *Sgt. Andrew Miller*
USNS *Sgt. Truman Kimbro*

Navy-owned ships carrying blue and gold stack colors are in service with the prefix USNS (U.S. Navy Ship) or are in commission (USS prefix); they have a hull number and are civilian-manned. Chartered ships retain normal colors and bear their normal SS, MV, and GTS and have no hull numbers.

Aboard the Task Force Ships

The Task Force 76 ships were assigned to pick up all the evacuees gathered during Operation Frequent Wind. They eventually picked up more than expected, not only F15 planes, helicopters, and even a Cessna, but also evacuees from boats.

Nguyễn Phúc Thiệu was a second lieutenant, South Vietnamese Air Force, stationed at Tân Sơn Nhứt Airport. The five-helicopter crew witnessed the airport bombing on 28 April. The following day, the American Marines landed and surrounded the Defense Attaché Office (DAO). After flying out refugees, they blew up the DAO. ARVN pilots, in the meantime, were still waiting for orders. They stayed confined in their barracks waiting for orders that never came. They did not even know their leaders had left them; they thought they were in meetings with the Americans. On the night of 29 April, they watched Kỳ on the local television stating he would stay back and fight. Then he left.

On 30 April, desperate and unable to wait any longer, they decided to fly to the delta to continue the fight. They went to their helicopters at 05:00 hours and found them vandalized. The batteries had been removed and the fuel drained. The pilots cannibalized some parts and took fuel from some helicopters and got two of them working. All the pilots got into the two planes and flew down to Cần Thơ in the IV Corps. The base was deserted, but some soldiers told them they should go to the Seventh Fleet.

They flew to the Seventh Fleet ships, despite being very low on fuel. As soon as they landed on a carrier, the soldiers took away their guns and led them aside. What they saw next astounded them. The Americans were systematically pushing their helicopters overboard to make way for other aircraft to land. A few screamed and ran toward the Americans, trying to hold them back. A Marine told them, "Stand back, boys. The war is over."

Some pilots started to cry. They wanted to fly back to Vietnam and fight again. Others wanted to pick up their families. Some tried to jump overboard, but the Marines stopped them. For them, the war was really over when they saw their helicopters sink into the ocean.[2]

People on the USS *Midway*, on 30 April, saw a swarm of bees coming across the water toward it. The bees became bigger with time and turned out to be groups of ARVN Hueys that converged toward the fleet. There had been no previous communication from them. The people on deck were frantically trying to wave them off, but they landed anywhere they could find places to set down. They then disgorged women and children ... and lots of them. One particular aircraft came in with fifty-three people. Some were too busy to say anything; others just shook their heads.

The Marines stepped in immediately to lock the rotors in place and to disarm all passengers. The Vietnamese were so small that they could be blown across the deck. Ropes were stretched out to guide them across the deck and down the stairs to a processing center. They were humble, grateful, and afraid. There was a lot of crying among the evacuees. They were the ones who had just lost their homeland.

Then there was this airplane: a little Cessna O-1 "Bird Dog" that buzzed the deck of the *Midway*. Each time he passed over the ship, he dropped something. On the third try, he dropped a wrench with a note. It said he was Major Bương, with his wife and five children, and he wanted to land on the deck. Order was given to clear the deck. He came in floating like a bird, made two bounces and came to a complete stop. Everyone broke into cheers. A crowd ran toward him, then somebody yelled. "Where in the hell did you learn to fly anyway?" The pilot turned around and said, "Texas." And the cheer got louder and louder.[3]

On the *Okinawa*, a press guy from the *Cleveland Press* was interviewing Harry Summers, an infantry colonel in the U.S. Army. Col.

Stuart Herrington, a counterintelligence officer, stepped in and asked, "Do you know what you just saw?"

"The fall of Saigon," answered the reporter.

"You saw betrayal of the worst order," retorted Summers.

Herrington thought that there had been no plans for any big evacuation out of the embassy, that it had only occurred by circumstance.[4]

By early morning on 30 April, the Marines who helped lead the evacuation at the US Embassy in Saigon destroyed the communication gear because they planned to complete the evacuation by 04:30. They left at 05:20 in the morning.[5]

Washington did not share the intelligence coming out of Vietnam both from the CIA and DAO, that there would be a major offensive in the central highlands in March 1975. They refused to believe it.[6]

Polgar once asked Kissinger of the value of CIA intelligence. After thinking for a moment, Kissinger said, "Well, when it supports my policy, it's very useful." This was the heart of the problem. American policy was not formulated in response to what the intelligence showed. The U.S. first formulated the policy and then tried to find the intelligence to support it.[7]

Fox Butterfield, a reporter for the *NY Times* in Saigon in 1975, was picked up at the DAO like other reporters and heli-lifted to the Seventh Fleet. As a graduate student from Harvard, he first went to Vietnam in 1962, where he witnessed the progressive American involvement there. He led some of the early antiwar protests at Harvard. In 1969, he was invited to visit Hanoi to witness the results of U.S. bombing in Hanoi. There, he did not see that kind of destruction; although the countryside was bombed, Hanoi was spared. That visit opened his eyes. He witnessed the very authoritarian Hanoi regime and the severe poverty of the North Vietnamese. He realized that the "North Vietnamese leaders were not interested in economic development or the well-being of their people; they were interested only in this nationalistic goal of obtaining complete power."[8]

When he asked Lê Đức Thọ and Phạm Văn Đồng about a list of American POWs, they gave him a blank stare. A Hungarian diplomat told him, "The Hồ Chí Minh Trail is a one-way street. People who were sent down the pike fight till they die or are just left down there. Nobody ever comes back."

This explained the widespread draft resistance in the North, which was completely suppressed in the press. This struck Butterfield deeply. He realized that on one hand, the leaders wanted to publicize the fact that going to war was a noble sacrifice; on the other hand, the people were not enthusiastic about going to war, but were forced to go to war.

The NVA prisoners in the South, when interviewed by Butterfield later, were very unhappy kids.

When asked about American POWs, Lê Đức Thọ and Phạm Văn Đồng would stare blankly, as if to ask, "What are you talking about? Two or three hundred men? Who gives a shit? We've lost 200,000 men going South and never seen them again and who cares?" It was a callous attitude, and at the same time, it was breathtaking. The reason why they did not care about a few hundred prisoners was that they had no way of knowing what had happened to millions of their people. That is what life was like to them.

New York Times reporter Fox Butterfield said, "I went to Hanoi being very antiwar and came home very anti–North Vietnamese. People like Jane Fonda who went to the North just didn't look around…. They were mesmerized by the banquets and the good cheer and so on.

Saigon was a wealthy city, and they were relatively free, and people told me how bad it was and how there were orphans on the streets. 'Yes,' I could tell them, 'but go to Hanoi and see how bad it can get.'"[9]

Keyes Beech noted, "I would say that the press did not lose the war, but they helped. Not because they were trying to, but the relentlessly negative reporting without any regard to perspective … contributed to an erosion of support of the war."[10]

Bruce Branson added, "We kept announcing in advance what we were not going to do. At every point the North Vietnamese took advantage of that. I think I felt like the others—by fighting a half-baked sort of war, with limits, we made almost impossible to win. As a result, it dragged out over years and years, and in the end cost far more lives, I think, than if we had gone in with a short, sharp attack and gotten it over with."[11]

USS Kirk

The USS *Kirk* was a World War II destroyer escort (DE) that measured 438 feet and displaced 4,250 tons, fully loaded. She was commissioned on 9 September 1972, and she carried the name of Vice-Adm. Alan G. Kirk, senior U.S. naval commander during the June 1944 Normandy landings. At twenty knots, she had a range of 4,500 nautical miles and used a single five-bladed, 15-foot-diameter propeller. Her freshwater evaporators could provide 24,000 gallons per day, which would be helpful later on. As her role was to detect and destroy submarines, she also carried a single SH-2F Seasprite LAMPS (Light Airborne Multipurpose System) helicopter to locate submerged ones.

3. Task Force 76 and USS Kirk

Kirk's mission was to provide surveillance, routine escort, and patrol, naval gunfire support if required, and anti-surface protection for the force.

On 29 April, many Vietnamese helicopters passed by *Kirk* without stopping. They were probably looking for a larger landing area on other ships. At 14:00 hours, the first South Vietnamese Huey landed on the *Kirk*'s deck. Eight adults and four children stepped out of the crowded aircraft. One passenger claimed he was the deputy chairman of the South Vietnamese Joint Chiefs of Staff. Another was a two-star general. The third was a Buddhist monk. The passengers were escorted away from the flight deck. The first aircraft was stored.

Fifteen minutes later a second Huey landed, disgorging twelve passengers. Since three more Hueys were waiting to land and no place was left for storage, the captain decided to ditch the aircraft. The sailors dragged the 2.5-ton aircraft to the edge of the flight deck and tipped it over into the sea. The Huey floated for about fifteen seconds before submerging. The procedure was repeated many more times the rest of the day, at a cost of a million dollars per aircraft.

Later a twin-rotor CH-47 Chinook arrived and tried to descend onto the flight deck, but it was waved away. It was too big to land on the small deck. The pilot also realized that the deck was too small for him to land. He lifted off, then came back. He positioned the aircraft about ten or fifteen feet above the deck and told the passengers to jump down to the deck one by one. Sailors tried to catch each one. The pilot then flew fifty feet away from the ship and ditched the aircraft while jumping out of it. He was rescued by the ship's crew. By the end of the day a total of twelve aircraft had landed on the ship, and all of them had been discarded except for one.[12]

The next day, Lt. Bob Lemke saw hundreds of dots appearing on the large radar screen of the USS *Kirk*. Each green dot signified the presence of a craft. Bob went to the flying bridge and scanned the horizon with the binoculars. What he saw amazed him: hundreds of boats, from small fishing vessels to rubber crafts, were converging on the *Kirk*. As they got closer, he could even see "a tiny wooden dugout with a man, woman, and two children clinging for dear life. They were simply paddling out to sea hoping to get to the rescue ships."[13]

On Tuesday 29 April, after talking the last time to Captain Đỗ in Saigon, the thirty-year-old civilian Armitage flew to the *Blue Ridge*, where he requested a meeting with Rear Adm. Whitmire, the commander of the Task Force 76. With the admiral's approval, he was sent at 9:00 p.m. that day to the *Kirk*, which would take him to a rendezvous with the South Vietnamese fleet at Côn Sơn Island.

Kirk headed to the island, which is thirteen miles long and five miles wide and covered with green vegetation. It was used as a penal colony for political prisoners and criminal offenders before housing VC prisoners. On 30 April, it served as a temporary sanctuary to thirty Vietnamese navy ships and boats and two civilian fishing trawlers. Besides those, fifty other vessels, including small river patrol boats and fishing vessels, were tagging along.

Kirk's whaleboat shuttled back and forth between the ships with food and supplies. The evacuees were missing all kinds of essentials, because for everyone concerned this was an unplanned departure in a most disorganized environment.

The overall condition on these ships was not good, because of lack of adequate food and water in a sizzling tropical environment with excessive crowding and virtually no sanitation. The overtaxed toilets stopped working, causing people to relieve themselves in buckets. Even though the decks were hosed, the smell from the ships was overwhelming. Dehydration and diarrhea were rampant, and conjunctivitis became an epidemic. Supplies of Kaopectate and Lomotil, used to stem the epidemic of diarrhea, rapidly ran out. And in four days, the supply of ophthalmic antibiotic ointment to treat the scourge of pinkeye was exhausted.

There were groups of armed soldiers among the evacuees on some of the merchant ships. Some of them sold scarce water to the evacuees. Rival soldiers fought for water and food. Separating them from the civilians would be difficult in the crowded environment. Some deserters hijacked MS *Greenville Victory*, causing the admiral to put squads of Marines onboard the merchant ships to protect the crews. Since there was no latrine for the passengers aboard MS *Trans-Colorado*, people just squatted where they were. The stench was unbearable. Once a woman died while delivering her baby on deck, and the bodies of the mother and infant were thrown overboard.

Some ships needed mechanical repair because in their rush to get out of Saigon, they did not take spare parts. Captain Jacobs dispatched members of his engineering department and his chief engineer to the Vietnamese navy ships for an overhaul. Some anchors stubbornly remained stuck to the bottom. Some rusty anchor chains had to be severed with an acetylene cutting torch.[14] By 14:00 hours on 2 May, the fleet departed from Côn Sơn Bay.

As the fleet was approaching his country, Filipino president Marcos told the U.S. ambassador in Manila, William Sullivan, that he would accept only 2,500 refugees into his country. When he realized that Vietnamese navy ships were arriving at Subic Bay, he warned Sullivan that

Subic Bay was reserved for U.S., not Vietnamese, ships. Marcos was probably thinking for himself and his country: he was torn between his alliance with the U.S. and his desire to be an integral part of a rapidly changing Southeast Asia. Sullivan retorted that as part of the Military Assistance Program (MAP), if any receiving nation no longer had use for donated equipment—in this case, American-supplied ships—the latter would be returned to U.S. ownership. When Marcos thought for a minute, then asked whether these ships could be transferred to the Philippines, Sullivan said that he would suggest that idea to his government. A handshake completed the agreement. A potential diplomatic confrontation had been avoided. To accomplish that goal, the Vietnamese navy ships had to be turned over to U.S. command and South Vietnamese flags would be removed and replaced by American flags. The ships would be disarmed and allowed to enter Subic Bay as U.S. Navy ships.[15]

Disarming the ships and reflagging them would take a day and a half. Disarming every passenger—there were more than thirty thousand of them—was time-consuming. But the reflagging was a painful and emotional act. As the South Vietnamese flag was brought down, everyone sang the Vietnamese national anthem. Following a moment of silence, the U.S. flag was raised. They all wept, because the act signified that South Vietnam as a country no longer existed. They had lost their homeland. They had lost their pride; their flag was no longer recognized. If they did not openly weep, they wept on the inside because they felt that something just got torn apart and could not be replaced.

The navy convoy finally entered Subic Bay on 7 May. Three ships were moved to a pier where evacuees were offloaded and immediately directed to Military Sealift Command ships for transportation to Guam, the second leg of their voyage. The evacuees on the other ships spent two nights in a temporary refugee camp set up on Grande Island before boarding other vessels to Guam.

The Philippines were just a stop on a long journey to the unknown, for no one knew their final destination at that time. Now that they had lost their country, who would open their arms to accept them?

The American Challenger

Phú Quốc Island, situated in the Gulf of Thailand, is about 120 kilometers (80 miles) east of the seaport of Rạch Giá, the largest town in Southwest Vietnam. Access to the island was through one of the many boats that ferried people, food and animals between Rạch Giá and the island. Phú Quốc was known for its nước mắm, a pungent fermented fish sauce that Vietnamese used to flavor their food. The rich fishing grounds offshore provide the anchovy catch from which the prized sauce is made.

The 50-by-25-kilometer island has been claimed by both Cambodia and Vietnam, although the Vietnamese had settled it since the eighteenth century during their southward migration. In the 1970s, its population was 30,000 people. With the communists invading South Vietnam, refugees from central Vietnam to Phú Quốc who were transported by ships, like the American Challenger, doubled overnight the population of the island. They were housed in camps that were once used to hold communist prisoners. These war prisoners having been released to North Vietnam after the 1973 Peace Accords, the camps were vacant.

On 30 April, after President Minh announced Saigon's surrender on the radio, islanders' reactions varied from utter disbelief to resignation, pain and anger. For the islanders who were used to travel from the island back to Vietnam or to neighboring countries, this would not be a new experience, although it would be a definitive one. They would cross the ocean for good and might not have the chance to return to Vietnam again. For many refugees coming from central Vietnam, they just shook their heads in disbelief for they had once been displaced already; the next trip should be a *déjà vu* experience. They knew that Phú Quốc was just a temporary stop, but what would the next objective be? They did not know or dared not think about it, because they were at that time at the southernmost end of Vietnam. Between the world and the island was the wild ocean. Would they be willing to take the next big step? It would be a step across the ocean, where they had never ventured before.

Torn between the call to remain in their homeland with their past and the fear of the communists, many did not know. Seeing other people rushing to the shore, they followed them. Once there, they boarded any boat that would take them—there was a lot of competition for the small number of boats available—to get out to the sea and to the unknown.

Close by, at the navy compound, officers, soldiers and their families could board speedboats that used to patrol the coastline watching for smugglers and communists who would transport armament and military supplies to the nearby port of Sihanoukville in Cambodia. By the time we (including the present author) arrived at the dock, only a few craft were left. With the skipper's permission, we jumped into one that was about to take off, and the boat darted away. Nearby was the military airbase, above which circled all kinds of aircraft that tried to land on the island's lone airport. From a distance, they looked like a swarm of locusts ready to land on a crop field. The place was already full of airplanes; some of them were even parked on the seashore. We had never seen that many planes trying to land at such a small airport.

Twenty-one years had passed since the partition of Vietnam into two states, during which the evacuees had grown up, studied, and worked in a war-ravaged country. Signs of war were everywhere: on the walls, in newspapers, in movies and songs, and especially on human faces. A feeling of sadness, despair, and fatigue could be perceived on each face, although it was hidden behind an Asian mask of serene acceptance. By escaping, they were without a country. An hour earlier, they were all connected and linked to a land called South Vietnam. Then, suddenly, there was no more South Vietnam. What they had called Motherland or Fatherland no longer existed. What they had cherished the most was lost.

They did not know where they were going or what their future would be. They did not know where this boat was heading to—Thailand, Indonesia...—but they did not care as long as it carried them out of reach of the communists. They were all attached to their country as long as it was free of communism. Now that this sacred land was turned over to the communists, there was no land to fight for. The choices were either to accept communism or to run away. Having known the communists and what they could do, they chose to escape.

The boat kept powering ahead. Even the roaring of the engine did not distract them from their deep thoughts. There was total silence besides the engine noise and the sound of waves crashing against the sides of the boat. The island gradually became a dot on the horizon. They had traveled for half an hour or an hour when suddenly in the middle of the ocean stood a four- to five-story-tall ship that was surrounded by a dozen small boats of all kinds: speedboats, fishing boats. It turned out to be—we realized later—the *American Challenger*, the boat that had been delivering the refugees to Phú Quốc a month earlier. She must have been lingering around and was finally ordered by the U.S. government to pick up the people from the area. The escapees were lucky to find her, otherwise they would have been forced to travel on this speedboat all the way to Thailand or Malaysia.

The sun was high in the cloudless sky. The sea was calm, and a light breeze greeted the evacuees. The speedboat docked against a row of boats that had arrived earlier and had not been moved away after their passengers moved to the ship deck. Each evacuee in turn climbed up the gangway. Since the crowd was of a reasonable number, there was no pushing or shoving. Elderly people and children were allowed to get up first. A few scarred women were helped up the ladder. For many, this was the first time they had climbed a gangway in their lives. The transfer proceeded slowly, and by the end of the day, everyone was boarded and settled in various places, either in the hold or on the deck of the ship itself. They were offered food and soon fell asleep, stressed and depressed by the turn of events.[16]

What a day it had been. The night before, they had slept in a warm bed in their homeland. That night, they were for the first time homeless and sleeping on a hard and cold deck somewhere on the ocean. The only thing they could claim was the starry sky as roof: a dark and silent sky dotted with scintillating stars that contrasted with their deep sorrow and anguish. In spite of the unusual situation, they slept pretty well because of the day's commotion and fatigue.

They woke up well rested and wondered about their location on the ocean. They realized that the ship had hugged the coastline during the night and was heading north, which they did not understand. A northward direction suggested a return to Saigon, while an eastward direction meant the Philippines, thus freedom. They just worried that the ship would turn them over to the new communist government.

By the end of the second day, they arrived in front of Vũng Tàu, at the mouth of the Saigon River but outside Vietnam's territorial waters and close to half a dozen of U.S. Seventh Fleet ships and a myriad of smaller boats. The area turned out to be the meeting place of all the evacuation ships before they headed for their final destination. The rescue work continued for a while, as flotillas of refugee boats kept coming from the Vũng Tàu area and converged on the anchored ships. Boats of all sizes and shapes, some civilian others military, filled with people, surrounded the ships. There were fishing boats, ferry boats, trawlers, tugboats, and military vessels. Anything that could float was put to use.

After picking up its share of people, the *American Challenger* sailed again, this time heading east with more than 7,000 people crammed on board. A heavy weight had been lifted off the evacuees' chests because an eastward direction surely meant freedom. The ship was crowded with anxious women holding onto their children, elderly people walking slowly, sad looking soldiers still in their uniforms, and people clutching their meager belongings in their hands. They would be fine if they were still actively walking or moving, but the majority huddled in groups or lay on the deck scattered here and there, staring at the horizon, submerged in their thoughts and barely speaking to one another, their minds a hundred kilometers away from that place and focused on the past, future, survival, and families.

This was the image of extreme despair and anguish: a group of defeated people who in the matter of a few days had lost everything:

houses, jobs, belongings, land, bank accounts, and country and were trying to assess the damage and to figure out the future. Who would have thought that they would have to leave everything behind for a bleak and uncertain future? There was no choice: although attachment to their lands, ancestral graves, friends, and possessions was strong, they had to think of their safety. Ancestral graves were the strongest bond for these people who cultivated kinship values like filial piety, family loyalty, and continuity of the family lineage. Abandoning the graves was tantamount to a desertion, because as offspring of these people, their job was to care for these graves. Who would care for the graves now that they were gone? The 1620 European pilgrims had been better prepared, for they at least knew where they were going. They planned ahead and brought provisions with them, while the 1975 Vietnamese evacuees just ran away with the clothes on them.

That night, they slept well again, certain they would not be returned to the new communist government. The following day, the ship sailed through a series of islands, which they believed to be part of the Philippines. The view was certainly beautiful and unique to this region. A few fishing boats were seen close to the islands' shores, while dolphins frolicked in the sparkling blue waters. Here and there another ocean liner passed the ship by. And people on the other ship must have wondered why this ship was loaded with so many people.

The evacuees settled into a boring routine broken only by mealtimes. The sea appeared immense, as no other ship was seen in the vicinity for many days. The skipper could have put his ship on automatic control, gone to bed for a few hours, and returned to the control room without seeing any change in the scenery. The days were hot, as the bright and shining sun cooked them like meat in the oven. They were totally unprepared for the ocean trip and the harsh sun: no one had thought about bringing hats or anything that could shield them from the sun. There was no place to hide except in the hold, where they could hide in the shade but not from the heat itself. At least on the deck, the cool ocean breeze brought some respite from the weather, while the lack of circulating air kept the heat steady and sometimes rising in the hold. Nights were tolerable and beautiful under the starry sky. The weather was gorgeous throughout the trip. The absence of storms prevented the evacuees from getting cold from the combined effects of heat and dampness. Toward the end of the trip, due to the closeness of the quarters, an epidemic of conjunctivitis (pinkeye) rapidly spread among the evacuees, who woke up with swollen, red, itchy, and teary eyes. Luckily, it was short lived, because the crowd was rapidly dispersed following their arrival.[17]

USNS Greenville Victory

The USNS *Greenville Victory*, which was launched in 1944, served as a commercial cargo ship during World War II. It was acquired by the navy in 1950 and assigned to the Military Seat Transportation Service (MSTS) for use during the Korean and Vietnam wars. She was sold for scrapping in 1983.

Since mid–April, Ambassador Martin had advocated the use of Vũng Tàu, one hundred twenty kilometers east of Saigon, as an escape site for a large number of Vietnamese, provided that the highway linking Saigon and Vũng Tàu was kept open. A Military Sealift Command had directed half a dozen merchant ships (among them, the *Contender* and *Greenville Victory*) to move closer to shore to pick up Vietnamese evacuees.

On 28 April, USNS *Greenville Victory* was anchored five kilometers south of Vũng Tàu. As enemy troops moved closer to Vũng Tàu, about 200 boats left the seaport at 10:00 hours but were intercepted by Vietnamese navy gunships. Some of these boats came through the blockade and were picked up by the ship. In early evening enemy troops bombarded Vũng Tàu, causing the ship to move further out to the sea for safety. Many more boats rushed to sea, forcing the *Greenville* to use cargo nets to lift the evacuees.

By afternoon the following day, the ship had picked up its assigned capacity of 6,000 people. It was forced to pull up the anchor and moved away, but boats continued to follow the ship. The captain received permission to pick up additional evacuees, the total of which rose to 10,000. They were pressed like sardines, spilling out of the hold into all corners of the ship.

It was estimated that 60,000 evacuees were picked up from Vũng Tàu by 2 May, when the evacuation ships were ordered to stop picking any more people and to head to the Philippines, leaving behind hundreds of abandoned and drifting vessels.[18]

Harold Murphy, a third mate on the *Greenville Victory*, which picked up six thousand people in Vũng Tàu and dropped them off in Subic Bay in the Philippines, said of the South Vietnamese,

> They are industrious people, great people; they work hard, they don't want welfare, want to work and send their children to school. One of them, I think, graduated top of his class at one of the military academies.... I felt very strongly when I was there that—you could almost see it in their eyes—"Why did you abandon us? Why did the Americans leave us?" But not with animosity. It was like a kid who would look at his father, "Why did you hit me?"[19]

On the afternoon of 30 April, Task Force 76 and the MSC group moved away from the Vietnamese coastline, all the while picking up more seaborne refugees. This effort continued the following day. Finally, when this human tide ceased on the evening of 2 May, the ships set sail for reception centers in the Philippines and Guam: Task Force 76, carrying 6,000 passengers; the MSC flotilla of *Sgt. Truman Kimbro, Sgt. Andrew Miller, Greenville Victory, Pioneer Contender, Pioneer Commander, Green Forest, Green Port, American Challenger,* and *Boo Heung Pioneer*, with 60,000 evacuees; and the Vietnamese navy group, with more than 30,000 evacuees.

The fully loaded *Pioneer Commander* and *American Challenger* set sail to Guam first on the early hours of 3 May. The *Pioneer Contender* had to unload 2,000 evacuees at Grande Island, the Philippines, before heading to Guam. The rest of the MSC ships followed later.[20] The *Pioneer Commander* would have been the first MSC ship to arrive at Guam except for an old naval tradition that allowed the senior skipper in a convoy to enter port first. En route, the *Pioneer Commander* was ordered to slow down to allow the senior captain, Bouchie of the *American Challenger*, to reach port first. The *Challenger* arrived at 01:15 on 7 May and dropped 5,200 evacuees before departing before dawn. The *Pioneer Commander* arrived at 08:00 the same day and deposited 4,678 passengers.[21]

Thus ended the U.S. Navy's role in the 21-year American effort to aid the Republic of Vietnam in its desperate fight for survival.

4

Guam's Preparations

The amazing fact was that out of this disorganized episode, 130,000 people escaped the communist conquest. That escape was validated years later by their avoidance of the terror and repression imposed by the communists on those who were unfortunate enough to remain in South Vietnam. An eastward escape through the open seas eventually landed them on the island of Guam.

Guam's History

The Papal Bull "Inter Caetera," issued by Pope Alexander VI on 4 May 1493, divided the world known to the Church between Spain and Portugal. It established a demarcation line one hundred leagues west of the Azores and Cape Verde Islands and assigned Spain the rights to acquire territorial possessions and to trade in all lands west of that line. This edict gave Spain the monopoly of the New World.[1]

The 1494 Treaty of Tordesillas reserved for Portugal the eastern routes around Africa, and Vasco da Gama and the Portuguese arrived first in India in 1498. To find a westward route to Maluku Island (Island of Spices), King Charles I of Spain in 1519 sent an expedition led by the Portuguese Ferdinand Magellan around Cape Horn to the Pacific Ocean. In 1521, Magellan first discovered the island of Guam, which is part of the Marianas, a series of fifteen islands that form a north-south archipelago 500 miles long. It lies 800 miles north of the equator, 1,500 miles east of the Philippines, and 1,500 miles southeast of Japan. It sits on top of a submerged volcano, the base of which is 37,800 feet below in the Marianas Trench.

Guam is 30 miles long and 4 to 8 miles wide, and is presently a territory of the U.S. Its population is 80,000, one third of which are military and their dependents. It has played a strategic role to maritime powers in the Pacific throughout history because of its topography and unique location. In the vast expanse of the northwest Pacific Ocean, it is the only high island with a protected major harbor and sufficient land for several airports.

The indigenous people called members of their high caste *chamorri*; the Spanish used the word *chamurres*, which over the years became *chamorro*. The old Spanish word *chamorro* stands for "bold" or "shorn" ("headless" in Portuguese), which described some natives who wore a topknot on an otherwise shaved head.[2]

Although Magellan discovered the island, he never gave it a name. Pigafetta, his recorder, noticing how swift the Chamorros were able to take a skiff away from one of the boats, called them "ingenious and great thieves." Magellan later, when pressed for a name, called the group of islands the Islas de los Ladrones (Islands of the Thieves).[3] The misunderstanding was due to cultural difference. The Europeans were not aware of the local Pacific custom whereby new arrivals present gifts to their hosts, who can take whatever they wish from the newcomers. On the other hand, the Spanish cherished their own properties, and in their customs, no one could take anything away without their permission. These cultural differences later led to tragic Spanish-Chamorro confrontations. Later, another Spanish explorer, Legazpi, referred to the island as *Goaam*, *Goam*, or *Guan*, as used by the natives. The name then evolved into *Guana* and *Guahan*. Finally in 1908, the Americans designated the island as *Guam*.[4]

Magellan's expedition left Guam and sailed westward toward the Philippines and then to the Indian Ocean, around Africa and back to Spain on 8 September 1522. Although Magellan did not complete the whole voyage because he was killed in the Philippines, he was credited as being the first European to circumnavigate around the globe.

Through the treaty of Zaragoza in 1529, the Spanish king Charles V, who was competing with the Portuguese for the rights to the Spice Islands, was able to claim the Philippines, Micronesia and Guam for Spain, leaving the Portuguese with the Spice Islands and most of Indonesia. From that time onward, the Spanish acquired then stored their oriental goods in Manila, the Philippines. The goods were transported in June and July by big galleons through the northern Pacific route to Acapulco, Mexico, and then across Mexico and the Atlantic to Spain. The safer alternative—from Manila to Spain through the Straits of Malacca, the Indian Ocean and around Africa—was blocked by the Portuguese under the Treaties of Tordesillas and Zaragoza. The Spanish westbound galleons began in March in Acapulco and went straight to Manila; they sailed through the Marianas, usually without stopping in Guam, leaving the native population almost undisturbed for another three hundred years until the nineteenth century, when whalers, traders and missionaries invaded the region.

The Spanish imprint on Guam would have ended right there had it not been for the zealous Jesuit missionary San Vitores, who upon seeing the free, untamed Chamorros, made up his mind to convert them to the Catholic religion. He first landed on Guam in May 1662 on his way to Manila. Once in Manila, he asked his superior to open a mission in Guam. When the latter declined because of lack of troops to protect the missionaries in Guam, San Vitores wrote to the king of Spain and Queen Mariana for support. Royal edicts supporting the Guam mission, written in June 1665, reached Manila in June 1666. It took two more years of preparation before San Vitores could land at Guam on June 1668 with a support group of fifty people. The missionary then called the archipelago the Marianas in honor of his supporter Queen Mariana, the name that is still used today.

In order to convert as many souls as possible, San Vitores baptized elderly and infants with or without consent of the children's parents. At the first mass in Agana, he baptized 23 children in one group, and 1,500 adults "converted," to be baptized later on after receiving doctrinal instruction. This rapid success drew the first negative reaction from the Chamorros: the Chamorri nobles thought that baptism, which they viewed as a special gift, should be reserved to nobles, not commoners. San Vitores refused to baptize anyone if he could not baptize everyone. Although the Chamorros backed down, resentment began to build up.[5]

To pay respect to elders who had passed away, the Chamorros kept their skulls in their huts. San Vitores began to initiate the destruction of ancestral skulls and carved idols, to the vehement objections of the Chamorros. The resentment slowly turned to hostility, and by November 1669, a year and a half after his landing in Guam, San Vitores realized he no longer could rely on the Chamorros' good will to protect his mission. Other tribes openly fought against the missionaries and the soldiers.

On 11 September 1671, the Chamorros attacked the mission with 2,000 warriors, using slingstones as their main weapons. As they were about to overwhelm the resistance, a typhoon smashed into Guam, causing grave destruction and leading to a peace settlement and the release of Hurao, one of the Chamorro leaders. Under Hurao, the Chamorros returned to the attack for another two weeks before calling for another peace settlement.

While many of the lower castes cooperated with the invaders, welcoming changes and the elevation of status they gained as Christians, the higher castes and women who feared losing their freedom—the

Chamorros are a matriarchal society—rebelled against the Spaniards. The Chamorros began targeting and killing isolated soldiers or priests, while soldiers burned native huts and killed the people in revenge.

In 1672, San Vitores went to the house of a chieftain, Mata'pang, to look for someone. Seeing a newborn baby, he asked for permission to baptize him. The chief refused, but the priest proceeded to baptize the baby. Mata'pang returned with a warrior and killed San Vitores.

San Vitores was both a hero and a saint for the Spanish empire and the Catholic Church. For the Chamorros, San Vitores brought them salvation through conversion but also death at the hands of the Spanish troops. He was viewed as a savior and a conqueror and their "attitudes toward him have all the ambivalence this paradox implies."[6]

The murder of San Vitores called for revenge and unleashed the Spanish-Chamorro War, which lasted from 1672 to 1698. Governor General Juan de Vargas y Hurtado once ordered Joseph de Quiroga, the head of the Spanish military garrisons in the Mariana Islands (1679–1720), to "be particularly solicitous about the pursuit and chastisement of murderers, rebels, and traitors who might impede the spread of the Christian religion."[7] The implacable Quiroga would fulfill these orders to the letter. He pressured villagers to turn in anti–Spanish ringleaders; the Spanish were summarily executed in public. When villagers (supposedly converted Chamorros) burned down a new church in Inapsan in February 1681, then sailed off to Rota in fear of Spanish reprisals, Quiroga went after them, burned their new village and forced them to return to Guam.

In April 1684, the Spanish conquered the island of Saipan, while disaffected Chamorros launched an attack on the Spanish in Agana. The attack was held off by friendly Chamorros from the hills of Sinajana. Battles continued back and forth, causing rapid depopulation of the island; infectious diseases brought by the foreigners contributed to the process. Of the 12,000 Chamorros who lived in Guam in 1668, only 2,000 were left in 1690. For each Christian killed, 100 or more Chamorros died in the war of conquest. As a consequence of their policies, the Spaniards found themselves in a paradox in 1689. They controlled Guam, which was then underpopulated. And despite the efforts of the Jesuits, the majority of Chamorros were not converted to Catholicism.

In 1604, the Spanish writer Miguel Agia described the incompatibility of the Spaniards and the Indians of Peru in words that could also applied to the Chamorros:

> The Spaniard and the Indian are diametrically opposed. The Indian is by nature without greed and the Spaniard is extremely greedy, the Indian phlegmatic and the Spaniard excitable, the Indian humble and the Spaniard

arrogant, the Indian deliberate in all he does and the Spaniard quick in all he wants, the one liking to serve and the other hating to serve.[8]

Quiroga continued to conquer one island after another until 1698, when the last hostile Chamorros retreated to the island of Aguijan. Aguijan has no beaches and rises straight out of the sea with stiff, high cliffs. Quiroga's men climbed the two paths leading to the top. One was blocked, while the Chamorros ferociously defended the other. The Spaniards finally overwhelmed the Chamorros, putting an end to a blood-drenched, thirty-year war. Some defiant Chamorros committed suicide by jumping off the cliffs. The surviving natives were taken to Guam for resettlement.[9]

Pax Hispanica thus descended on the land of the Chamorros for the next two centuries until 1898, when new conquerors would make Guam part of a new empire.

In the meantime, the natives were stripped of their lands and worked as laborers for the crown ranches. Many were forced to do heavy labor at minimal wages (two to three leaves of poor-grade tobacco for a full day's work). Communal ownership by Chamorro families of ancestral properties under Spanish rule devolved into the hands of the new *principalia* class that replaced the old *chamorri* families. Poverty, malnutrition, despair, and loss of work thinned down the native population. Worse, the Chamorros, who did not have any immunity, could not resist the new infectious diseases brought to the island by foreigners. A chicken pox epidemic in 1779 and a flu epidemic in September 1794 killed many natives but few Spaniards or Filipinos. The 1783 census revealed for the first time that there were more non–Chamorros (1,623 people) than pure-blood Chamorros (1,608) in Guam.

The governors, who were not well paid, rewarded themselves from the work of the natives and the markup of imported food items (sugar, tobacco, chocolate, wine, and the like) as well as uniforms and cloth. They also extended loans to Chamorros and soldiers at usurious interest rates.

Governor Tobias (1771–1774) was one of the exceptions. He improved the island's agriculture and encouraged production of cotton, sugarcane, mangoes, pineapples, and vegetables. Seeds and seedlings were brought in from Mexico and the Philippines. He established small cotton gins and looms to make cloth. He brought in a herd of deer from the Philippines and set them free. The deer survived and are still hunted on Guam. He created a 200-man militia, paid them a small but regular salary, and had them raise crops on crown lands in place of the forced labor by the Chamorros.

4. Guam's Preparations

A French explorer, Crozet, whose crew recuperated from a severe episode of scurvy on Guam, dutifully noted the work of Tobias. A French priest, Raynal, in Paris, read Crozet's notes. As an antimonarchist, he incorporated the notes into his book decrying the Spaniards' ruthless exploitation of the Chamorros but praising Tobias as a model exception. Raynal's book, published in 1778 became a bestseller. When Manila became aware of Raynal's history in 1785, the Spanish dismissed Tobias, whose wife left him because he fell out of favor. Tobias was reduced to despair and returned to Spain in total obscurity. The moral of the story is that no good deed goes unpunished.[10]

"In the long sweep of Guam's history, Joseph de Quiroga ranks second only to Father San Vitores among the individuals who had the most direct personal impact on the tragic destiny of the Chamorro people."[11] Without Quiroga, the Spanish would never have been able to control the Chamorros of the Marianas.

By 1798, one hundred years after the Spanish resettled all the Chamorros from the northern Marianas to Guam, the traditional Chamorro culture had changed a lot, although the language and maternal control of family life endured. The natives, who were no longer allowed to roam freely on the seas on their proas, became docile peasants who slowly lost the art of sailing. On Guam they were known as "lazy, indolent, and ignorant," but once abroad they became "good workers ... the Chamorro away from his island is a lamp brightening a stranger's door."[12]

Because Spain was engaged in the Napoleonic wars with France from 1806 to 1814 and had to deal with its revolution-convulsed South American possessions from 1808 until 1824, its other colonies were more neglected than before. Guam was left in the hands of incompetent and often abusive governors who drove the economy further downhill. The island survived by welcoming supply ships, a few whalers, and some scientific expedition ships.

In February 1856, an American merchant schooner arrived at Apra Harbor from Manila. Although one passenger had died of smallpox aboard, the ship was only quarantined for three days before releasing its passengers. Unchecked, the disease spread rapidly on Guam despite frantic efforts by the Spanish to contain it. By August it had spread to the whole island. By November 1856, the epidemic had wiped out 5,534 people of all ages, or over 60 percent of its population of 8,775. The whole island was in visible despair.

Then came a royal order in 1857 to build a prison on the island for civilian convicts. The governor dutifully transformed the old barracks of the Agana presidio into a prison. The Philippines then sent 63 convicts, so "violent, sick, and weak" that they were returned to Manila. In the 1870s, Madrid, being convulsed by severe internal political problems, sent 1,200 political prisoners to the island. Since it was difficult to escape from the island, they were allowed to roam free, living, working, and spreading dangerous political ideas among the unsuspecting Chamorros. An investigation into the killing of an unpopular governor by a Chamorro guard revealed a plan to overthrow the government.

Insurrections in the Philippines in August 1896 sent scores of political prisoners to Guam. As some of them knew the weakness of the penal colony, they tried to escape through the roof of the barracks in December. Caught the first day, they tried again the following day. This time the scared guards panicked and blasted volley after volley of fire into the prisoners. The carnage ended with eighty dead and forty-five wounded.

As the Spaniards were limping toward the end of their second century of colonization of Guam, their main legacy remained Catholicism, which became the bedrock religion that allowed the natives to survive through the neglected and incompetent Spanish system of government. However, behind the *patron* system with its privilege and elitism—family ties and macho enthusiasm for military service—the Chamorro identity, with its language and matrilocal orientation, still persists.[13]

Bitten by a colonialist fever, the U.S. Congress declared war on Spain on 25 April 1898, following which Commodore Dewey destroyed many Spanish warships in Manila Bay on 1 May. Captain Glass, USN, captured the Island of Guam on 21 June before leading a convoy of troops to the Philippines. President McKinley annexed Hawaii in July 1898 (American businessmen overthrew Queen Liliuokalani in 1893) and in December made an offer of $20 million to Spain for all the Philippines. The Treaty of Paris, signed by Spain on 10 December 1898, granted Guam to the United States as a colony. There was, however, no mention of Guam's sovereignty or the rights of the Chamorro people.

The same day, Spain turned over to Germany the Marshall and Caroline islands, including Palau and all the Marianas other than Guam. During World War I, Japan declared war on Germany on 23 August 1914 and seized the islands of German Micronesia. Japan would use these islands to launch their Pacific war during World War II.

For the next four and a half decades, until 1941, Guam languished as an American outpost under the control of the Navy Department and was led by "hardworking, sometimes capable, sometimes obtuse naval officers" as governors and acting governors of Guam.[14]

The 1940 census showed a total of 23,067 people, of which 21,502 were of Chamorro descent. Agricultural production had increased. There was electricity and other amenities, although the island possessed only eighty-five miles of roads, all of crushed limestone. The majority of the people depended on government support. Illiteracy increased to 17 percent in people over age ten. Use of the Chamorro language in public school was forbidden. The death rate fell from 27.8 per 1,000 persons in 1905 to 11.7 in 1940, but the navy failed to improve local civil liberties, governmental standards, and strategic defense of the island. That failure in the end rested on the U.S. Congress, which has the "authority and responsibility to ensure democratic government in all U.S territorial dependencies."[15]

On 8 December 1941, Japan began bombing Guam, then sent 5,000 troops on 10 December to invade the island, which was guarded by a few hundred navy troops. The Japanese were brutal, bayoneting everyone on their path: men, women, and children. Guam surrendered the same day. The American prisoners were sent to concentration camps in Japan, while native men were forced to do heavy construction, to build roads, bunkers, and an airport and to work as stevedores or miners; women and children were used as field workers.

The Americans counterattacked on 21 July 1944 with a 3:1 advantage in troops (54,891 against an estimated 18,500). The bloody battle lasted almost three weeks, during which the Americans suffered 1,769 casualties compared to 18,377 Japanese. Another 1,250 Japanese were taken as prisoners. During the next three decades, 114 stragglers surrendered. Sergeant Shoichi Yokoi, the last straggler, surrendered in January 1972, twenty-six and a half years after the war ended.[16]

The rapid demobilization following the end of the war drastically changed the landscape. There were 201,718 military personnel and 21,838 civilians on 31 August 1945. By mid–June 1946, military personnel dropped down to 36,923, an 82 percent reduction. Military surplus items such as Quonset huts, barracks, jeeps, trucks, weapons, fuels, canned food, and supplies were auctioned off. Vehicles and military trash, abandoned because the cost of disposing it was too great, transformed the island into a huge junkyard.

The navy wanted 75,700 acres, or 55 percent, of the island to be able to provide defense and security for the area. It already owned 28,345 acres and wanted to acquire 29,460 acres at $54 per acre. The remainder of 17,895 acres was to be leased from Guamanian owners for $0.60 per acre.

On 7 September 1949, President Truman formally transferred administration of Guam to the Department of the Interior effective 1 July 1950, ending 277 years of military government on the island since the death of Father San Vitores. The 1950 Organic Act of Guam (an act of the United States Congress that establishes a territory of the United

States) was signed into law by President Truman on 1 August 1950 but made effective as of 21 July.

Guam Memorial Hospital (GMH) was separated from the Naval Hospital in 1950, and a new GMH was dedicated in 1956. It was only in 1972 that English and Chamorro were accepted as the two official languages in school. U.S. citizenship was granted to natives born after 11 April 1899. The Organic Act of 1950 granted limited self-rule to Guamanians. The new Guam International Air Terminal was dedicated on 5 March 1966.

In 1892, Asan Beach was the site of a leper colony, which was utilized for eight years until it was destroyed by a typhoon. Then in 1901, this land turned into a prison camp for exiled Filipino insurrectionists. In 1922, Asan Point became a U.S. Marine Corps camp with a quartermaster depot, a small arms range, and barracks. It was used as headquarters and barracks for the U.S. Navy Seabees who helped to reconstruct the island. Then from 1948 to 1967 it was the "Civil Service Camp." In essence, it was a small military base with housing, an outdoor theater, tennis courts and a fire station. In 1968, the navy converted the buildings into a hospital annex for use during the Vietnam War.[17]

The site had been a leper colony (1892–1900), the Presidio of Asan (1902–1903), a Marine camp (1922–1931), Camp Asan (1945–1947), a civil service camp (1948–1967), a navy hospital annex (1968–1975), and finally a Vietnamese refugee camp (part of Operation New Life, which relocated South Vietnamese after the fall of Saigon) in 1975. All of the buildings once located here were destroyed by Supertyphoon Pamela in 1976 and subsequently removed. In 1978, the property was acquired by the National Park Service and turned into the War in the Pacific National Historical Park.

The Asan Beach Unit consists of 109 land acres and 445 water acres and is the site of the northern landing beaches. It was here that the Third Marine Division came ashore on 21 July 1944 for the initial assault and was met by troops of the Japanese 320th Independent Infantry Battalion. War-related structures and sites, all associated with Japanese defenses, are located at Asan Point and Adelup Point.

Battered by the 1973 worldwide Arab oil embargo, Guam—like the U.S. and South Vietnam—sank into recession in 1974 when oil and gasoline prices rose and the flow of tourism to Guam dwindled.

Late in 1974, Paul Bordallo was elected governor of Guam. When taking office in January 1975, he imposed a 25 percent cut in all department budgets and a freeze on government hiring. New investments evaporated, the consumer price index rose, and unemployment jumped to 8.3 percent in May 1975. This was the time when the Vietnamese evacuees reached the island. Federal subsidies kept the island afloat financially in the middle and late 1970s. By 1978–1979, these funds totaled $424.3 million or $4,000 for every man, woman, and child.

The first planeload of Vietnamese evacuees on a Flying Tigers Airline jet landed at the civilian international terminal in mid–April. The aircraft was impounded. After a week of bureaucratic confusion, Washington authorized the evacuation of Vietnamese through Guam. The flow of evacuees began arriving at Andersen Air Force Base on 23 April 1975.[18]

Preparations and Action

On 5 April 1975, as the war was winding down in Vietnam, the Commander in Chief, Pacific (CINCPAC), asked its representative in Guam and the Trust Territory of the Pacific islands (CINCPACREP GUAM/TTPI) about its capability for accommodating refugees pending onward movement. The number of refugees was estimated to be 100,000.

The Guam representative answered that bedding and support could be available for 12,900 people for ten days at Camp Asan and Andersen Air Force Base (AFB). The small staff of CINCPAC GUAM/TTPI, which consisted of 24 officers and 51 enlisted men, turned to on-island commands for assistance and resolution of planning objectives. On 7 April, it was asked again about the availability and location of refugee support material.

On 13 April, the Joint Chiefs of Staff (JCS) authorized CINCPAC to assist in the evacuation of Americans and other evacuees from Vietnam to safe havens designated by the secretary of state. On 18 April, CINCPAC GUAM/TTPI issued the tasking for evacuation planning actions, including the roles of the staff.

On 21 April, the JCS outlined a planning concept for logistics including medical support. CINCPAC was also advised about the typhoon season from 1 May to 30 November and the rainy season from 1 July to 30 November.

The withdrawal of U.S. nationals and eligible parolees was by aircraft from Saigon to Clark AFB in the Philippines, where they were held pending onward processing. On 23 April, CINCPAC advised that Guam was the designated staging area for evacuees from Guam and that flights to Clark AFB were to cease. Planning then became execution.[19]

In Vietnam at that time, the battle of Xuân Lộc on the outskirts of Saigon had just ended but Saigon had not fallen yet.

The Guamanians did not know much about the arrival of the Vietnamese on the island until the *Pacific Daily News*, the local newspaper, leaked excerpts of a letter sent by Secretary of State Henry Kissinger to Governor Richard Bordallo:

> There is no reason to believe large number of Vietnamese will remain on Guam.... We have already secured parole authority from Congress for the admission of large groups of these refugees to the United States, and are rushing immigration and consular officers to Guam to process these people as rapidly as we can.... Representatives of American humanitarian volunteer agencies will be arriving to assist in locating sponsors for the [evacuees]. We are also actively engaging organizations such as the U.N. (United Nations) High Commissioner for Refugees and the International Commission for European Migration to arrange resettlement in third world countries for many of these refugees....[20]

The Guam legislature, after an intense and emotional debate, passed a resolution on 18 April offering Guam only as a temporary safe haven. On 25 April, it passed another resolution requesting Governor Bordallo to "reconsider and reassess" his offer for permanent residency to 25,000 evacuees.[21]

The local newspaper also found out that a certain number of Americans, while they were in Saigon, had been offered bribes ranging from $600 to as much as $7,000 to help the Vietnamese get out of the country. There were also reports that evacuees had brought gold plates sewn into coat linings through customs. Unofficial sources also claimed that some people could not pass through the airport metal detector and were later found to have gold bullion shaped into cylinders hidden in their rectums.[22]

CINCPAC GUAM/TTPI terminated all leaves and vacations and recalled personnel to work. All except the most vital tasks were suspended. A communication system was established to keep all commanders informed.

The Naval Construction Battalion (Seabees) stopped all work and reported to the two major areas: Orote Point and Camp Asan, where camps were being built or renovated. The first contingent, at Orote Point, began clearing 600 acres of tropical jungle that had been growing on the old Japanese airfield.

The second contingent headed to Camp Asan to renovate the twenty abandoned barracks-type corrugated tin buildings. Deserted and abandoned for three years, the buildings had missing electrical fixtures, broken plumbing and appliances, and were cluttered with tons of trash and debris. It was estimated that it would take the crew ten days of around-the-clock work and half a million dollars to fix them. First, they had to clear the debris in and around the buildings and tear down all the damaged walkways. Civilian engineers from the Power and Water Company reconnected all the wiring, installed plumbing, and strung up telephone lines. Work was speeding up, with the goal of delivering four ready buildings the following day, 24 April by 18:00 hours.

At the other end of the island, Air Force personnel rehabilitated the forty galvanized tin buildings comprising "Tin City." The camp would eventually house four thousand evacuees.[23]

As Guam and Wake Island were chosen as safe havens in the Pacific, the army was tasked with providing necessary forces to handle the largest refugee group ever settled on Guam. The Orote Point camp, as it was called, eventually processed 112,000 refugees and at its peak housed 40,000 people. The air force also managed a center at Andersen AFB and the navy, several sites in Guam. The Wake Island refugee center was operated by a civilian contractor under the supervision of Commander in Chief, Pacific Air Force.

Two thousand army personnel along with two hundred members of the Women's Army Corps (WAC) participated in the reception and triage effort. The First Medical Group, from Fort Sam Houston, Texas, arrived on Guam on 26 April, followed on the next day by the 25th Infantry Division Task Force, the 45th Support Group Command Element, and the First Battalion, Fifth Infantry. It was this group that erected the tents, the mess halls, the aid stations, and hospitals and other support facilities that would become the Orote Point refugee center.

Guam, which housed only 80,000 people, would double its population in just a few weeks. The islanders, who depended on the U.S. mainland for most things, from food to cars, must have thought that the doubling of the population could lead to potential scarcity of food, utilities, and jobs. This period, therefore, would forever change the lives of the Guamanians, as it would test their hard work, resilience, good will, and generosity.

For navy captain Richard (Dick) Wyttenbach, that period was unique, as civilians and military personnel in Guam were overwhelmed by the sudden flow of people that descended on the tiny island that spring and summer of 1975. Guamanians—who were used to catastrophic natural disasters—were surprised and afraid that the island would "sink" under the weight of new arrivals. In fact, many had expected that the evacuees would stop and get screened at Subic Base, an American navy base in the Philippines, which was strategically closer to Vietnam than Guam. As a port, Subic Base was also much bigger than Apra Harbor, Guam, and could easily handle thirty of the evacuee ships without any problem. However, they did not expect the strong objection of Filipino President Ferdinand Marcos to the arrival of the Vietnamese evacuees.

In 1975, Captain Wyttenbach was the liaison between Rear Admiral G. Steve Morrison (the representative of Commander, Naval Forces Marianas (COMNAV-MAR), CINCPAC, on Guam) and Guam's civilian government, led by Governor Ricardo Bordallo. He first witnessed the arrival of children from Operation Baby Lift, who were dazed, disoriented, and frightened. Then on 23 April 1975 came the word to execute Operation New Life, a program designed to receive, support, and process evacuees as they came out of Indochina. No one, however, knew the exact number. He then wondered how to execute the order when he had no money to embark on necessary preparations and pay for their expenses. As Congress had not appropriated the needed funding, Morrison told Wyttenbach to keep the planned arrival quiet and to meet with Bordallo.

When the excited but nervous Wyttenbach drove to the governor's mansion that morning—it was 05:00 hours local time—he found the governor already awake. As he began explaining about the arrival of the Vietnamese evacuees, Bordallo told him that Secretary Kissinger had already contacted him the night before to ask him to allow the Vietnamese to transit on the island before heading out to the mainland. Bordallo, without hesitation and without even contacting the island's legislature, responded affirmatively. A highly charismatic politician and businessman in the first year of his governorship, he showed no fear and strongly believed he could do it. A success could only burnish his image locally and nationally.

Wyttenbach was elated, for he did not have to explain to Bordallo the many details concerning Operation New Life, which was not only a significant event for the tiny island but might also pose a major economic burden for the local economy. Since the U.S., Guam included, was in a recession at that time, many mainland governors were reluctant to support Operation New Life, and some had openly refused to take the evacuees.

When Wyttenbach told Bordallo about his need for funds, the governor assured him of the local government's financial assistance. How could the good-hearted governor be so bold as to commit himself and his legislature to a mission that Guam was not used to nor prepared for? Kissinger expected the arrival of 20,000–40,000 people; the final count of 130,000 would dwarf everyone's imagination. Had the governor known the true numbers, he probably would have asked for more details before committing himself to the mission.

Armed with the governor's assurance, Wyttenbach began running around looking for ways to house thousands of evacuees. He found one

4. Guam's Preparations

vacant hotel and requisitioned unused civilian and military buildings and commercial buildings, especially Butler buildings, which were used to house temporary workers. But Guam, as an isolated island in the Pacific Ocean with an average-sized naval station, did not have a lot of vacant buildings. He also asked the companies who owned these buildings to absorb the cost of feeding the evacuees until he could get the food service in place and running and acquire the funds from Washington, D.C.

The Tokyu Hotel was one of the first buildings requisitioned. Closed a year earlier, in 1974, it was rented by the navy. Cleaned, stocked and reopened by personnel from the Navy Communications station, it soon housed close to 1,000 people.

Camp Asan—a World War II hospital annex located on the western side of the island and comprising 15 barracks—was built in the shape of an arc and overlooked the beach. It was in a state of disuse and ill repair, with debris littering the streets and overgrown grass. The walls needed painting and the light fixtures were missing. The Seabees[24] arrived at Camp Asan on 23 April and began cleaning the camp, the barracks, and reconnecting the light fixtures. By working all night, they were able to fix and deliver four barracks the following day to allow the first evacuees to move in.

The new occupants were processed, oriented and assigned living areas depending on the size of their families. They also found blankets, sleeping gear, and food awaiting them. Those who were tired were allowed to sleep, while others were led to the mess hall to soothe their hunger pains. In the meantime, the Seabees continued their work, and the following day, 25 April, Camp Asan had 5,000 people.

These areas, which had a total capacity of a few thousand beds, were rapidly taken by the first arrivals. As in any military town, not many buildings stayed unused for a long time. Next, Wyttenbach looked for a place to raise huge tents, some of which could house a hundred people. Orote Point on the western side of the island, along with the abandoned World War II Japanese airstrip, were selected as sites for a large tent city.

To a directive from Washington that RADM Morrison respond by the "close of business," Wyttenbach simply responded, "We never close here—we function 24 hours a day." Local citizens were urged to volunteer to help the newcomers in some way or another. The Red Cross lent its assistance. Drivers were requested to transport the evacuees from one place to another. They soon had to work overtime because of increasing demands and arrivals that came at any time of the day or night. Although tired, they did not mind, because they were happy to help out. Teachers were called in to teach hygiene, reading, writing, math, geography, and especially English.

Đào Đức was a merchant marine and a navy reservist from Saigon. He knew it would be bad for him if he were captured by the communists. He got on a ship that departed when President Minh surrendered on 30 April. He went to Singapore, then to Subic Bay, before arriving on Guam. He found a job on the island and became a Guamanian.

Tony Hua left Saigon with his brother and his brother's son and arrived in Guam on 24 April. Because his brother worked for DAO (Defense Attaché Office), they were able to leave Saigon early. Tony stayed at Camp Asan for more than four months. At age 14, he was young and innocent and did not know anything except that his country was at war. When his brother pushed him into the C-130 that took him to Guam, he thought he was going for a ride before returning home.

When he finally landed in the U.S., he was glad to have left Vietnam for the land of milk and honey. In 1990, he mentioned that he owed a lot to the U.S. military for evacuating him and his family and that he had looked forward to the freedom and challenges he faced in the new country.[25]

On 28 April 1975, the last American airlift of Vietnamese evacuees resumed at Guam after a 36-hour lapse to give officials the time to prepare for the arrival of 8,000 more people a day. During that period, all flights had been diverted to Wake, swelling the local population from 200 to 8,200 people. With the arrival of 821 evacuees in 60 minutes at two Guam airports, immigration officials vowed to improve efforts to move the 20,000 evacuees already in Guam to the mainland. So far, only 1,300, most of them American citizens, had left the island.

About 700 Guam citizens had offered to house refugees in their homes. But officials of the Immigration and Naturalization Service, which had only five representatives in Guam, had confined the evacuees to their camps. Officials estimated that they could clear about 3,200 people in an eight-hour day. But that would leave the evacuee population expanding at the rate of 2,800 a day. Evacuees had to complete forms that could potentially exclude them from entering the U.S. if they had serious criminal records, or a history of subversive activity or insanity. With the completion of these forms, including fingerprinting, refugees would be issued "paroles," which were, in effect, temporary United States residence permits.[26]

Within days, in the place of a vacant jungle rose rows and rows of tents on both sides of the runway. As each tent looked like the other, even with the numbering in front, the evacuees could easily get lost and enter the wrong tent. A new city was born, appropriately called the "Tent City." At its peak, it was bustling with people and housed almost 40,000 evacuees.

Although they were assigned to certain tents, the evacuees often moved to another one to be close to their families or friends. In the new land and with their lack of fluency in English, they found strength and help in numbers. The rapid turnover—once registered, they were moved rapidly either to Camp Asan or the tin city to get ready to catch the plane to the mainland—allowed the rapid reshuffling in the tents. Once assigned to a tent, the first thing the evacuees did was to go to the showers, which many had missed, especially if they came from the big ships. They then lined up at the field kitchens to get their meals. The kitchens at Orote Point were open only twice a day: from 7 to 11 a.m. and 3 to 8 p.m. One cannot blame the administration for not having enough staff to deal the sudden inflow of evacuees and their erratic arrivals. Although the lines were always long, even under the hot tropical sun, the evacuees rapidly learned to line up after the last person in line, which was not their habit in Vietnam.

The drawback of offering only two meals daily in the beginning at Orote Point—without any other place to provide or sell food—was that it may have induced hoarding and extra trips to the dining halls to store food for lunch or a late-night snack. In the tropical weather, the food spoiled fast and got thrown away, causing unnecessary food wasting. This may explain the problem of excess consumption of food above allowance in the beginning, along with food wasting.

Major General Charles F. Minter directed air force activity on the island, while Rear Admiral G. Steve Morrison, the CINCPAC representative on Guam, coordinated the whole program.[27] Daily press conferences were conducted by RADM Morrison. It was a tense time, as no one knew the scope of the mission. A massive coordination between the various branches of the U.S. Armed Forces and the local government, as well as Washington, had to be fine-tuned, a master plan drawn out and vast manpower mobilized. Everyone was in sense "drafted" for this huge endeavor, and the response by volunteers was staggering and remained so throughout the entire operation. "This assignment, even taken in steps, was sheer insanity; how could shelters be built for 100,000 people and an infrastructure including massive medical care and food to feed these people, be put in place in only weeks, then only days, then only hours?" asked Wyttenbach.[28]

Arrivals

The first planeload of evacuees landed at 15:15 hours on 23 April, the same day Wyttenbach reached out to the governor of Guam for help.

When the passengers disembarked, Andersen AFB and Naval Air Station (NAS) Agana personnel had just finished setting up their processing area. Soon the aircraft were landing faster than the processors could accommodate them.

By the end of the second day, 8,162 people had arrived and rapidly filled Andersen AFB's Tin City and NAS Agana's rapidly converted barracks.

Around the clock, planes landed alternatively at Andersen Air Force Base (AFB) and Naval Air Station to unload people rescued by operation Frequent Wind. The flights from Saigon would not end until 28 April. Some 5,000 people arrived each day. Processing included the usual custom clearances, immigration questions, and medical screenings before the tired travelers were served soup and crackers by volunteers and loaded aboard buses for trips to the assigned camps.[29]

By 25 April—the war in Vietnam had not officially ended—more than 14,000 evacuees from Saigon had arrived on Guam, saturating its lodging facilities. On Andersen, they were housed at Tin City, Chapel #2, the gymnasium, the bomb squadron building, the engine shop, the religious education center, Chapel #1 annex and the fabrication shop. Two thousand people were bedded down in the open-air nose docks. At NAS Agana, two thousand more people were housed in BEQ barracks 5, 6, 7 and 8 and in two hangars.

During Operation New Life, the Media Assistance Center issued 328 media passes to members of the major television networks, wire services, and other newsgathering organizations around the world. On 25 April, CINCPACREP GUAM/TTPI began giving daily, then three times weekly, briefings about the operation. The briefings continued until 27 May.

The first refugees arrived at Tent City on 26 April. The first order of business was a bath, by whatever means available. With eight field kitchens in use, there were still long lines. On an average day, nearly $64,000 was spent on ham, pork chops, canned meat, and other foodstuffs for the Orote Point kitchens.[30] In a gesture of friendship, the citizens of the village of Merizo planned a Chamorran fiesta for the refugees at Radio Barrigada, which allowed them to meet local people and Governor Bordallo.[31]

On 26 April, the flow of inbound evacuees exceeded the pace of construction and restoration of shelters. With 20,000 evacuees present on the island, flights were diverted to Wake, which served as a temporary shelter. Three private construction company barracks were leased and immediately occupied by evacuees. Other new camps were opened at sites including the NAS Gym and the Seabee Sports Arena.

After a week of navy operation, army units from the 25th Infantry Division arrived to administer Tent City. Army cooks, engineers, corpsmen, typists, and infantrymen—nearly 2,000—provided support and security for Tent City, while the Marines took care of camp Asan.[32]

By that time, all military personnel and Department of Defense civilians were working on 12-hour shifts, seven days a week. Their wives and teenagers were also volunteering in the camps and processing centers. Many family members, therefore, did not see each other for one whole month.

Rumors began circulating among the local population that Guam food supplies were being depleted because they were diverted for evacuees' needs. Some Guamanians rushed to the stores and bought enough supplies to empty some stores. Military commands took great pains to explain to them that supplies used by evacuees were flown in from off-island and were separate from the civilians' supplies.[33]

By 1 May, the 22 field kitchens at Orote Point Camp were combined to form three large dining areas. Site preparation was 85 percent complete; 77 telephone lines were in operation and 1,800 tents had been erected.

By 7 May 1975, 12 refugee camps were operating across the island. The largest, Tent City at Orote Point, housed 30,427 evacuees. Asan had 5,632 evacuees, Andersen's Tin City had 3,297 evacuees, and 3,175 were spread among other camps. About 3,000 evacuees a day were moving to stateside camps, about 4,000 were arriving on Guam by air, 6,822 had arrived by sea and another 14,000 were en route in other ships. There was a constant influx and outflow of people. To keep a current daily number of evacuees was tricky, if not daunting, especially on an island that was not used to such a large number of simultaneous arrivals and departures. Some ships arrived in the middle of the night and others during daytime, while the arrival and departure times of the military and civilian planes were also unexpected.

By 7 May, the daily influx of refugees reached staggering proportion—13,071 on that date alone—as merchant ships of the Military Sealift Command arrived on Guam.[34] This was one of the largest single-day arrivals of refugees on Guam—enough to overwhelm the handling capability of the reception centers. Each of the ships was loaded to the gills with people who were picked up off the coast of Vietnam and transported directly to Guam. There was no stop in the Philippines, for the reception centers there were already overcrowded. The evacuees were tired and dazed and showed evidence of severe exhaustion, fatigue, and despair after living in cramped and primitive conditions in the cargo holds or on the decks of the ships for one whole week or more.

They were lucky if they were not sick with diarrhea, constipation, or conjunctivitis.

It was hard to live confined to area less than six feet square for a whole week, with no end in sight. There were the same stony faces that looked at them day and night. They could not avoid these unpleasant gazes, to say the least, because of the confined space they were in. After one or two days of getting to know one another, even if they still had the strength or were kind enough to converse with each other, there was nothing else to talk about. The confinement, the insecurity, and the lack of privacy finally weighed on them and put them in a sour mood. There was no place to stretch out, and it was easy to bump into a neighbor. The bed was the hard floor covered with at most a piece of paper or cardboard. They were lucky if they had brought some bedding with them and luckier if the floor was not soiled. Unfortunately, these were not luxury cruise ships, but simple cargo ships that used to carry containers. In this postwar period, the evacuees were handled as human cargo.

There was no explanation from or communication with the ship's crew about the duration of the trip, for the 30-person crew was overwhelmed just to prepare food for 6,000 or 8,000. They managed it pretty well, as there was no officially reported riot or fight. Some evacuees carried Buddhist shrines; two men suffered under the weight of a ten-foot crucifix. No one knew how they managed to carry their loads on the planes later for the trans–Pacific flight.[35]

The evacuees were glad to arrive in Guam. Dockside administration was established to clear 800 people an hour as the ships unloaded. Soldiers and sailors were given civilian clothes. The Vietnamese military personnel hit the portable showers first and were given new aloha shirts and jeans by the hospitable Guamanians. Each family was given a small bag containing soap, needles and thread, combs, and other essentials donated by military wives. Children were fed cookies and Kool-Aid.

On 11 May, the USS *Midway* (CVA-41), with decks overflowing with 101 VNAF and Air American aircraft that had been landed on board by pilots fleeing with their families, arrived at U.S. Naval Station, Guam. Her stay lasted a day and a half, enough to offload 96 evacuees picked up in the Gulf of Siam and the 101 aircraft.[36]

On 13 May, Guam received the 100,000th refugee, and the next day the resident evacuee population peaked at 50,430, which was a more than 50 percent increase in Guam's normal population at the time. On 15 May, Tent City hit its population peak of 39,331.[37]

On 15 May, the first of twenty former RVN military and civilian ships filled with evacuees arrived in port from the South China Sea.

How would Guam screen and find lodging and transportation for the 14,000 new arrivals on an island of 80,000 people? How to feed or assist these evacuees? Imagine a small county of 80,000 people on the U.S. mainland being asked to find provide lodging, food, and transportation for 14,000 people. It would be a logistical nightmare for the local government. In the end, the Guamanians handled it superbly. At the end of the day, each evacuee had a place to settle in, a cot to lie on, and something to eat. It took the dedication, good will, and unselfishness of the workers and volunteers who put in long hours to help the newcomers. Many workers toiled for twelve to sixteen hours each day, went home to take some rest, and returned the next day for more work. No one complained of the hard work, although they had to put aside their daily regular work to get involved in this new project.

On one occasion early in the resettlement process, arriving evacuees had to be diverted to Wake Island because repair had to be done on Camp Asan. Overflowing plumbing, exposed wiring, and long waits outside the dining halls made moving into Camp Asan a stressful, if not risky proposition. Therefore, the decision was made to divert the planes to the nearest hospitable place: Wake Island. Wake, with two nearby islets, occupies a total of three square miles and is situated 1,500 miles northeast of Guam.

While the resettlement was in full swing, the governor's office pushed for legislative approval of special powers, for without them, the governor thought he could not deal with the evacuees quickly or effectively enough. The rapid influx necessitated quick and bold decisions that sometimes had to be made on the spot. *How many evacuees would Guam have to accept? 50,000? 100,000? How long would they stay in Guam? What would be the short and long-term impact on the island? Who would pay the bills?* In the meantime, the Guam legislature, as part of its due diligence work, tried to understand the evacuee problem and continued to probe the State Department about its overall impact on Guam's economy, society, and environment. Secretary Kissinger finally advised Governor Bordallo in a cable to "plan initially for ninety days with the possibility of a longer period."

Legislative speaker Joseph Ada was worried about Guam becoming another Miami, with the Cubans staying for life. The deputy liaison officer for the State Department had to affirm to local officials that the situation was temporary and that Guam was only a staging area to hold the evacuees pending further movement.

After clearance by the Immigration Service, refugees were moved to Tin City at Andersen AFB to await departure on a chartered plane to one of the stateside camps and the next phase of their new lives.[38]

It was the largest military effort on Guam since the day in the

Vietnam War when B-52 bombers filled the sky, heading to Hanoi. It allowed the reception, screening, lodging, feeding, training, and resettlement to the U.S. mainland of more than 130,000 evacuees, all within the span of three short months. To coordinate, move and feed so many foreign individuals without preparation and practice was itself an achievement.

5

Operation New Life

Operation New Life, which dealt with the reception and outbound shipment of evacuees, could be split into two components that were intimately linked together. One was the shipment of the evacuees to the mainland U.S. and Third World countries (23 May–26 August) and the other, shipment back to Vietnam (3 May–16 October). As the second part was the spinoff of the other, it will be discussed separately in chapter 8, covering the repatriates.

Resettlement Health Problems

The main goal of the Operation New Life was the resettlement of the evacuees from Southeast Asia, which included a heterogeneous group of people: Cambodians and Laotians, Chinese-Vietnamese as well as Vietnamese. They did not speak the same language, nor share the same faith or belief, and therefore did not mix as a group. They spoke at least four main languages: Cambodian, Laotian, Chinese, and Vietnamese. Most did not even know how to write their own names.

The resettlement of this diverse group of evacuees also implied solving a myriad of simple as well as complex problems from all levels: administration, coordination, and logistics, food delivery and distribution, education, entertainment, security, and so on.

Evacuees were quartered in camps that were administered in the spirit of the Geneva Convention, with attention paid to the health, welfare, education, recreation, religious affairs and discipline of the evacuees. Although most of the evacuees were well behaved, a small group of returnees resorted to violence to highlight their demands. This will be discussed in chapter 8.

The sudden influx of 130,000 people was bound to raise controversy and problems not only locally, but also on the national and international levels. The impact of the group, which turned out to be larger than the native island population, on health, food, water, and sewage on the island raised concern among the local people, especially when it was found out that Dengue hemorrhagic fever was present in the Saigon area before the people left Vietnam.[1]

The locals were no doubt affected by the arrival of evacuees. School buses—the only readily available means of transportation large enough to hold large numbers of people, and available in large numbers—were used to transport the evacuees from the civilian airport, air base, and docks to the camps, from one camp to another, then back to the air base. Buildings were requisitioned to house the newcomers. Bus drivers were asked to work twelve hour-shifts. Builders and electricians were enlisted to upgrade old buildings and add new telephone and sewer lines, while others were asked to volunteer as helpers and greeters. Traffic doubled or tripled in volume, congesting the island roads. Locals had to share their highways with buses filled with evacuees and trucks hauling food, construction materials, tents, pipes, and so on.

Within two weeks of the first arrivals, the existing evacuee camps were full, requiring the creation of new smaller camps or housing complexes, each holding 200 to 1,000 evacuees. This created administrative as well as communications trouble. The chain of small camps was especially wasteful of administrative staff.

The arrival of the evacuees also impacted the island's health care system, because they had not been screened or vaccinated prior to their departure. It raised the fear of an epidemic to the level of a public health concern.

Dengue fever is a mosquito-borne tropical disease caused by the Dengue virus. The virus is transmitted by several species of mosquitoes within the *Aedes* group, especially *Aedes aegypti*.[2] Symptoms include fever, headache, joint pain, and a characteristic skin rash that is similar to measles. In a small number of cases, the disease can turn into a life-threatening Dengue hemorrhagic fever. The death of a few evacuee children in Guam from Dengue fever evoked the specter of epidemic. It was feared that local mosquitoes coming into contact with diseased children could acquire and spread the disease to the local population.

The decision was made to fight potential mosquito-borne disease on the island after discussion between the civilian authorities in Guam and the U.S. Navy. A decision was made to do four sprayings at two-week intervals. Specially designed aircraft flew in from the U.S. to spray malathion, a pesticide that was used to eradicate mosquitoes.[3] The insecticide was to be delivered as an ultra-low volume (ULV) spray that consisted of extremely fine droplets not visible to humans, dispensed at the rate of one-fourth ounce per acre.

The first aerial spraying of the island began on 23 May. Mosquito traps scattered around the spray area indicated a 99 percent reduction in the number of adult mosquitoes per trap. No complaint of eye irritation or other health problems from the population was noted. The second aerial spraying took place on 30 May. Except for some dead fish and bees, no major problem was encountered. The third and fourth sprayings took place on 6 and 13 June 1975. No new case of Dengue fever was confirmed on Guam after the spraying. The potential malaria vector *Anopheles* also were controlled by the malathion applications.[4]

Overall, there were six confirmed cases of Dengue, one fatal and one unstated, but a small number of malaria cases among the evacuees. Ten cases of typhoid were found. About 20 cases of pulmonary tuberculosis were diagnosed. In addition, subsequent studies revealed active tuberculosis in a number of children. Many children were immunized against measles, German measles, and poliomyelitis.[5]

There was a constant need to explain to the evacuee population about the need for outside resettlement, for there was nothing like idleness, boredom, and confinement in a walled camp to invite discouragement, unhappiness, and disorder. Even if food and shelter were provided daily, confinement remained a big problem for people who used to roam free. Once the belly was full, the mind would kick in and ask for changes. The lack of freedom to get out of the camp, the lack of news from the family—especially if they remained stuck in Vietnam—and uncertainty about the future tended to sap the morale of the evacuees. The longer the confinement, the more these reactions would manifest in the open.

The weather had to be monitored closely, as the Guam area was prone to high winds and typhoons. The large population, housed in flimsy tents, would be susceptible to the effects of weather. A simple tropical storm, let alone a hurricane or a typhoon, could easily knock down the flimsy rows of tents, soak the evacuees, and render them homeless for some time. Luckily, the period of 23 April to 25 June 1975 was the one of the driest in the history of the island. The sun was shining high and bright on the evacuees.

Processing Difficulties

There were many problems with food distributions on the supply side as well as on the consumer and the kitchen sides. In the beginning, the food supply got backlogged at Travis AFB while camp equipment moved to Guam ahead of the food. The first increment of food, which was due on 7 May, was stuck at Travis AFB and delivered only on 21

May. One ship carrying rice for some Asian country was diverted to Guam to increase the rice supply.

Rationing in the beginning was impossible because of lack of control over evacuees in the food serving lines and because of the rapid fluctuations in the numbers of evacuees due to new arrivals and departures. Consumption from April through May was 1.5 times the standard ration. With daily inspection of feeding operations, consumption was brought down to the standard allowance.

Most food receipts lacked adequate documentation, complicating the maintenance of adequate stocks. Material was received in a confusing order. Partial orders or partial shipments were split into as many as twenty receipts for one single order.[6]

In addition to scheduled, regular deliveries to 3,200 troops, the influx of 3,000 additional troops placed huge demands on the operation. Receipts and deliveries for the military and evacuee had grown 16-fold (from 3,200 to more than 50,000). The need was compounded by the urgency. With evacuees coming in droves, these deliveries of food, flatware, cots, tents, and so on were required on the spot, otherwise the evacuees would be sleeping on the ground or would have no food to consume.

On 22 April, Operation New Life was provided a $500,000 reimbursable operations target (OPTAR) as initial funding. This was raised to $2,000,000 on 25 April and $10,000,000 later the same day. In late May it was raised again, to $14,000,000.

As to the storage of the 101 Vietnamese aircraft brought back by the carrier *Midway* from Vietnam, meetings were conducted to identify resources and ways to deal with the problem. *Midway* arrived on 11 May and within 24 hours, 25 F5s, 27 A37s, 48 helicopters, and one O-1 were offloaded on barges, transported to piers, and arranged in their storage locations. Arrangements were then made for proper cleaning, preservation, and storage for eventual shipment.

From 23 to 28 May, the 48 helicopters were loaded aboard the SS *Green Wave*. The F5 and A37 were transported to Naval Air Station (NAS) for loading and transporting to CONUS.

On 24 June, under direction of JCS, the number of evacuees on Guam was decreased to 10,000, leaving behind cots, tents, and mess halls. This began the phase-down period of Operation New Life. The main problem at Orote Point was to determine the disposition and ownership of the many tents, cots, and other pieces of equipment that had been rushed to Guam to meet the demands of incoming evacuees. All New Life materials had to be either returned or reimbursed. All unused materials also needed to be returned and all bills paid.

> **Table 5-1. Operation New Life**
>
> *Military Functions*
>
> 1. Conduct initial evacuee processing
>   —identify name, nationality,
>   —record time, place of arrival
>   —do a gross medical screening
>   —assign a number unique to evacuee
>   —customs inspection
>   —create roster of all arrivals and departures
>   —establish a locator to allow family contact
>
> 2. Direct center organization and management
>   —transport to reception centers
>   —present orientation briefings
>   —provide food/shelter
>   —take care of personal needs
>   —educational and recreational activities
>   —provide information and other common services
>   —manage allocation of volunteer assistance
>
> 3. Arrange for resettlement in the CONUS camps

Processing the evacuees was a crucial part of Operation New Life, not just to document the operation but also to allow the matching of family members and determining, for the benefit of the evacuees, who had made the trip and who had not made it. For example, a lady with three children was looking for her husband. If he was not among the people registered, it was likely that he did not make the trip, although there was a small chance that he could turn up later at another camp. If a person looking for his siblings and the rest of his family found only one sibling but not the rest of his family, he could be pretty certain that the others did not make the trip.

The staggering number of evacuees led to confusion, disorganization, and disruption, which eventually could undermine the operation itself. Thousands of evacuees, young and old, looking for their relatives, could despair if they were turned away from the information centers in the camps because no one knew anything about their relatives. Thousands of youngsters could be placed in foster homes if their families were not found.

Without a common recording or filing system, it would have been very difficult, if not impossible, to reconnect a person to his family, leading to unnecessary searches that could lead to more disruptions. Reconnecting members of a family became extremely important, not only for the family but also for U.S. society.

Authorities established a roster of arrivals and departures along with a locator to allow family members and friends to make contact. With people landing in different places, at Clark AFB in the Philippines, Andersen AFB or NAS in Guam, or at Wake Island Airport, different numbering systems were used, making reconciliation of the numbers difficult. Even on Guam, evacuees landing at NAS and Andersen AFB were under different numbering schemes, both starting at #1, causing further confusion. In addition, other organizations—like the Immigration Naturalization Service, hospitals, camps, the government of Vietnam, and the U.S. Embassy in Saigon—used their own numbers. Guam authorities, therefore, decided to look for a simple method to identify the evacuees. They found it in the "Clark system," which was instituted by the 43rd Combat Support Group at Andersen AFB. It was only on 27 April that all the navy and air force files were merged into a single island-wide system.

When the first planes landed at Andersen AFB, the evacuees were led to the passenger terminal for medical screening, customs, and personal processing. At first everything worked as planned, because official workers and volunteers had been trained in their specific duties. However, the arrival of four successive planeloads of evacuees confused and stressed the terminal workers, causing long delays in the processing lines. Interpreters fluent in French and Vietnamese had to be brought in to assist with translation.

A decision was made to open more space and to use more workers and volunteers to help speed up the process. The evacuees were brought to holding areas first, where they were allowed to rest and eat, for many had not been eating regularly for some time. It was found that feeding them first helped them move faster through the lines. Military wives, teenage dependents, and volunteer servicemen cooked, served food, changed baby diapers, and kept the terminal clean. Officers and NCO clubs brought steamed rice and donated their own kitchen supplies. Commissary personnel brought food and personal hygiene items. Workers installed additional portable toilets and showers.[7] There was overwhelming enthusiasm and help from military personnel and volunteers who gave away their time and effort to assist and provide whatever help was needed. Many easily put in twelve- or fourteen-hour shifts.

Dealing with the evacuees meant dealing with Vietnamese culture and society. In a country that followed the lunar calendar and used the lunar New Year to mark the birthday of every citizen, the Vietnamese viewed age differently than the Americans. A child when born was considered to be one year old. On lunar New Year's Day, he would turn two, while in American terms, he might be counted as only a few months old. Vietnamese is a monosyllabic tonal language. *Ba*, for example, means *three* or *father*. Adding a diacritical mark above the vowel changes the meaning of the word. Since there are five diacritical marks, *ba* can have five other meanings. Therefore, Nguyễn Văn Ba could be the name of six different persons, depending on what diacritical was added. However, since the computers of the times did not allow the use of diacritical marks, these names tended to cause a lot of confusion to screeners, workers, and helpers. There could be five people named Nguyễn Văn Ba, with five different birthdates.

To make matters worse, there were only 21 common family names in Vietnam compared to the 151,761 last names in the U.S., according to the U.S. Census Bureau. This resulted in a lot of similar names: there were 68 Nguyễn Thị Hoa on Guam at that time. Also, because they use a different order of names, the Vietnamese confused the Americans a lot. A name in Vietnamese starts with the family name and ends with the personal name. These differences gave data systems more trouble than any other aspect of Operation New Life. It made mail delivery difficult and camp administration extremely complicated. These differences "did not manifest themselves until a great deal of damage had been done."[8]

The other problem that surfaced was that of multiple wives in Vietnam, a practice that was prohibited in 1963. A man could have secondary wives. Younger ones were needed because the older ones could no longer work in the fields or have children. The younger wives were considered to be sisters to the main wife. When elder men came to the U.S., they claimed these secondary wives as "nieces" or "daughters." A 50-year-old man with his wife was often seen accompanied by some "nieces" or "daughters" in their thirties or forties.

Transportation was the next important item and was taken care of by the navy. Captain Wyttenbach, on behalf of the navy, had to negotiate to get Guam's school buses to transport the Vietnamese. The latter would arrive at irregular times. As a matter of fact, most of them arrived in the middle of the night, especially on the night of May 7, when 10,000 people arrived aboard two different ships. The sudden influx of new arrivals necessitated drivers to work overtime to transport them back to their compounds. Since bus drivers were working overtime—beyond their standard 8 hours of government contract—they were legally responsible for any accident they had, as one driver remarked: "If an accident happened, the burden was on the fatigued drivers despite the fact they were doing a favor to the Navy."

Black Construction provided 10,000 lapboards to be used for the educational program. These were 8.5-by-11-inch mahogany sheets that provided instant classrooms for the new refugees. Wyttenbach, who wanted to provide some basic orientation to the refugees prior to their departure to the U.S., enlisted the help of the Department of Education's

> **Table 5-2. Task Force New Arrivals**
>
> *Civilian Functions*
>
> 1. Conduct initial refugee processing
>   —determine proper immigration status
>   —provide social security documentation
>   —match refugee skills with job opportunities
>   —supervise civil affairs operations
>   —maintain refugee locator system
>   —enter refugee data into computerized files
> 2. Direct center organization and management
>   —support infrastructure in the refugee community
>   —educational and recreational activities
>   —provide information and other common services
>   —manage allocation of volunteer assistance
>   —establish liaison with public and private sectors
> 3. Arrange resettlement in the United States or abroad
>   —evaluate sponsors
>   —approve clearance and release
>   —provide travel and relocation services
>
> *Military functions*
>
> Coordinate frequency of refugee flight arrivals
> Transport refugees from airhead to reception centers
> Present orientation briefings for the refugees
> Determine identity of refugees and issue ID cards
> Develop personal information for refugee data base
> Provide housing, food, health care and security
> Execute civil affairs operations as directed
> Perform required medical vectoring and screening
> Furnish necessary logistic support

teachers. He went on the radio asking for their help. The DOE also supplied 14,000 textbooks in "English as Second Language." Topics taught include hygiene, sanitation, the United States, geography, climate and a little English.

Other instructions followed. Refurbished sewing machines were put to use in so-called "Klinger Sewing Centers," named after the character in the TV series "M.A.S.H." Refugees could go to these centers to learn about sewing or to use these machines to mend their clothes. To alleviate boredom, water sports were taught by Vietnamese instructors.[9]

Local Problems

Problems abounded in the camps for officials as well as for auxiliaries. These were usually minor problems, cultural in nature, that required flair and tact to solve. There was an elderly man who refused to leave his tent, even for meals. Upon further enquiry, it was found that he had a small stash of gold he needed to protect against potential thieves. How he was able to carry his gold from Vietnam to Guam undetected was unknown to officials. How he was able to safeguard it by himself remained puzzling to officials, who decided to help him as much as possible. Wyttenbach had the brilliant idea to call on the Vietnamese Boy Scouts for help. He provided them with distinctive kerchiefs and asked them to stand in for elderly people in food queues as well to monitor the wellbeing of others. This gave the youngsters something to do and freed officials from meddling in the cumbersome personal affairs of the evacuees.

As to the gold some refugees had brought with them, there was no safekeeping available in the camps. They carried it around in their bags, which were left under their cots in the view and reach of other roommates. Since Vietnam was a country at war, paper money had rapidly became worthless due to inflation. The Vietnamese saved the value of their property by buying taels of gold,[10] the price of which was pegged to the U.S. dollar. Gold, therefore, in Vietnam never lost its value and became a commodity years later.

Wyttenbach then suggested bringing in some banks that would convert this gold into cash. This became a tricky idea, as it required the Guam legislature to approve the authority of the camp management to set up banking tents in the compounds. After the approval, the big banks did not want the business because they thought the amount of trade would be too small to be worth the travail. That left a local banker, Deak Parera, free to deal with the Vietnamese. He in the end reaped all the rewards of doing business alone. As to the Vietnamese, once their money was safe in the bank vault, they were free to sleep without worry.

The gold wafers became popular in Guam as jewelry, investment pieces and collectors' items after the Vietnamese brought them there in 1975. Deak Parera bought a total of 98 pieces, which were later traded and sold in many local jewelry stores. Things became complicated from then on, because after the fall of Saigon, both North and South Vietnam were designated as foreign countries by the Foreign Assets Control section of the Treasury Department. Importing gold taels to the mainland became illegal, and they could be confiscated by the U.S. customs. However, since Guam is outside the U.S., U.S. customs laws do not apply to it. In short, Guamanians could own taels in Guam but could not take them to the mainland U.S.

In December 1981, the State Department gave an exception to Deak

Parera Guam to buy gold taels from the Vietnamese refugees, thus making the 98 wafers certified by Deak Parera eligible for entry into the U.S. To qualify for entry, the taels must be for personal use only, not for resale. The owner must have an original, serial-numbered invoice from Deak Parera Guam showing name of purchaser, date of purchase, and purchase price along with an accurate description of the article.[11]

Wyttenbach also thought that the Vietnamese should police themselves and that each section should elect its own representative. This would not only boost the morale of the refugees but also give them a say in the daily management of the camp. In the process, the Americans would save themselves a lot of headaches, as minor problems would be ironed out by the Vietnamese themselves, leaving only the major ones for the management to solve.

After seeing four tiny old ladies clad in black pajamas sitting on the pavement at Asan Camp and chattering away in their native tongue, question was raised about what to do with these four ladies and thousands of their fellow citizens.

General Nguyễn Cao Kỳ, former South Vietnamese premier, who was in the camp at that time, wanted to start a cooperative farm where he could employ thousands of his fellow refugees. The news reached actor John Wayne, who immediately offered Kỳ 17,000 acres for such a project. However, the American system did not lend itself to a labor-intensive farming system like the one in Vietnam. Everything was mechanized in the U.S. for the simple reason that human labor was very expensive in terms of wages, insurance, and health care costs. The climatic and soil conditions are different, and the crops too are different.

A civilian coordinator of the largest refugee camp in the U.S., at Fort Chaffee, suggested three options:

    1. A long-term camp with special on-site programs for language, rehabilitation, vocational and other training leading to relocation.

    2. The traditional course, using volunteer agencies like the U.S. Catholic Conference and the International Rescue Committee, which placed the Hungarian and Cuban refugees through relocation camps.

    3. Returning the refugees back to Vietnam. This solution could take care of a few thousands of refugees, but sending them back home would not be easy, as the *Thương Tín* affair would later prove.

Joe Murphy, editor of the Guam *Sunday News*, however, argued that the Vietnamese are different. They not only are a gentle and patient people willing to wait in long lines without complaint but also are eager to learn and highly educable. He turned out to be correct in his assessment, and all the mainland camps were closed by December 1975. The Vietnamese moved quickly into mainstream America faster than the Polish, the Irish and the Cubans before them. As for the four ladies in question, they were in the twilight years of their lives and the U.S. can afford to allow them to live that life in freedom and dignity.[12]

6

Life in the Guam Camps

While the majority of the evacuees just passed through the various Guam camps on their way to the United States or other countries, some did stay there for many months; many simply wanted to wait for their missing relatives. Therefore, the experiences of the evacuees varied depending on the length of stay, the size of the family, their personal habits, and so on.

Twelve Guam refugee camps ranging from large military buildings (Andersen Air Force Base's ten buildings, Orote Point's "Tent City," Camp Asan's fourteen refurbished buildings) to smaller residential centers like Black Construction, J & G Construction, the Hawaiian Dredging company, and the Tokyu Hotel were upgraded or modified to serve as lodging areas for the evacuees. Two of the most important Guam camps were Orote Point and Asan, for any evacuee had to pass through one of these camps before being allowed to migrate to the mainland.

Orote Point Camp

The main base at Naval Base Guam, also referred to as "Big Navy," lay on the west side of the island, about midway between its northern and southern ends. During World War II, the Japanese took over the naval base and built an airstrip close by. When World War II was over, the Japanese airstrip was abandoned. Over the decades, the vegetation had become luxuriant and taken over the entire area, leaving only the two transected runways still visible from the air.

The camp was first called Camp Fortuitous. There was even a big sign in front of the camp flouting these words. Fortuitous can be defined as "happening by chance." Had the Vietnamese not arrived in Guam, there would have been any camp there. Fortuitous, for non–English speakers, can be a strange and difficult word to pronounce. It appeared to be too intellectual for the Chamorros, soldiers, and truck drivers who

6. Life in the Guam Camps

preferred the simple words Orote Point. Eventually, no one called the camp "fortuitous" any longer.

On 25 April 1975, Seabees of the Thirtieth Construction Regiment began the task of clearing 600 acres of bushes and undergrowth.[1] Crews from the USS *Hector* and the USS *Proteus* joined the Seabees to put up the tents. Working without sleep, they put up 350 tents each day in ground so hard that jackhammers were used to drill stake holes. A total of more than 3,000 tents were thus erected in record speed. More than 20 miles of pipes were laid to bring in water for drinking and showers in additions to miles of electric and telephone wires.[2]

People worked in shifts as long as 16 to 18 hours, although no one had asked people to do so. They just saw the huge need and would not stop responding to it. That was how the Guamanians responded and raised themselves up to the challenge of Operation New Life.

The pressure of the 20,000 refugees already on this island taxed the authorities and the facilities. Sanitation problems were a concern, as the tent camps were overflowing. At Orote Point, site of the new tent city being carved out from an old Japanese airbase, refugees rushed into tents even before sweating sailors finished erecting them.

The following day the site was aswarm with humanity—crying, laughing, sleeping, playing, staring and holding hands. Baggage lay unclaimed in large batches on the old runway. The route to the camp took the evacuees along Guam's main street past El Play Boy Club, the Genghis Khan Furniture store, and the world's largest McDonald's, a sprawling 24-hour establishment where the manager had painted a sign of welcome to the Vietnamese refugees—in English.[3]

Long Trần, a Guam evacuee, wrote:

> The next morning [following his arrival], after an early breakfast of diced ham, scrambled eggs and toast, our eldest son Jim and I started exploring the camp. It consisted of rows and rows of olive drab canvas tents erected on a large stretch of sand called Orote Point, not far from the seashore. We went to the centrally located tent that served as the camp administrative headquarters and received a copy of a sketchy map of the camp. We scanned hundreds of messages pinned on bulletin boards set up in this administrative tent.

It was a camp built up in a few days to solve a logistical problem, and the uniformity of this camp no doubt struck all the evacuees. The irony of the situation certainly did not escape them either. After trying to flee a war-torn country, they ended up into the hands of another military machine. It was the same picture everywhere: rows after rows of "olive drab canvas tents." But it did not matter because it solved two problems: providing food and shelter to the mass of evacuees.

Long Trần further wrote:

> The news of Vietnam we read in the magazines and newspapers [at the Tent City] was not good. I had naively hoped for a peaceful reunification of Vietnam under the communist regime. I was wrong. The communists coined the term "ngụy" (pseudo, false, sham) to label all those millions of Vietnamese closely or remotely associated with the former regime. All these "pseudo–Vietnamese" were required to present themselves to the communists and were placed in concentration camps to be "reeducated." We later learned that tens of thousands of these prisoners, condemned to hard labor, languished for years in captivity and some finally died in these reformation camps.[4]

At Orote Point Camp, eight mess halls were built to serve almost 40,000 evacuees. The halls served 5 million pounds of food during Operation New Life, with each hall serving 10,000 meals a day. The number of meals served was staggering. Hours were 07:00 to 10:00 a.m. and 03:00 to 11:00 p.m., although one mess remained open at night to serve evacuees who arrived after hours.

The odd opening hours of the halls favored hoarding and extra trips to the kitchens. With only two feeding times a day, evacuees were forced to save some breakfast food for lunch, otherwise they would go hungry from 10:00 a.m. to 03:00 p.m., which would be a long fasting interval. Hungry evacuees might return to the mess hall for a brunch at 03:00 p.m. and a supper between 07:00 and 08:00 p.m. For some, a two-meal day could thus turn into a four-meal day. There was no time to do anything else except stand in lines for meals. Another factor that led to hoarding was the absence of large dining areas at Orote Point, which forced evacuees to bring the food back to their tents for consumption.

Other problems with the mess halls were the lack of a varied diet, shortage of eating utensils, policing of the eating area, control of mess lines, and construction of sumps. Hoarding of consumable utensils was a continual problem. The use of 8 plates, 8 cups, and 6 sets of flatware per evacuee per day for the month of May rapidly depleted military supplies and forced authorities to cut down to three of each per person per day. It was not until the lines were forced to stop feeding because of lack of utensils that the evacuees realized the need for conservation. Providing for the special needs of this particular population for chopsticks and rice was helpful in alleviating theft or hoarding.

The food allowances were set at 1,200 calories minimum and 1,600 calories maximum per day. Minimum requirements[5] were established for rice, powdered milk, pork, poultry, fish, fruits, bread, soy sauce, and utensils:

- Rice—50 kilo bag per 200 people per day
- Dry milk—50 kilo bag per 300 people per day

- Meat—5 kilos per 100 people per day
- Bread—5 kilos per 100 people per day
- Fruit—5 kilos per 100 people per day
- Water—2 gallons per person per day

In addition, there were two water purification teams capable of generating 6,000 gallons of water per hour with a storage capacity of 18,000 gallons; two quartermaster laundry detachments capable of 2,600 pounds of bulk laundry per week; nine quartermaster of clothing and bath detachments with a capacity of 27,000 people per week.

Governor Bordallo, who allowed Guam to be used as reception center for the evacuees, one day visited Camp Orote Point. He was seen passing in front of hundreds of evacuees who lined up to greet him. They looked clean and fairly well dressed, considering that they had left their country in a hurry and were just allowed to take a small bag with them. These were mostly youths, males and females, not elderly farmers or bar girls, as described by the news at the times. There were also children and a row of teenage girls in their flowery *áo dài* (Vietnamese tunic). They were serious, somewhat lost in their thoughts, probably not in a mood to parade in front of anyone.

Asan Camp

Asan Beach has a rich history that mirrors the history of the island. Located in the western part of the island, it was the site of a leper colony from 1892 to 1990, when it was destroyed by a typhoon. In 1901, it served as a prison camp for Filipino insurrectionists who fought against the Americans who were taking over their country. In 1922, Asan Point became a U.S. Marine camp with a quartermaster depot, a small arms range, and barracks. This was where the U.S. Marines landed during World War II to retake the island from the Japanese.

After World War II was over, Asan Beach became known as Asan Camp. From then until 1947, the camp was used as headquarters and barracks for the U.S. Seabees, who helped to reconstruct the island. From 1948 to 1967, it was a small military base with housing, an outdoor theater, tennis courts, and a fire station. During the Vietnam War, the navy converted it into a hospital annex, which was used until 1975, when it served as a refugee camp for the displaced Vietnamese. The camp was completely destroyed by the Supertyphoon Pamela and in 1978, the National Park Service bought it to establish the Pacific National Historical Park.

Marines, prior to their departure for Vietnam, used to stay at Asan Camp. This was the place where they recovered from their wounds and war traumas prior to being released back to their communities. Asan Camp had been unused for some time when the evacuees arrived. The barracks had to be upgraded and refurbished prior to accepting the first evacuees. They were arranged in a curved row, each with a housing capacity of 200 people. Each barrack had two floors, with bathrooms, and offered a sense of security against weather and storms. The barracks, which were built along the beach, offered a beautiful and idyllic view of the area. The camp had a movie theater, messes, soccer and basketball fields, a library and a reading room. There was even a church, and later a place where Buddhists could gather and say their prayers. It was a calm, quiet, and soothing place where evacuees finally could relax and find release after suffering through a two-decade war. It was different than a crowded and hurried place like the Orote Point tent camp. It felt like a high-end or "chic" place in Guam, compared to the low-income housing at Orote Point. It was everything that the evacuees needed and more.

Refurbishing the old hospital annex in less than 24 hours was a nearly impossible undertaking. Formidable as the job appeared, no other choices existed, and the Marines and Seabees on Guam turned all their attention to meeting this deadline. When the first busloads of refugees arrived the next day, the Navy and Marine Corps team had four of the fifteen barracks ready. The new occupants also found blankets, sleeping gear, and food awaiting them.

The initial buses took their passengers to Building 502 for processing and orientation. Next, the Marines showed the refugees their new living spaces, with their dimensions and assignment based on the size of the family. From here, the new occupants moved to blanket issue, after which the Marine hosts gave them the choice of going either to bed or to the mess hall. At Building 548, hot rice and tea awaited their arrival. This process would be repeated thousands of times before Operation New Life ended and Camp Asan closed its doors. By the following day, 25 April, Camp Asan had a population of 5,000 people. On that Friday, the first departing group left Camp Asan for Andersen Air Force Base, and a flight from Guam to the United States. After that, a continuous flow of arrivals and departures became the routine.

Colonel McCain later related that by the time the first refugees arrived at 18:00 on 24 April, he had established a complete camp organization to provide full support including administration, billeting, baggage handling, messing, medical, transportation, clothing, and location of relatives. By 11:30 on 26 April, the organization administratively processed 6,420 arrivals, adding them to the camp rolls. This effort involved not only the Marines on Guam but also their families. Marine wives assisted with the initial reception and processing of evacuees, including the collection and distribution of clothing and baby supplies.

Asan Camp was closed for repair on 26 April. Its 30-year-old hospital, with its overflowing plumbing, exposed wiring, and hour-long waits outside its dining-hall, irritated the 5,000 refugees already there. This caused thousands of new arrivals to be shifted to Wake Island camps.[6]

Asan Camp, like all military camps, was enclosed by a fence, which simply served as a divider between the civilian community on the outside and the military personnel and evacuees on the inside. It was a simple fence that people could climb without difficulty. There was no question that this was necessary, as latter demonstrations by groups of evacuees would point out. Still, a divide is a divide, and for some evacuees, especially those who remained in the camp for a long time, the fenced camp appeared like a prison.

In the evenings, Guamanians, who are kind and good-hearted people, came by, stood outside the fence and slipped candies and cigarettes through the mesh to the evacuees on the inside. They usually communicated with each other in broken English, for not many escapees spoke English fluently at that time. But this was enough to melt the ice and break potential barriers between hosts and newcomers and make each other comfortable again. At Orote Point, Guamanian and evacuee children swapped comic books through the mesh.

Local chapels were designated as centers through which hundreds of volunteers were channeled to serve. Duties included leadership roles or simply sorting out mounds of clothes given by the local people throughout the island. About 30 tons of relief material passed through chapels' collection centers.

Surveys by chaplains showed that 50 percent of the people at Orote Point and Agana were Catholics. Therefore, masses were scheduled regularly. The first baptism was performed in Guam on 8 May for two-week-old Hoa Thị Nguyễn. On Saturday 17 May, Bishop Felixberto Flores celebrated a field mass at Orote Point assisted by army and navy chaplains and 36 Vietnamese priests. Eleven thousand Vietnamese worshipped during the Saturday Mass. On 4 June, Bishop Flores officiated again at Orote Point; 698 children received confirmation and 293 first communion. Vietnamese priests baptized 20 children. Weekday masses were attended by 15,000 people.[7]

Small-scale educational programs were initiated by volunteer groups like the Kiwanis Club ladies at Asan, local Red Cross volunteers at Tent City, and Australian volunteers at Asan and Orote Point.

Celebrating their first fourth of July in America, the Vietnamese evacuees at Camp Asan hosted CINCPACREPGUAM/TTPI and the governor of Guam with extensive festivities. The activities included a flag raising ceremony, a beauty contest (all contestants were judged winners), sack races, tug-of-war, bike races, and a fishing competition.

Tin City

From 23 April to 19 August 1975, the 43rd Airlift Wing (AW) or Strategic Wing (it was then a bomber wing under Strategic Airlift Command) took part in Operation New Life at Andersen AFB, Guam. With only 18 hours' advance notice, the 43rd AW handled direct support for up to 10,000 evacuees, with the majority being cared for on the navy installation. This number would be vastly exceeded during the course of the four-month operation.

The 43rd Civil Engineer Squadron (CES) re-opened and renovated an area called Tin City. Tin City was a barracks area used for storage. The 43rd CES invested an extra 21,000 man-hours to get these buildings back in shape, including over 600 plumbing repairs. They reopened a dining facility capable of feeding up to 5,000 people. The CES worked up to the last minute, literally leaving the buildings when evacuees were entering to occupy them.

Each evacuee was screened by qualified medical personnel. People with contagious diseases were quarantined. The seriously ill were routed to one of two field hospitals constructed for the evacuees. Attention was given to exterminating flies, mosquitoes and other disease carriers to reduce the potential for serious outbreaks in the evacuee population.

The personnel office devised a simple data form for evacuees to fill out, sometimes with the assistance of translators. This information was then given to data processing personnel who transferred the data to key-punch cards for input on the base computer. There was one computer for the entire base.

Tin City, which was originally intended to handle only 2,900 of the 10,000 total evacuees estimated for Guam, found its numbers increased to 4,400. To make matters worse, it was peak tourist season on Guam and local hotels that might have been used to house evacuees were already full.

Aircraft maintenance personnel had to take care of their own B-52s and aircraft bringing evacuees into Andersen as well as maintain aircraft that were taking refugees to the U.S. Fuel specialists distributed 25 million gallons of fuel to non–SAC aircraft and 11 million more gallons to SAC aircraft.

Transportation specialists moving people from one area to another carried a total of 315,000 passengers for a total distance of 157,000 miles with only minor vehicle damage from accidents and no personnel injuries.

Thousands of personal bags were brought into the base. Each one was inspected and, while many people were separated from their baggage in the chaos of transportation and lodging efforts, by the end of the operation there were only a handful of unclaimed bags left in the terminal.

Chaplains, family service workers and Red Cross volunteers helped "feed the body and soul" of refugees. Their efforts reunited countless separated families and soothed feelings of fear and uncertainty.

The 43rd Security Forces Squadron faced numerous situations while dealing with the influx of people. Some issues were the potential for infiltration by Communist agents, dealing with immigrations and customs regulations including anti-hijacking procedures, black marketing, prostitution, profiteering, and theft and vandalism in housing areas. They also performed customs inspections and aircraft inspections for contraband.

Evacuees swarmed onto the island. While the vast majority of them descended on the navy base, practically every one of the evacuees was processed through and flown out of Andersen. There were as many as 3,700 evacuees processed and airlifted in a day.

Toward the end of June, the leadership became concerned about the welfare of evacuees in the event of a typhoon. With typhoon season just around the corner, the 43rd AW was directed to surge operations to evacuate all but 10,000 refugees from the island by 24 June 1975. Since 10,000 was the number of people who could be reasonably protected from storms, this meant a significant increase in efforts. Even while this surge was going on, morale problems increased.

Numerous refugees had been sent to Wake Island and had become separated from families. They became upset that they had not yet been reunited. In an effort to assist these people they were flown from Wake Island to Guam prior to being sent to the U.S. In some cases, this meant that people would get off one plane, get processed in short order and proceed directly to another plane to fly to America. In one case a flight was literally held over to ensure a family was reunited prior to leaving Andersen. The 43rd airlifted 109,805 refugees to the U.S. and elsewhere.[8]

Outside the camp and only one month into Operation New Life, officials and reporters were already discussing the placement of refugees with modest skills and assimilation handicaps, like farmers and elderly ladies who just squatted and chatted in Vietnamese among themselves.

Hearing Nguyễn Cao Kỳ suggesting that Vietnamese farmers should be helped to return to their rice farming business, actor John Wayne was gracious enough to offer 17,000 acres of land for the Vietnamese to start a cooperative rice farm in the U.S. Although this was a lot of land for farming, it would not be enough for all the farmers lingering in the camps. Besides, farming conditions were different in Vietnam than in the U.S. And it was argued that since everything was mechanized in the U.S., there was no need for the Vietnamese intensive style of farming.

For those with modest skills, three options were raised:

- To create a long-term camp with on-site programs for language and vocational training, leading to later relocation. The proposed location would be Ft. Indiantown Gap camp.
- To use volunteer agencies like the U.S. Catholic Conference and the International Rescue Committee that had experience placing the Hungarian and Cuban refugees.
- To return those to Vietnam who were willing, for one reason or another. A total of 1,546 people opted for this choice.

As to the young Vietnamese and those with skills, it was thought that they would move quickly into mainstream, as they are "gentle and patient, willing to wait in long lines without complaints."[9]

Below are stories about some of the evacuees.

The Camp Manager

On the first day of their arrival at Asan Camp, the refugees were greeted by Marine Colonel Eugene "Jinx" McCain, who stressed, "We [the military] want them [the refugees] to run the camp." He said that the "only way I know how to organize it is like the military."

This was probably Col. McCain's brightest idea, because the South Vietnamese refugees—a complex, non-homogeneous, disparate, on-the-edge and stressed community—after dealing with a two-decade war and a twelve-year military government, had enough of things "like the military"—although they might not want to loudly acknowledge it. They could be animated or extroverted among themselves, although not all the time. They often kept everything inside themselves until the high pressure generated over time caused a sudden blow-up, which could be catastrophic, as exemplified by the *Thương Tín* case (see chapter 8).

But who would be that leader? How would he be chosen? For every single Vietnamese wanted to be a leader, although not everyone had the required experience and qualities to do the job. That was why at the 1967 South Vietnamese presidential election, sixteen candidates competed for that single position. Not five or ten people like in another country, but sixteen.

The leader should have a fair to good command of English to deal with the administration; he should have been a leader and possibly have worked with Americans before or know the American system. He should be willing to work long hours without interruption and with complete dedication. Above all, he had to put on hold any thought about his family and future. How that person was chosen remained a mystery. But it turned out to be Tony Lâm, who had worked as a contractor for the Americans in Vietnam for eleven years.

For ninety days, Tony worked nonstop at Asan Camp for "as many hours as it takes." He mentioned that he had not been to bed before 2 or 3 a.m. for "the last 27 days." His days were spent shuffling from one place to another, from one meeting or briefing to another with his crew, the military, or giving out interviews. Tony, reflecting on his three-month experience at Asan, said that although the job was "thankless," he and his men did it "because of moral obligation." Life was hectic for the camp manager. Besides going to meetings, he had to solve the daily problems of the camp. Below was his typical day.

He made some physical improvements to Asan, like building a Vietnamese-style bamboo cabana near the shore, covered with a thatched roof of palm fronds. The cabana could be used for citizenship education or personal enjoyment.

A barbershop was opened to serve refugees. A barber came to the office each morning to pick up the towel and shears, which he and his partner used to give 25-cent haircuts. He kept 15 cents and the remaining dime went into a fund to buy newspapers for the radio broadcasters to keep abreast of world news in their daily telecasts. The 25-cent haircuts, although inexpensive, were out of reach for the majority of the refugees, many of whom did not possess even a single dollar in their pockets. In their rush to escape, many did not have time to go to the banks to take out their money. Even if they carried cash, it consisted of worthless Vietnamese piasters that no one used in the U.S.

Then American officials came to Tony to ask for two more interpreters to speed up the work of the Immigration and Naturalization Service. Later during the day, he had two briefings, one with the COM-NAVMAR chief of staff and the other with a representative of Sen. Edward Kennedy's subcommittee on refugees. Dr. Nguyễn Thanh Phước, who took the job of maintaining hygiene in the camp, came and visited him. Every day, Dr. Phước began the day at 06:30 hours with a hygiene and sanitation lecture delivered over the public address system. He advised the refugees to clean the insides and outsides of their homes and use the toilet correctly: sitting on instead of squatting on the toilet seat.

Next, Tony strolled toward the mammoth Asan mess hall, where 1,000 loaves of bread were consumed daily. About 18,000 plates were also used daily by the Asan refugees, and thanks to Dr. Phước's lecture, not a single plate was seen lying on the floor. Next was a visit to the dispensary, where 18 Vietnamese doctors, 8 Vietnamese nurses and 5 Air Force medics took care of up to 600 patients a day.

Tony confided that he was worried about the future. After two decades of working in Vietnam, he had saved enough to buy a house and a boat. And then with the sudden collapse of the country, he had lost everything. And then he had to provide for seven children, which would be simple in Vietnam but not in the U.S. Besides, the U.S. being in a recession, jobs were not easily available.[10]

The Story of Nguyễn Tài Ngọc

Ngọc left Vietnam on 30 April 1975 on a battleship of the U.S. Navy's Seventh Fleet. Five days later, he landed in Subic Bay, the Philippines, where he rested for a couple of days. He was then flown aboard a C-130 cargo plane to Guam, where he was transferred to Orote Point, then Asan Camp in preparation for the long trip to one of the four mainland camps in the U.S. As the C-130 was a cargo plane with a cavernous interior, there were no seats for the passengers, who were forced to sit on the floor. The trip on the C-130 was scary for many Vietnamese civilians, who were not used to sitting on the floor of an airplane without being strapped down. Still, he was among the lucky few who were flown to Guam instead of being ferried on one of the U.S merchant ships where passengers had to brave the bright sunlight, sleeping on the deck or in the cargo hold, with minimal amenities for about a week.

This was the usual route taken by the refugees: most of the Vietnamese picked up by the battleships of the U.S. Navy's Seventh Fleet landed in Subic, then were flown to Guam; later, all the other ships were directed to sail straight to Guam.

The early arrivals at Guam wrote a motion to the government and the people of the United States, which said,

> We, the undersigned intellectuals who have been evacuated to Guam, recognize the great efforts of the American Government, the Governor, and the People of Guam in securing our safeguard.

However, most of the highly qualified professionals are still stranded in Vietnam. We therefore urgently entreat the Government and the People of America to continue the effort in bringing them back to Freedom. We who have been more fortunate in being brought here before, are ready to share our place and the little we have in order to save as many of our fellow-countrymen as possible with us.
Guam, April 28, 1975.

The letter was signed on 28 April, which was a turbulent time because people were still looking for ways to get out of the country while the communists were shelling the city. Among the signatures, we recognized those of Dr. Lê Quốc Hanh, chairman of Pulmonary Diseases, Hồng Bàng Hospital, University of Saigon; Dr. Lộc, a plastic surgeon; the artist Mộc; and Dr. Nguyễn Lê Hiếu, who would later become a family practitioner in the Midwest. Dr. Hiếu recounted that when asked how he would like his name to be spelled out, as Hiếu is his given name and Nguyễn his surname, he stated that he would like to keep his name in the same order as on his birth certificate. The judge then asked what would be his first name. He took a minute to think and opted to go with Bacsy as the first name (Vietnamese for doctor). He was later known as Bacsy NguyenLeHieu, combining and Americanizing his surname and given name.[11]

An Entrepreneurial Artist

On 6 July 1975, Nguyễn Văn Mộc, an evacuee, opened an art exhibit at Asan camp in Guam, where he lived. He was able to sell at least two paintings for one hundred and fifteen dollars, which was a large sum of money for a refugee. The receipt, which he himself scribbled on paper, read:

I have received a sum of money: one hundred and fifteen US dollars (115$US).
About the painting n#7 (MOTHER & CHILD) and n#23 (PARADISE LOST).
Now they are belonging to Mr. and Mrs. …
Sighned [sic]
Nguyễn Văn Mộc
Artist Painter
Asan, 6 July 1975.

"Mother and Child" was a silk painting depicting a Vietnamese mother breastfeeding her baby. Nguyễn Văn Mộc held his second exhibit at the local Megg's Department Store.

Nguyễn Văn Mộc, who was born in Hanoi, North Vietnam, in 1948, moved to Saigon with his family in 1954. That was the time of the first exodus, when almost one million northerners moved south following the Geneva Accords to stay away from the communists who took over North Vietnam. He attended grade school and high school until 1965, when he moved to Bordeaux, France, to study painting. He returned to Saigon in 1967, where he graduated from high school. He attended two years of college, one year as a law student and the following year as an architecture student. "But he did not succeed in neither law nor architecture," he said with his big smile.

As the military draft came calling, he enrolled in the South Vietnamese navy while continuing to paint and hold art exhibits. He had won many awards, which he listed in his hand-written program: this included a silver medal at a spring painting exhibition, the National Painting Award in Saigon in 1974, a gold medal at a Catholic art exhibit, and a bronze medal at the Esso (later known as Exxon) Painting Exhibition in Saigon in 1975.

He was a lieutenant in the Vietnamese navy (VNN) when Saigon fell and came to the U.S. with his three-year-old daughter, leaving behind his wife and three other children. He stated that he jumped onto his ship with "only his uniform, a watch and started with a big zero." He left Vietnam on 29 April with the big convoy of 32 Vietnamese ships, aboard the VNN DER#1, on which he was the navigator. He arrived in Guam on 13 May.

He spent a lot of time painting at Asan Camp, trying to depict "the spirit of human being" and the "view of the Vietnamese people." It took him one-half hour to do an oil painting, three hours for a silk painting, and two hours to carve on wood. He did 80 paintings in a 40-day span while in the camp, which was a lot of work even for an idle evacuee. Luckily, he was on his own except for a three-year-old daughter in tow.

He held his third and final exhibit in Guam at Government House at the request of Madeleine Bordallo, Guam's First Lady. On exhibition were 40 silk paintings, 25 oil paintings and 6 wood carvings. He painted in "cool, dark, quiet hues using expressionistic and surrealistic styles." He hoped to go to California first, then to attend school in New York.[12]

Of the hundreds of artists arriving on Guam at that time, Mộc was probably the only one to be able to profit from his stay there. Instead of thinking about his bleak future or worrying about whether he would be able to earn a living in a new country, he simply plowed ahead and began painting while he was in the camp. He managed to get paper and paints and sketch out one painting after another. Of course, he was well known in Vietnam as a painter prior to coming to the U.S. He talked to officials to let him hold exhibitions. Then the First Lady of Guam called on him to hold another exhibition at Guam Government House. He created opportunities for himself, while others just complained about one thing after another. It seems like society is willing to open doors to those who are ready to engage with the world.

Lipman saw the Guam camps as detention centers, relics of the U.S. colonial empire; she also extolled the virtues of the repatriates who managed to force their way back to Vietnam.[13] Others saw these camps as necessary places to screen and educate the evacuees and to serve as "immersion centers" into American society, the eastern "Ellis Island" from where the evacuees would emerge as law-abiding and productive citizens of a new society.

7

First, Second, and Third Wave Arrivals

Although they arrived on Guam a few days before or after 30 April 1975, three distinct groups of evacuees have been noted. The first and second groups were the dependents of Americans, third country nationals (TCN), Vietnamese who worked for the U.S. government or U.S. companies or Adventist Hospital, and those who bought their way out. They formed the 8,000 people who were heli-lifted from the U.S. Embassy and surrounding area. The rest belonged to the third group: those who were able to get on the Vietnamese navy ships and the MCS[1] ships.

The First and Second Waves

The first- and second-wave arrivals had special relationships with the Americans: they were American citizens and their dependents, and Vietnamese who worked for Americans. They had been selected by the Americans for early departures and left Vietnam before 30 April. They flew aboard C-130s from Saigon to Subic Bay, the Philippines, then from Subic Bay to Guam. They were well dressed and would not become a burden to the government. While some carried only a suitcase, others had their arms loaded with everything from flight bags heavy with gold bars to stuffed animals and golf clubs. They were fluent in English and willing to talk with reporters if their names were not mentioned.[2]

The second wave consisted of employees of the U.S. government and firms or those who had saved American lives. They, too, would cause few problems for the government. Not all Vietnamese who were invited to evacuate left Vietnam. Some refused to leave, while others were restrained by the crowds at the assembly points or by Vietnamese police at the docks.

7. First, Second, and Third Wave Arrivals

Because he had saved Americans by warning them of the sudden withdrawal from the central highlands, Colonel Lê Khắc Lý was advised by the Americans he would be the second person to leave Vietnam after General Cao Văn Viên. Lê Khắc Lý said, "We flew out of Vietnam on a C-130.... That was on the twenty-fifth of April. I knew when we left that everything was lost.... I thought that when Kissinger went to China and shook hands with Mao Zedong that was the end of Vietnam.... If you are Vietnamese and you love your country, then you must ask why the Americans did this. Many people say we were sold out. And sadly, I have to agree."[3]

One refugee who was very fluent in English recounted:

> We left Asan Camp on Saturday morning [3 May] and were moved to a staging area [Black Construction Company] where we stayed for about 44 hours before being transported to Andersen Air Force Base on Monday morning 5 May. We were served breakfast, rested for a while, then taken at 17:00 to the theater on the base to have our papers and boarding passes checked. We waited for our plane sitting in the theater, watching four movies in a row before being called to a bus at midnight.
>
> Our plane took off at 01:00 on 6 May and after a smooth seven-hour flight landed in Honolulu at 10:00 on 5 May. We took off again at 13:00 and landed at Fort Smith Regional Airport at 02:00 on 6 May. We were then driven by bus to Fort Chaffee, Arkansas fifteen miles away. The night was peaceful and cold and the breeze was blowing hard. All of us were tired and sleepy but were told to get on with the red tape right away.[4]

In 1975, the Adventist Church, with the assistance of Loma Linda University, operated a private hospital in Saigon about a mile from the airport to care for U.S. dependents as well as Vietnamese nationals who could afford the service. As the Seventh Day Adventist Hospital was closing down when the communists threatened Saigon, Pastor Watts on the evening of Wednesday 23 April asked Pastor Giao to draft a list of Vietnamese workers and their families who would be allowed to leave the country. After agonizing the whole night about whom to take and whom to leave out, Giao and his aides came down with 225 names instead of the 175 allowed. On Thursday, Watts, after shaking his head in disbelief, took the list to Mr. Johnson, the liaison for the evacuation at the Defense Attaché Office, and was told to return in a couple of hours. Johnson later handed him a letter that read:

> Embassy of the United States of America
> Defense Attaché Office
> 24 April 1975
>
> To whom it may concern:
>
> The attached manifests are dependent of individuals who have closely associated

with the United States government. Because of this close association with us, their lives may be in danger.

H.D. Smith, Jr.
Major General, United States Army.[5]

With the list approval in hand, Watt told Giao at 16:00 hours to have his people available for departure from the hospital by 19:45 hours the same day. Since Saigon was under curfew from 18:00 hours until 07:00 hours and to avoid the crowd, it would be easier to take the locals to the airport after the curfew took effect, since ambulances would not be stopped by the police.

Watts and a co-worker returned to the airport to submit the manifests. They found the staging area filled with more than 300 people waiting to register for check-in at three stations. He decided to bypass the lines and go directly to the supervisor, whom he helped write the manifests. With three people working together, it still took an hour and a half to complete the project.

Multiple trips from the hospital to the airport had to be made to transport the group of 225 travelers. In the meantime, six or seven young Chinese Vietnamese approached Watts during one of the loading sessions at the hospital and demanded to be allowed to fly out; they continued to harass him. A frustrated Watts told them to wait until he had completed the transfer of official people before taking care of them. Later Giao told Watts that two other families—a total of fifteen or sixteen people—had been inadvertently left off the list. Watts got the names and added them to the manifests when he arrived at the airport. At 01:30 hours on Friday, the transfer was completed with the last two families on the last trip. The tired Watts went back to the hospital to take a shower and a nap.

By 3:30 hours he returned to the airport, refreshed and ready to take on another day, when Giao told him he had missed another family: Chiêu, a Chinese-Vietnamese who lived in the Chinese section of Saigon. Giao called the last traveler to tell him to be present with his family at the airport by 07:00 hours. They stepped out of the airport gate to look for Chiêu while people began to gather at the gate. They failed to find him, unaware that Chiêu had managed to get into the airport by himself. When they tried to get back into the airport, they realized that they had forgotten to take the manifest with them. Without it, Giao was not able to get through the security booth outside the airport until they thought to put Giao on the passenger side of the ambulance and have him turn his head the other way. Wyatt managed to drive through the security lane while the policeman talked to another person.

The C-141 transport plane took off at 13:00 hours on Friday 25

7. First, Second, and Third Wave Arrivals

April. It was only in Guam that Watts realized that the group of 225 people had grown to 410 people. The group was sponsored by Loma Linda University and left Guam a few days later.[6]

The first arrivals on Guam were in general better off than the subsequent arrivals; they were well prepared and got out in style with their belongings, paperwork, money, and clothing. They knew where they were going and had friends or relatives (sometimes their children) waiting for them. They were accompanied by their families. They flew in by planes, whether by commercial or military aircraft, carried with them elegant sets of matched luggage, and did not have to fight to get out by sea.

One could see them waiting in an orderly manner for food in Guam. Having arrived earlier, they got the best lodging places on the island: the Tin City, the Tokyu Hotel, private construction camps and un-crowded living areas. They were well dressed in tailored outfits or dresses and as a group, looked like they had gone out on a vacation. They walked in sync with one another despite not having known each other before. For them, nothing had changed, except for the scenery.

In Vietnam they were pampered, with maids to serve them, and in Guam someone would attend to their needs. It was not that they had lost nothing—they did—but their loss was much smaller than that of the second arrivals. They still had money, gold, accounts stashed somewhere; above all they had connections and families in the U.S., while the majority of the second arrivals had nothing. Since they arrived early, they were flown to Camp Pendleton in California and tended to remain in that state because of the nice weather. They came in and got out as fast as rules permitted and had the best sponsors, most often their connections.

The second-wave arrivals consisted of the bulk of arrivals to the island. In a dispatch to the *New York Times*, Andrew Malcolm wrote that three merchant ships arrived on the island in the early hours of Saturday 10 May 1975. They were the *Transcolorado* and the *American Racer*, which are under contract with the Military Sealift Command, and the *Thương Tín I*, a 476-foot cargo craft operated by the former South Vietnamese government. The arrivals were doctors and fishermen, priests and farmers, importers and soldiers. They were not all from professional occupations, as earlier arrivals seemed to be. But neither were they all simple country folk. More of them were elderly persons than in the previous group.[7]

The newest arrivals brought the island's refugee population to 48,000, almost a third of Guam's civilian population. A total of 38,000 had departed for the continental U.S. The list of refugees was expected to swell with the arrival of 20,000 more South Vietnamese on the last six refugee ships due on the island from evacuation camps in the Philippines.

The *Transcolorado* docked at Guam with one more passenger than when she sailed from Subic Bay. The addition, John Colorado Than, was born on the United States flagship in international waters and would likely be eligible for American citizenship.

Others, however, died on the way, including a 2-year-old baby and a 67-year-old man, both of whom had been injured in a communist rocket attack as the *Thương Tín* hurriedly left Saigon. One explosion killed five people, including Chu Tử, a prominent Saigon journalist.

The Third Wave Arrivals

Those in the third wave left Vietnam on their own, usually because of lack of connection to Americans. They made up the majority of those who came to the U.S. They were lower-level Vietnamese government officials, teachers, rank and file members of the Vietnamese army and navy, petty traders, farmers and fishermen. Many spoke little English and had few skills usable in the United States. They consisted of persons many American officials believed should have stayed in the country.

They managed to escape from Vietnam either with the Vietnamese navy or through their own means. The latter were not well organized and had no plan: seeing or watching their friends or neighbors rushing to the sea, especially those living along the coastline or at the seaside resort of Vũng Tàu, they just followed them. They used motorized boats, barges, sampans, fishing boats, tug boats, and other small craft to get out of Vũng Tàu, a village at the mouth of the Saigon River. They took with them their families, friends and some paying guests and were picked up by ships from the Seventh Fleet, which was luckily anchored twelve miles off Vũng Tàu.

Many had to make the 2,600-mile trip between Vietnam and Guam by sea, which took them a week or more. Others were lucky to stop at Subic Bay, the Philippines, then be loaded onto a plane at Clark AFB. Others still had to make the second leg from Subic Bay to Guam by sea. By riding ships, they arrived on Guam a week or two after the fall of Saigon and therefore were designated as second arrivals at Guam for Operation New Life. In reality, they were the first "boat people" out of Vietnam in 1975.

Crowding and poor sanitation aboard the MSC ships facilitated person-to-person spread of infection. Many came down with a form of

7. First, Second, and Third Wave Arrivals

conjunctivitis (pinkeye) which was initially resistant to viral identification. The disease affected 29,000 evacuees in Guam and was characterized by conjunctival injection (100 percent), lid edema (84 percent), eye irritation (81 percent), and sub-conjunctival hemorrhages (45 percent). The illness lasted six to 10 days. Conjunctival swabs with paired serum specimens in a small number of patients implicated enterococcus 70 as the primary virus and adenovirus 11 as a less frequent agent. Forty-three percent of a subgroup of 604 evacuees were affected. Only 13 out of 1,300 Americans who were in frequent contact with the affected evacuees during that period got the disease.[8] Isolation, continuous disinfecting, spraying, and washing took care of the problem.

The late arrivals represented the masses of people who got out at the twenty-fifth hour, just in the nick of time. They most likely ran around from one place to another in Saigon before getting onto one of the boats going out of the country.

> Many of them were barefoot and ragged; they were confused, tired, and hungry. A few of them arrived with a small bundle or basket with all their earthly possessions. Most had nothing more than the clothes on their backs. Most had not eaten for days. For those of us who boarded the ships, the stench was almost overpowering. Sanitary facilities and bathroom facilities were almost non-existent. There was no water on board the ships for washing or bathing.[9]

They looked dazed, bewildered and lost. They wondered why and how they had gotten to Guam and what this country was about. Many had never traveled abroad before. Because of leaving by themselves, they often had missing family members: husbands, wives, siblings, grandparents, sons…. Usually, either the head of the family or the spouse had gone out with one or two children. The rest were lost or scattered somewhere.

The tents on Guam were the solace of the evacuees, whether they were in the first, second, or third wave. They gave them a moment of respite and peace in their search for freedom. Tents and cots were better than sleeping on the deck or being crowded aboard the ships. They gave them privacy and shelter from the prying eyes of neighbors and strangers.

But when they stood in lines for their meals, the differences between the two groups were visible. While the first and second waves were well organized, wore matched outfits, and stayed in lines, the third wave people did not seem to have energy left; they moved slowly, deep in thought. They wore different outfits: some in soldiers' garb and others in mismatched shirts and pants. Some wore flip flops instead of regular shoes. There were elderly people and youngsters in the group; and women attending to young children. Although there were intellectuals in the group, the group represented a broad section of Vietnamese society, including farmers, fishermen, soldiers, and housewives. As a matter of fact, the fishermen were well represented because they were the ones who owned the boats or had access to them through kinship, friendship, or work.

They tended to stay longer in the camps for various reasons: because they were waiting for missing members of their families, or because they had large families, or because they were unaccompanied or had no education, which made placement difficult. Having no connections, they did not know where to go to get information, or which course of action to choose. The unfamiliarity of the country and the people, as well as the American lifestyle, forced them to make difficult and sometimes incorrect choices. Should they go to New England, the Midwest, or the South? All these places were unfamiliar to them. Coming from a country the size of California, the huge expanse of the U.S. began to daunt them. Would they want to be sponsored by churches or private citizens? Since most of them were Buddhists, it was hard for them to accept the sponsorship of a church.

Refugee Profiles

Even the best-planned scenario could go wrong in time of war and in the face of unexpected adverse factors. The evacuation plan, designed in a calm environment, probably had in mind a stable South Vietnamese government that maintained law and order, a population that did not get panicky when the city was shelled or bombed or under siege, and an orderly departure of 5,000 or 10,000 people. None of these factors, however, were present in Saigon during the last two weeks of the war. In that situation, it was almost impossible to design an ideal evacuation plan for an unstable and unsafe area when the definition of instability could not be spelled out. There was an almost total collapse of the South Vietnamese government, and complete absence of policemen and firefighters to enforce peace and stability. The top military brass had left town. The ministers of the new government had not been sworn in yet, except for the president. The city and the airport were shelled, rendering the runways unusable.

Civilians mobbed the U.S. Embassy, and enemy troops had positioned themselves all around the city, blocking all the exits and ready to attack. Artillery was aimed at downtown, ready to launch its deadly rounds. People were restless and panicky. Disorder was rampant. Fires

7. First, Second, and Third Wave Arrivals 103

broke out at many places, with firefighters nowhere to be seen. In the meantime, more than one hundred thousand people frantically fought to flee the country. The mood was fearful, although luckily there was no military revolt yet. To look for the right people to evacuate from this disorderly environment would be impossible.

Overall, the majority of first- and second-wave evacuees in Guam were from the educated elite of the country: 20 percent had attended a university, 40 percent were Catholic and 35 percent spoke some English.[10]

On paper, 26 August was the official date of closure of the island camps.[11] (Some people in special situations remained in Guam until 1 November). The four months most spent on Guam (23 April–26 August)—were crucial not only to the stabilization of the postwar exodus from Vietnam, but also to resetting of the mood and minds of the evacuees. That period allowed them to settle down: it gave them time to think everything over and look more at the future than the past. Of course, they could not stop thinking about the past, because it kept haunting them by remaining as part of their identity for the rest of their lives.

For most of these people, this was the first time in their lives that they had ventured abroad. If someone had asked them what they thought of being on foreign soil, they would not be able to answer, because this was completely new to them and there was nothing to compare it to. Facing the future at that time did not seem as important as looking at the past. They knew they had lost the past, but they were not ready to embrace the future because it remained a mystery.

The evacuees, however, seemed less upset, anxious, and nervous about the past and future as time went by. They settled down and later were dispatched throughout society. The stay in the camps, therefore, helped smooth out the resettlement process. It introduced the Vietnamese to the American way of life and culture. It re-channeled their negative forces and redirected them toward rebuilding a new life in another country.

Because of their traumatic past, the evacuees were later found to be traumatized, psychologically and mentally. They had lost not only all their worldly possessions and personal belongings, but also their friends, families, ancestral graves, and their country. They were moneyless, jobless, homeless, and stateless, and by that time had reached the bottom of society. Above all, they had lost their own identity and nationality. Their old way of living might not be comparable to that of the U.S., but it was better than nothing. It was that way of living that they were hanging onto, not that of the U.S. that they could not foresee and had not been introduced to yet.

Of the 138,869 evacuees processed through the system, 129,792 (93.46 percent) were resettled in the United States; 6,632 (4.77 percent) were resettled in third countries; 1,546 (1.1 percent) were repatriated to Vietnam; and there were 403 births (0.69 percent) and 77 deaths (0.59 percent).

Vietnamese who came to the United States tend to be young, part of a family group, and Catholic. In table 7–1, 45.9 and 80.5 percent of all refugees were under the ages of 18 and 35, respectively. Table 7–2 indicates that only 16,810 out of 124,493 came to the U.S. alone. About 40 percent of refugees were Catholics, compared to 10 percent of the South Vietnamese population.

Table 7-1. Age and Sex of IndoChinese Immigrants

Age	Male		Female		Total	
	Number	Percent	Number	Percent	Number	Percent
0–5	10,572	8.6	9,817	8.0	20,389	16.6
6–11	9,704	7.9	8,611	7.0	18,315	14.9
12–17	9,519	7.7	8,296	6.7	17,815	14.4
18–24	13,591	11.0	9,105	7.4	22,696	18.6
25–34	12,063	9.8	8,821	7.2	20,884	17.0
35–44	6,364	5.1	5,068	4.1	11,432	9.2
45–62	4,706	3.8	4,569	3.7	9,275	7.5
63+	980	0.8	1,515	1.2	2,495	2.0
Total	67,499	54.7	55,802	45.3	123,301	100.0

SOURCE: US Department of Health, Education, and Welfare. HEW Refugee Task Force. Report to the Congress. Washington, D.C., DHEW, March 15, 1976, p. 25.

Table 7-2. Immigrant Household Size

Household Size	All Households			
	Number of Households	% of Households	Number of People	% of People
1	16,819	44.45	16,819	13.51
2	4,524	11.96	9,048	7.27
3	3,166	8.37	9,498	7.63
4	2,952	7.80	11,808	9.48
5	2,537	6.69	12,685	10.19
6	2,185	5.77	13,110	10.53

7. First, Second, and Third Wave Arrivals 105

Household Size	All Households			
	Number of Households	% of Households	Number of People	% of People
7	1,663	4.39	11,641	9.35
8	1,357	3.59	10,856	8.72
9	960	2.54	8,640	6.94
10	620	1.64	6,200	4.98
Subtotal	36,783	97.20	110,305	88.60
>10	1,061	2.80	14,188	11.40
Total	37,844	100.00	124,493	100.00

Table 7-3. Educational Levels of Immigrants

	Heads of Household Only		All Immigrants 18 Years of Age or Older	
	Number	Percent	Number	Percent
None	407	1.3	1,384	2.1
Some Elementary	5,120	16.7	11,979	17.9
Some Secondary	14,632	47.8	25,432	37.9
Some University	7,004	22.9	11,150	16.6
Post-graduate	1,375	4.5	1,955	2.9
No Information	2,090	6.8	15,133	22.6
Total	30,628	100.0	67,033	100.0

SOURCE: *HEW 15 March 1976, p. 26.*

Table 7–3 reports educational levels according to whether refugees had entered primary, secondary, or higher education. It does not indicate that they completed primary, secondary, or higher education. Although these educational levels look average by American standards, when compared to those of all South Vietnamese, the immigrants emerged as an educated elite.[12]

Table 7-4. Primary Employment Skills of Household Heads (N=30,628)

Skill Categories	Number	Percent
Medical Professions (MD, Dentists, Pharmacists, Midwives, Nurses)	2,210	7.2

Skill Categories	Number	Percent
Professional, Technical, Managerial	7,368	24.0
Clerical, and	3,572	11.7
Sales Services	2,324	7.6
Farming, Fishing, Forestry, and Related Areas	1,491	4.9
Agricultural Processing	128	0.4
Machine Trades	2,670	8.7
Benchwork, Assembly, Repair	1,249	4.1
Structural and Construction	2,026	6.6
Transportation and Misc.	5,165	16.9
Did not indicate	2,425	7.9
Total	30,628	100.0

HEW, 15 March 1976, p. 27.

Table 7–4 does not indicate the jobs individuals held in Vietnam; rather, it lists the skills they possessed as translated into U.S. Department of Labor job skill categories. It shows that 31 percent of immigrant heads of household had professional, technical and managerial skills, followed by transportation (16 percent), and sales skills (11.7 percent). These skills made them part of the Vietnamese elite.

From the above analysis, it is hard to understand why various American officials mentioned that the "wrong" Vietnamese were evacuated.[13] The statistics point to the immigration being composed primarily of the South Vietnamese elite and their families.

Reaction to the New Refugees

Guam's civilian community had mixed reactions to the airlift. The governor's office was pushing for legislative approval of special powers. The Guam legislature continued its questioning of the State Department to find out if Guam would suffer under the influx of Vietnamese. Secretary of State Henry Kissinger told Gov. Ricardo Bordallo in a cable to "plan initially for 90 days with the possibility of a longer period." Speaker Joseph Ada mentioned, "We don't want this to be another Miami with the Cuban refugees staying for life." Doris Flores Brooks, a senator of the 20th Guam Legislature, argued that the U.S. could not force Guam to be a refugee center unless Guam voluntarily agreed to it.[14]

7. First, Second, and Third Wave Arrivals 107

Other Guamanians' worries were simpler and more down to earth. They worried about their island sinking under the weight of the newcomers, especially when the number of refugees kept increasing in number. They worried that camp managers would go out and buy food, vegetables, meat from local food stores, causing a lack of food on the island.

The presence of evacuees raised questions about their eventual resettlement. As the U.S. asked other countries for their help in resettling the evacuees, Australia answered that it would accept only a few hundred people, mostly spouses and children of Australians in Vietnam or relatives of Vietnamese students attending Australian universities. The prime minister of Singapore said Singapore would not take any evacuees. Thailand, which had accepted 60,000 Vietnamese when the French left Vietnam, refused to accept any Cambodian or Vietnamese refugees. West Germany said it would take a few thousand who would be carefully selected.

The U.S. mainland was also not receptive to accepting the evacuees. California threatened to throw legal roadblocks in any plans to relocate Vietnamese evacuees to that state. "I propose that no refugees be accepted until definite plans are proposed by the federal government," stated Mario Obledo, California secretary of health and welfare.

Representative Richard White of Texas suggested that the evacuees be settled in the Trust Territory instead. "They would be in a location quite similar to their own climate and terrain and with people of similar ethnic strain." Mackie argued that White had probably never been to the Trust Territory. Guam is the southernmost of a chain of islands called the Marianas Islands. Because of a historical technicality, the remainder of the Marianas Islands became a part of the Trust Territory, while Guam is a U.S. territory. But ethnically, culturally, and linguistically, they are the same people, who had been impacted by the influx of Western culture for centuries. They are technically Western cultures, much akin to Texas.[15]

Although many Americans welcomed them with open hearts and sponsored them, some were opposed to the resettlement of the Vietnamese in the U.S. due to the difficult economic conditions worldwide at the time and the recent opposition to the war in Vietnam.

Norman Sweet, senior coordinator with the Agency for International Development (AID) refugee task force, stated that he was "happy" with Guam's efforts on behalf of the refugees, despite the fact that the legislature and the general populace had "no uniform view on this [refugee] matter." In fact, one poll showed that 52 percent of Americans were not happy about the refugees.[16]

In a department store close to the Ft. Indiantown Gap refugee camp, one woman loudly asked, "Why don't we just ship them back to where they come from? ... We don't want those dirty peasants." Another evening after watching a news broadcast featuring the refugees, one middle-aged man shouted an obscenity and told his neighbor, a soldier stationed at the base, "Why the hell did they send them here? They'll never be Americans." The soldier answered, "All of them dope peddlers and whores are coming in."[17]

Civilian officials at the camp were aware of the hostilities the Vietnamese could face and they planned to cover the subject during orientation courses. The refugees were not expected to be sent to areas with high racial intolerance.

Negative perceptions in the community about the evacuees continued to persist and in some cases led to violent confrontations, including death. Such was the well-known case of the Ku Klux Klan and the Vietnamese fishermen.

Fishermen who had been shrimpers in Vietnam settled in the Galveston Bay area and pooled money together to buy boats and engage in the shrimping business. As strangers and newcomers, they got the worst possible deal: they had to buy boats in poor condition for high premiums. Undeterred, they fixed their boats by themselves and got into the business by working hard to try to get ahead. White men reacted by pressuring local shops to boycott Vietnamese catches. The legislature was successfully lobbied to decrease the number of new shrimp boat licenses. Competition was fierce. Over time, the increased fishing activity caused a decrease in shrimp harvest in the Gulf of Galveston. An additional rise of shrimp imports kept the wholesale price low. Many had to cut their costs to survive, and others went out of business.

Between 1979 and 1981, several Vietnamese boats were burned and investigation revealed that they were intentionally set on fire, although no one was caught in the act. Crosses were burned near Vietnamese fishermen's homes. On 3 August 1979, in the town of Seadrift, Texas, several Vietnamese boats were burned and a vacant house was firebombed. A fistfight between white and Vietnamese fishermen left one white man shot to death. Two Vietnamese were tried for murder but later acquitted on the grounds of self-defense. This incident led to hard feelings against the Vietnamese community. Some mistook the refugees as North Vietnamese they had fought in the past in Vietnam. Others believed that the refugees should leave the area.

On 14 February 1981, white fishermen and the Ku Klux Klan organized a rally against the Vietnamese and gave the government until 15 May to get the Vietnamese out of the area, otherwise the Klansmen would take "laws into their own hands." The rally was covered by local news media. The Vietnamese, operating from a stretch of docks dubbed "Saigon Harbor," outnumbered the Americans. On 15 March, hooded Klansmen paraded in boats in the waters near Seabrook, displayed weapons, and made threatening gestures at the Vietnamese. An effigy of a Vietnamese was hung on the deck of a boat.

On 16 April 1981, Morris Dees, a civil rights lawyer, filed a lawsuit on behalf of the Vietnamese against the Klansmen in federal court, seeking a court order against the Klansmen's campaign of harassment and intimidation during the 1981 shrimping season. During a four-day trial, several Vietnamese fishermen took to the stand to testify before an audience that included many robed Klansmen. Judge McDonald also heard testimony of the defendants, law enforcement officials, and the reporter who accompanied the Klan on the 15 March boat parade. An injunction was issued on 14 May preventing the Klan from harassing or intimidating the Vietnamese fishermen. In July, Judge McDonald issued a written opinion that the Klan violated the Vietnamese fishermen's rights under Texas contract law and federal antitrust law.[18]

8

Repatriates and the *Thương Tín I* Odyssey

The other problem of Operation New Life was the repatriation of some evacuees who were homesick and wanted to return to Vietnam at any cost. This happened in the period from 3 May until 16 October 1975.

The Thương Tín I *Odyssey*

The Repatriates

The problem of those refugees on Guam who wanted to be repatriated, although short, was at times violent, and brought a lot of worries and headaches to the camp managers and the Guamanians, all the way up to the governor of Guam, the secretary of state, and the hopeful repatriates themselves. It also reveals the interdependence of local, national, and international institutions, like Guam, the U.S. government, the United National High Commissioner of Refugees (UNHCR), the southern Provisional Revolutionary Government (PRG) and the northern Democratic Republic of Vietnam.[1]

The number of returnees, in fact, was small: 1,546 out of the 120,000 moving to the U.S., or a little more than one percent of the evacuee population. They were, unfortunately, people who changed their minds at the last minute.

From the beginning, this one percent minority debated in their minds about whether to follow the crowd and go abroad with them. They did not have any idea of what life abroad entailed—neither did those who forged ahead—since the majority had not traveled abroad before. But they were, on the other hand, very familiar with Vietnam, its way of life, its fields of rice and swamps, and the small hamlet they lived in. Would they want to trade a field of rice for a field of wheat, rice for bread? Probably not. But seeing other people rushing to the shore and

8. Repatriates and the Thương Tín I *Odyssey*

jumping on boats, and not wanting to stay behind to face the communists alone, they followed the crowd.

Each personal attempt to get out of the country was unscripted and unplanned, except in the case of those who worked with the Americans. However, the best scripted evacuation plan can turn into disarray and failure. No one had forced these people to get out. They were the ones who sought to leave the country, with or without the permission of the government of South Vietnam. A crowd hung around Tân Sơn Nhứt Airport and the U.S. Embassy, waiting for the chance to get in. Each person who got into one of the departing ships or boats meant one place less for others.

In one ARVN platoon, a lieutenant gathered his men around him for the last time to bid farewell to them. It was 30 April 1975. The war had ended, as President Minh had surrendered to the incoming communists and had asked each soldier to lay down his gun. The lieutenant thanked his soldiers and asked whether any of them would want to follow him abroad. All his men, being from the Mekong Delta area, only wanted to return to their hamlets and follow the life of their forefathers. None of them wanted to go abroad. The lieutenant wished them good luck and joined a group of officers who also headed for the shore to get out of Vietnam.

But people changed their minds often, especially when they were under stress. And there was no more stressful situation than the imminent fall of Saigon. When enemy divisions were surrounding the gates of Saigon, when Americans were leaving Saigon in droves, when the future of the South Vietnamese under the communists was the big unknown, to leave or not to leave the country was the main question. But *how* to get out was next, because there were not many routes open to get out of the besieged country. Although the planes and ships could be stuffed with evacuees, the helicopters at the U.S. Embassy in Saigon and the civilian and navy ships could only hold so many.

One photograph in the *Army After Report*, snapped from the deck of a huge American ship, showed on one side the deck of the ship filled with evacuees, and on the other side, three Vietnamese boats closing in on the ship to allow some evacuees to get aboard. Between them was a 50-yard space of open sea where two or three Vietnamese were swimming.[2] It turned out that they had jumped off the big ship trying to get into the small boats. They had changed their minds and wanted to return to Vietnam instead of going abroad.

Guam Protests

On the island of Guam, some potential repatriates first identified themselves on 3 May—that was just three days after the fall of Saigon.

They were among the early arrivals, who most likely were well connected to or had worked for the U.S. in Vietnam. Facing the problem, the U.S. had asked UNHCR (United Nations High Commissioner for Refugees) to step in and to help with the negotiation process, since the U.S. had no consular connection with the Hanoi government or the PRG (People's Revolutionary Government). On 17 June, the potential repatriates demonstrated against a proposed move to Wake Island. When all the CONUS potential repatriates were transferred to Guam for consolidation on 5 July, the stage was set for new rounds of civil and military confrontations.[3] While negotiations continued with the Hanoi government, peaceful protests occurred on 17, 24 and 25 July and 19 August.

The protests, which were benign in the beginning. rapidly turned violent because, without reason or proof, the repatriates believed that the Americans were dragging their feet. They did not realize that Hanoi did not want to take them back at that time, having too many problems to deal with. Therefore, they staged hunger strikes, then shaved their heads in protest. They vowed not to eat until they died, and one of them even threatened to cut off his finger. Their rhetoric also changed: if in the beginning, they wanted to go home to be reunited with their families, they later framed their return as a nationalistic duty. They still wanted to be reunited with their families, but that purpose was no longer their primary goal. They claimed "they did not lose their country; but a new regime had taken over the government." The main goal of returning home this time was to help rebuild the country. To make matter worse, one of the protesters who was an artist drew a picture of Hồ Chí Minh, which they prominently displayed and saluted; they stood at attention under it with a banner declaring "Tinh Thần Cụ Hồ Chí Minh Bất Diệt," or "The Spirit of Ho Chi Minh is indomitable." In all probability, the painting was a signal directed at the PRG and designed to stress to the PRG that the potential repatriates would be loyal members of socialist Vietnam.[4]

In his memoir, Trụ, despite also being a repatriate, dismissed the aggressive actions of the protesters. He commented that it was a bad idea to use the picture of Hồ Chí Minh to fight against the Americans and Guamanians. Trụ believed the protesters were opportunists who used any tool in their hands to push their agenda forward—but they did not mean to propagandize for the communists.[5]

On 31 August and 3 September, the repatriates escalated the tempo of their fight by burning two barracks, damaging several vehicles, and injuring four United States Marshals who were sent to contain them. This was followed by demonstrations with hunger strikes, head shavings, and other forms of protests. They slowly realized that the problem rested with Hanoi, which on 30 September was still unable to give a firm date for their return. Upset at the lack of breakthrough, the repatriates asked the U.S. authorities to simply give them a ship so that they could go home on their own. They were willing to accept total responsibility for their actions.

The U.S. refitted, refurbished, and restocked the *Thương Tín I*, which had been sitting in the harbor since its arrival at Guam in early May. The cargo ship had to be refitted to house the 1,546 repatriates and restocked for a 30-day trip, in case the repatriates changed their minds. A one-way trip would take only from seven to ten days. Some repatriates were trained to run the ship. The conversion, training and organization of the crew into an efficient, responsible unit capable of running the returning ship, estimated to take three weeks, were accomplished in twelve days. The new crew was tested for docking, sea trials, and seaworthiness.

On 16 October, the *Thương Tín I* pulled anchor and set sail toward an uncertain future with Trần Đình Trụ as its captain.[6]

Trụ wrote in his 1994 memoir, nineteen years after he departed from Guam, "I felt utter sorrow flooding over me and tears welled up in my eyes, unsure if I was coming back to my family and my homeland or journeying into the netherworld."[7]

Captain Trần Đình Trụ

Trần Đình Trụ conceded, when he landed in 1991 at the San Francisco International Airport sixteen years later, after applying for immigration to the U.S. through the Humanitarian Operation (HO) program, that all his "energy has been sapped by the communists"[8] during his thirteen years in communist reeducation camps and he was only looking forward to raising his children and giving them some education that was missing in Vietnam. He eventually settled in Dallas on 12 December 1991.

This concluded a sixteen-year ordeal for a man who arrived in Guam in 1975 along with the first 120,000 refugees, only to decide to return to Vietnam to be reunited with his family, who had remained in Vietnam. This time, he came with his full family. He concluded, "Rage boiled up inside me. Had I chosen to remain in America [back in 1975 when he was In Guam], I would have been able to support my family. And now [1991], it was too late. I could only blame it on my fate."[9]

He should have blamed himself, instead of blaming his fate, for he was the one who made the fateful decision on 16 October 1975 to returning to Vietnam from Guam despite his friends' advice to the contrary.

In early 1975, he assumed the position of deputy commander of a naval base in the fifth naval region in Nam Căn, Cà Mau, South Vietnam. On 23 April 1975, his wife and three children flew from their home in Saigon to the naval base, being too afraid to stay home in Saigon by themselves.

What transpired between his wife and him that day at the Nam Căn Naval Base is not known, but he made the unfortunate decision of returning to Saigon the next day to pick up his children's belongings. With Saigon in turmoil, he was unable to get a flight back to his naval base and remained stuck in Saigon. He got out of Saigon aboard the navy fleet on 29 April at 20:00 hours. The convoy took off under the direction of Admiral Hoàng Cơ Minh and arrived at Côn Sơn Island the following morning.[10] After a day of preparation, the whole convoy headed toward the Philippines.

Trụ made two crucial mistakes: he returned to Saigon in April to pick up his children's belongings and was evacuated with the VNN ships while his wife and children were stuck in Nam Căn Navy Base, and from Guam he returned to Vietnam in October 1975 to rejoin his family.

The Demonstration

In Guam, Trụ enlisted with UNHCR to return to Vietnam despite repeated urgings from friends to the contrary. He lost the power to think because of his feelings for his family.[11]

By the end of August, Orote Point began to close and the 3,000 remaining evacuees were moved to four different camps: Black Construction, J and G, Hawaiian, and Barrigada. These camps had previously been reserved for civilians working for private companies that supported army and navy troops stationed on the island. Amenities were plentiful and included sleeping halls, bathrooms with showers, messes, offices, gymnasiums, and movie theaters. These amenities suggested they had to settle for a long wait before being allowed to return home. As a result, they became depressed by the long waiting period.

The routine was good. A bus took them to the marketplace every day to run errands and buy stuff for the return trip. Fresh fruit and meals were available and found to be better than those available at Orote Point Camp. Each evacuee was provided with five packs of cigarettes per week. The Red Cross also gave them extra clothing, footwear, and daily household needs. They were well cared for, and whoever changed their mind about returning home was well taken care of.

Among the potential returnees were three lieutenant colonels, 20 majors, 70 officers, from aspirants (the lowest officer rank in the Army of the Republic of South Vietnam) to captains, even doctors, dentists, and the rest from all the branches of army, navy, and air force. They even had access to newspapers published in France, England, Canada, and Australia sent to them by courtesy of their relatives from these countries. However, there was no news about South Vietnam and what was going on there. But rumors, which abounded in the camp, caused the evacuees to meet privately in groups of three or four to discuss and comment. This was what idle people would do. There were rumors about refugees returning from Singapore who were warmly welcomed and about communists who hunted down those who tried to escape but welcomed the returnees. One navy man who claimed to be Huỳnh Tấn Phát's cousin had received a telegram advising him ironically to "stay put and study." Huỳnh Tấn Phát was one of leaders of the communist National Liberation Front (NLF). The laconic message was dissected endlessly, although it did not provide any clue about the situation in Saigon and South Vietnam.[12]

The returnees from the four camps on Guam Island got organized and elected their representatives. They hung up banners expressing their desire for a speedy return to Vietnam. As no response was forthcoming, they began a hunger strike.

Lê Minh Tân led a group of 251 evacuees who crossed the camp gate of the Naval Communications Station where they were housed and proceeded to walk downtown. They carried banners and their belongings in bags and boxes and walked half a mile before being caught. They were herded back to Orote Point by the police and marshals. Their goal was to create a commotion in the island community. The following day, the group at Hawaiian Dredging Company marched with their hands tied behind their backs and stood in front of a pizza store during rush hour. A group of 500 simultaneously walked out at the Black Construction Company, wearing signs saying, "We are not prisoners of war." U.S. authorities responded to these protests by consolidating the potential repatriates at Camp Asan for easy monitoring.[13]

The majority, however, had remained silent. They just wanted to go home, not actively participate in the fight. As the protests escalated and became violent, dissention broke out between the two repatriate groups. On one side, the moderates who did not want to antagonize their hosts urged for more patience while solutions were being worked out, and on the other side the aggressive ones vowed to continue to fight using violence as a tool. This was reflected in the competing signs erected by the repatriates within the camp. One sign mentioned, "Dear Guamanian and American People. Our desire is only to go home. We don't want to disturb you and to be lost your sympathy [sic] that would be reserved for us. Please understand that how painful we are now and try to support our repatriation." Another sign said, "Hunger strike till die." One protester even threatened to immolate himself.

Facing potential violent confrontations, U.S. authorities brought back retired Army General Herbert, who made the rounds of the camps to talk to strikers. He explained to them that repatriation was not easy because of lack of cooperation from the new communist Vietnamese government that was dragging its feet. Therefore, the U.S. had asked UNHCR for help, and in turn he asked for more patience from those who wanted to return to Vietnam.[14]

Two new leaders had emerged at Asan Camp. Lê Minh Tân had previously worked for the U.S. military in Saigon for 6 or 7 years. From Guam, he was sent to Ft. Chaffee, Arkansas, where he asked the Americans to prioritize the rapid transfer of the repatriates back to Vietnam. He wanted to go home immediately. "The American government is very rich and has very, very many planes," he said.[15] Tân was later transferred to Guam for repatriation. The other, Như Văn Úy, was a former South Vietnamese representative. From Guam, he opted to move to France. Once there, he changed his mind and wanted to return to Saigon; therefore, he was transferred back to the camps on Guam for repatriation.

The following day, Guam governor Bordallo and General Herbert, the Washington representative, came to the camp for a discussion with the refugees. Bordallo told them that he understood their grievances and was working very hard to solve them. He asked them to be patient and to conserve their energy for the trip home. He warned them that any disturbance that created ripples in the local community would be dealt with. The camp representative explained that worries and frustrations about not being able to return home led to the demonstration that in his view was justifiable, although no harm was intended. The refugees just wanted to know how soon they would be able to return home. Herbert counseled the refugees to be patient. He explained that Washington was doing everything it could, including asking UNHCR for help, to speed up the return process. He had even notified Washington about the demonstration. The refugees apologized to the governor for the incident. Everyone seemed to be understanding.[16]

UNHCR sent a representative (Ali Khan) to Hanoi to discuss the evacuee problem. Following his return to Guam, Ali Khan gave the refugees a report about his trip. He had spent three days in Hanoi and two in Saigon. He had witnessed the devastation of the country, which was poor and had huge economic problems. Communications were scarce and difficult, with bridges and roads not yet repaired. Although peace had settled on the country, Hanoi had no rebuilding plans. Even if the

8. Repatriates and the Thương Tín I *Odyssey*

country could rebuild, the process of repatriating the evacuees would take a long time. Hanoi did not have enough people to take over the administration, vacant offices, and factories in the South. Hanoi officials had told him that rebuilding the country and administering the South were their priorities before they could take on the evacuee problem. At this time, they did not even have enough housing and jobs for everyone in the country. Once the problem had settled down, they certainly would welcome the evacuees back. They hoped the evacuees would understand them.

Ali Khan then suggested that UNHCR was ready and willing to help with the resettling of the repatriates if Hanoi could not take care of them. As an intermediary organization, UNHCR had the responsibility to make sure that the refugees would be well treated and resettled on their return. Hanoi, however, argued that the responsibility to care for returning Vietnamese rested on the Hanoi government, not on any outside organization. They, therefore, suggested the refugees be patient. The report threw the refugees into despair. How long would they have to wait, and how long would they be willing to wait?[17]

Herbert flew back to Washington to make his report. Ali Khan did the same with UNHCR in New York. On his return to Guam, Herbert had a talk with the refugees. He again suggested that the refugees should be patient. Violence would not achieve anything. During his absence, the returnees in Barrigada and Hawaiian had destroyed some properties in the camp. They asked to be given a ship to prepare for the trip home and suggested Captain Trụ as the potential commander. They told Herbert that the five or six ships that had brought them to Guam were still anchored in the harbor. Herbert asked Trụ to begin setting up a crew for the ship.

Trụ asked potential volunteers in the camps to list their navy experience on a piece of paper. There were plenty of seamen in the camps who gladly signed up for the job because at least there was some hope on the horizon. From the list of 300 volunteers, he chose 120; this included 12 officers. He turned over the list to Herbert, who flew to Washington for his usual report. The news spread to all the camps and the evacuees were elated.[18]

Hunger Strikes and Negotiations

Following Herbert's return, all the potential repatriates from the four camps were transferred to Asan Camp. They numbered about 2,000, down from 3,000. Some of them had to make many trips to transport all the belongings they had acquired on Guam; these things had been given to them by the Red Cross and other volunteer organizations. As for Trụ and many others, they did not care for the things, for their only goal was to return home; they, therefore, did not intend to acquire stuff, except for necessities like soap, toothpaste, and toothbrush.

A new election was conducted to promote unity of leadership within the new group. A new leadership was voted in. Lê Minh Tân and Như Văn Úy of Barrigada and Hawaii camps were elected to the fighting unit (a local leadership unit created by the refugees for the purpose of dealing and negotiating with the authorities in Guam and Washington, D.C.); according to Trụ, they did pretty much what they liked and sometimes without the knowledge of the leadership. No one would interfere with their work because people feared repercussions when they returned home. They asked for cloth and paint to draw banners for future hunger strikes.

Among the group was Bình, an artist who was already famous when he was in Saigon. He did quite a few paintings while he was on Guam. The paintings were eagerly sought out by certain islanders who appreciated his art and were willing to shell out hundreds of dollars for some of them. He could have made money had he stayed in the U.S., but he gave the money away, stating that he painted only for art, not for money. Bình then started painting a portrait of Hồ Chí Minh and the northern communist flag. No one knew whether it was his own idea or someone else had planted the idea into his mind. He might have thought that this action would win him leniency from the government in Vietnam when he returned home. However, he was just acting, for he did not know what communism was about and what the communists would do or how they would react to his painting.[19]

A few days later, the fighting group set up a stall for fifty people, close to the camp entrance gate and facing the street. The following morning, fifty people sat down and began their hunger strike, holding banners opposing the U.S. and demanding their return to home. On display was Bình's drawing of HCM. The overall atmosphere was quiet, and the rest of the people in the camp remained neutral. There was no violence noted. Trần Ngọc Thạch, the newly elected camp representative, knew the strike—which was the work of a small group of people—was not approved by the leadership; he still had to notify the authorities so that the rest of the evacuees would not be held responsible for future events.

By the fourth strike day and as the authorities took no action, the Lê Minh Tân group decided to act aggressively. At 20:00 hours, a fire broke out from the last barracks, which was unoccupied. A few nearby barracks were also vandalized. Thạch and the leadership were taken by surprise by the action of Lê Minh Tân's group. A group of youths armed with clubs and sticks stood in front of the burned barracks, ready to prevent firefighters from coming in. Roughly ten minutes later, firefighter trucks, ambulances, and police cars arrived at the gate with their sirens on. Police with guns, masks, and bullet-proof vests came in. The police chief told the evacuees to stand aside so they could control the fire. As youths armed with sticks were blocking their paths, they decided to throw tear grenades. Youths reacted by throwing rocks and sticks, injuring a few policemen. More tear grenades were thrown in, causing everyone in the camp to break into tears. The youths dispersed and within five minutes, the fire was under control. Women and children broke into tears because of fear. The firefighters and police pulled out of the camp and told the potential returnees to go back to their barracks, which they did a few hours later because of the lingering smell.[20]

Three days later, Herbert called for a general meeting with all the potential returnees. He brought with him Professor Sauvajeaut from the University of Virginia. Sauvajeaut introduced himself as Nguyễn Hữu Hải. He explained in Vietnamese that because of his role as a U.S. adviser during the war and because he married a Vietnamese woman, he had been given a Vietnamese name. Vietnam was for him a second homeland. Although he understood the goals of the returnees, he told them the communists were not ready to accept them back. Having taken over a whole country, they had problems managing it. If the returnees went back now, they would only create more problems for the communists. He therefore asked them to take it easy and wait for a while. Having no intention to hold them back, the U.S. just wanted to make sure that the potential returnees would return safely in their homeland. He was holding talks with the Vietnamese with the help of the United Nations and would soon resolve the problem. He told them there was no need for more fighting, burning or destroying barracks. These actions would not speed up the return process. And he was always willing to listen to their ideas. These words soothed the spirits of the returnees.

Thạch stood up and told the U.S. envoy that if the U.S. and Vietnam found it difficult to solve the problem, the refugees were willing to take their chances. They asked to be given a boat—one that had brought them to the island—on which they could sail home by themselves. They assumed all the consequences—imprisonment or death by the communists. The crowd agreed with the remarks and gave Thach a good round of applause. The U.S. representative responded that he would transmit the wishes of the returnees to Washington and would get back to them.[21]

A few days after the U.S. representative returned to Guam, a meeting with all the potential returnees was convened in the presence of a few U.S. congressmen who flew all the way from Washington to hear the wishes of the returnees. The camp representative again suggested that they be provided with a ship so that they all could sail back to Vietnam. They also would assume all the consequences from that time onward. While the discussion went on, a few refugees continued their hunger strike "till death," as suggested by banners that were hung outside the camp fence.

A week later, another meeting was convened at 19:00 hours with all the potential returnees. Present at the meeting were Herbert, many high Washington officials, Mr. Smith, the high commissioner from the United Nations, and Governor Bordallo. After a short introduction, Herbert explained that despite all his admonitions, the returnees had continued their strikes and demanded a ship to sail back to Vietnam. Washington, he said, had been working feverishly with Hanoi on this matter through UNHCR; however, the problem rested with Hanoi, which continued to refuse to accept the returnees.

Mr. Smith objected to the return by ship and told the returnees to be patient while he was working on a solution. He thought that it was not safe to return home at this time, and UNHCR felt it was its responsibility to safeguard the lives of the returnees. He suggested that the returnees could temporarily settle on this island and learn some crafts that would be useful for them in the future. They could then return home whenever Hanoi gave the green light.

Governor Bordallo added that despite all the strikes and demonstrations, his administration understood the refugees' motives and had made life in the camps easier for the refugees. He suggested that they remained patient until they could safely return home.

The camp representative then stated that they had made their final choice, which was to return home on their own ship. Herbert conferred with UNHCR representatives, who soon left the camp, somewhat upset about the lack of reception for their plan.

Facing a potential public relations disaster from continuing confrontations with the repatriates, and indefinite detention camps on Guam or Wake Island, Washington finally agreed that the ship option was the course of action. More than that, it ordered its officials to remain on the sidelines and let the Vietnamese "run the show." It knew the PRG viewed the repatriates with suspicion, seeing them as tainted by the U.S. imperialists. It warned that there should not be any official send-off ceremony by U.S. or Guamanian officials. Washington's suspicions proved to be correct. The PRG framed the repatriates' return as a violation of its sovereignty and power. Angered that the U.S. did not recognize it or negotiate directly with it, the PRG denounced the repatriate ship as having a "sinister role." Hanoi also called the move an "adventurous and irresponsible action."[22]

After the departure of Governor Bordallo and Mr. Smith, Herbert mentioned that the ship solution seemed to be taking form, and in principle, Washington had agreed with this option. He also warned that the returnees would be fully responsible for their actions and future should anything happen to them once they were back in Vietnam. He would have to confer with Washington one last time before announcing the final decision. As it was 21:00 hours, he would get back to them in a couple of hours.

The crowd seemed to be elated, as suggested by a long round of applause that followed. For the first time, the potential returnees saw some rays of hope shining. Although it was late, they would not mind waiting for a couple of hours, for as long as they had their wishes, they would be happy. Some even held each other and cried. The end of an agonizing wait seemed to be close.

The two hours slowly passed. Although it was late, the crowd packed the courtyard, eagerly waiting for the final news. The representatives slowly walked into the meeting room ten minutes prior to 23:00 hours. At the scheduled time, General Herbert walked in, followed by just a few people. He said that he had talked to Washington, which had finally agreed to the wishes of the returnees, including giving them a ship.

The camp representatives loudly applauded the news. Outside in the courtyard, people shouted, "We got the ship. We got the ship." They threw hats and even shoes into the air. Some people even tore up their clothes. They were crazy with happiness. The dream had finally been fulfilled.

The *Việt Nam Thương Tín*

The discussion, however, continued. Herbert said that *Việt Nam Thương Tín*—or simply *Thương Tín I*—would be the chosen ship. It had come to Guam in early May and had not been used since. It would need a lot of repair and maintenance before it could sail again. The U.S. would appropriate a million dollars to upgrade it and make it seaworthy again. Herbert would meet with Trần Đình Trụ and his crew the next day to work out the details. The time would be announced later.

The representatives applauded and jumped to their feet to bid farewell to Herbert and his entourage. Herbert was smiling and shook everyone's hands. He had completed the first part of his job, and everyone seemed to be happy.

Outside, a few youths continued their rampage. This time they took on the stall that had served as the sitting place for their hunger strike. They were so happy that they smashed and tore it apart. They too had succeeded and no longer needed to go on strike.

Although it was midnight, people were still standing around and talking in the courtyard. They were so happy they did not feel like going to bed. They hung around, talking. Happiness was showing on their faces. Smiles were seen everywhere.[23]

At 07:00 the next morning, as Trụ was sipping coffee and talking to friends in his barracks, a policeman entered the room and told him Herbert would like to see him immediately. As the policeman did not know anything else besides his instruction, Trụ got dressed up and followed him.

In the office, Herbert handed to Trụ a communiqué issued by the Hanoi government and intercepted by the FBI. It said,

1. The U.S. is trying to subvert Vietnam by returning the Vietnamese abroad on a ship.
2. This action gravely affects the sovereignty of Vietnam.
3. The Vietnamese abroad should hold off their return and refuse to accept the ship until officially authorized by Vietnam.
4. The Vietnamese on Guam should be careful not to fall into the wicked ploy set up by the U.S. to destroy Vietnam.
5. The Vietnamese on Guam are fully responsible for their unilateral decision to return home without the expressed consent of the government of Vietnam.
6. The U.S. are responsible for this act of aggression against the sovereignty of Vietnam.

Trụ felt dizzy after reading the communiqué. Although he and the returnees had willingly accepted any untoward consequences of their action, the bluntness of the message did shake him up for a while before he could recover. As best he could, Trụ responded that these were Hanoi's decisions. As far as he was concerned, he had made up his mind to return to Vietnam. However, he would like to relay the message to all returnees for them to see. Herbert told him it was his duty to convey the message to all the returnees. He also advised Trụ to take his time to consider all the options, although the ship would be available any time he wanted it. He had always respected the opinions of the returnees. Trụ bid him goodbye and returned to the barracks to inform the other representatives who were anxiously waiting for him.

As he informed them of the message, the other representatives were also shaken by the news. After last night's elation, they felt like they were receiving a cold shower early in the morning. They all dispersed, deep in their thoughts, not knowing what to say or how to react.

In the evening, Thạch gathered the returnees in the courtyard for a plenary session. Trụ explained how he was made aware of Hanoi's communiqué, which was translated and read in its entirety before the crowd. He again stated that he was willing to return to Vietnam despite all the potential risks as mentioned in the message. Everyone, however, had to make his or her own choice, and the U.S. would respect it. He would meet again with Herbert the next day to convey the decision of the crowd and to proceed with the refurbishing and refitting of the ship. The process would take at least one month, during which the returnees would have plenty of time to think about their options. He would also work with the crew so that everyone would be aware of his duty.

Thạch then said that the final decision, however, would be a personal one for each returnee. The U.S. was willing to let them go home, although Hanoi did not want to accept them at this time. According to him, the message was just a normal diplomatic reaction of Hanoi to having been left out of the final decision-making about the refugees' return. He felt, after discussing it with the other representatives, that it was safe to return to Vietnam.

The crowd's loud applause signified their approval and the meeting ended soon thereafter. Everyone, however, was to a certain degree affected by the message. And some of the 2,000 potential returnees would change their minds.

The next morning, Trụ gathered his crew to hear their decisions firsthand. All opted to return to Vietnam; all being young males thrown into a particularly challenging and sad situation, they chose to stick with the group that would give them identity and a goal to achieve. Both these factors had been lacking since they left Vietnam. The job was much simpler than during the war because they only had to take care of the sailing part without having to think about fighting.

He then divided the crew into groups dealing with a certain duty on the ship (mechanical, sailing, supply, medical, security, etc.), each under a seasoned former officer. Each officer would sit down with his group to make the appropriate assignment. In the afternoon, he reported to Herbert about his work and assignment and told him he was ready to take a look at the ship.[24]

The next day, Herbert took Trụ and some of his crew to tour the ship. *Thương Tín I* had been idle in the harbor for more than six months. It was Vietnam's largest civilian boat: 12,000 tons, 140 meters long, with six holding areas.

The refitting and refurbishing of the ship took four weeks. Sleeping berths were made available for 2,000 people. A kitchen large enough to accommodate and serve the same number of people was built. On Monday of the fifth week, a Vietnamese crew of 200 people came aboard to test the ship and take it for a 24-hour training exercise at sea around the island. The test went fine, and the ship returned to the dock without any problem.

Since the distance between Guam and Saigon is 2,575 miles and the speed of the ship about 11 miles per hour, it would take approximately ten days to make one-way trip. The refugees were given ten extra days of supplies in case something happened during the trip; in addition, General Herbert decided to add another ten extra days of supplies should the refugees change their minds and turn around. Therefore, 30 days of food and fuel were loaded aboard the ship. As far as water was concerned, each individual was allotted a 5-gallon can per day for personal use: drinking, washing, tooth brushing. That would make 2,000 cans per day, or 60,000 5-gallon cans, for all the passengers.

At 08:00 on 15 October 1975, buses lined up at Camp Asan to pick up the returnees. They were driven to the Guam Port Authority and led to booths for final processing. The U.S. wanted to provide a last "bail-out" option for repatriates who secretly might want to remain; therefore, they were asked about their final decision: either return to Vietnam or change their minds. In the first case, they were directed to the door on the right; in the second, they went through the left door. At the end of the door on the right, a bus was waiting for them. When full, the bus drove the returnees to the ship.

Twenty-eight opted not to return to Vietnam. Among those was Lê Minh Tân, the repatriate leader who had led successive hunger strikes and protests. Trụ in his book suggested that he was a CIA spy all along, although some repatriates accused him of being a communist infiltrator because of his combative tactics.

At 18:00 hours, Herbert came aboard the ship and told Trụ that he could begin his journey the next day. About 30 people from the U.S. continental camps would arrive late at night and join them to return to Vietnam. A total of 1,652 people, including 250 women and children, left Guam to return to Vietnam. Someone had raised the NLF flag on the mast of the ship. The ship took off at 13:00 hours on 16 October.[25]

Reeducation Camps

The ship arrived in front of Cam Ranh Bay, central Vietnam, inside Vietnamese territorial waters on 24 October. As the captain did not see any Vietnamese ships except for a few fishing boats, he made the decision to head south toward Vũng Tàu. They arrived there the following morning at 08:00. Vũng Tàu, which was crowded and vibrant with activity before 30 April 1975, looked dead, as no activity was noted at all on the streets. There were only a few people occasionally riding on bicycles, and all the shops were closed.

Three patrol boats met them at sea in front of Vũng Tàu and directed them to Nha Trang, central Vietnam, where upon landing Trụ was interrogated by a group of ten Công An (security agents) sent in from Hanoi. One of them told the repatriates that all the southern soldiers had reported to the reeducation camps and had been free to return home. This was not true, although the repatriates did not know it. The security agents kept on interrogating Trụ and asked him one question after another, making him feel like he was being judged before a tribunal. They told him he was not authorized to return, but he still went ahead. They tried to force him to say what they wanted to hear. After a lengthy interrogation process, he was returned to the ship and all the returnees were confined in jails.[26]

Trụ and two other pilots were thrown into a 2-by-4-meter jail cell with a straw mat placed at each corner of the cell, one for each prisoner. That was on 27 October. The prisoners had two meals a day and outdoor showers with water from a pit. They were strip searched and all belongings were confiscated, except for two pairs of clothes. They slept on the floor while waiting to be interrogated.

On the second day, they were led to an auditorium where sitting on the bare floor, they listened to the first of many reeducation lessons, followed by interrogation sessions in the afternoon. These interrogations by seasoned interrogators were designed to lead toward what they wanted to hear, not what had happened in reality. They asked Trụ why he had fought against the fatherland and the revolution. He told the interrogators that he fought for his ideal of freedom, not against the fatherland. But they countered that the revolution personified the fatherland, and therefore, Trụ was wrong for having fought against the revolution. They then wanted to know what ploy the U.S. had used to try to destroy Vietnam that involved sending the refugees home. On the third afternoon, Trụ was ordered to write his biography from age 10 onward, including his military work, duty, grades, promotions, his family, and what he had done wrong against the fatherland. The interrogation sessions and the writing of his biography continued daily for over three months. Trụ went through more than one hundred interrogators, who had asked him the same questions over and over again. And the answers had remained the same.

The returnees thought they would be able to see their families in a week or two, but three long months passed by without anyone being allowed to see his family. One day, the chief warden gathered them in the courtyard and told them they had learned the basics of the revolution. The time had come for them to do labor. They would be sent to a new area, larger and better than this place, where they would have plenty of opportunities to learn about labor. It would be through labor that they would become good people.

Everyone was shocked to hear the news. Each of them had expected that they would be released once they had learned the basics. But no, this was only the beginning; there would be labor time, but what kind of labor? And where? The warden was really a crooked person: he did not tell where they had to go and what they needed to do. The returnees knew as much then as when they landed on Vietnamese soil.

They were ordered to go back to their cells, take their belongings, and get ready. The door swung open, and they were called out one by one. The place was full of guards armed with AK-47 machine guns. Thirty returnees, shackled in groups of two, were shoved into each truck. They finally realized they were prisoners of the state.[27]

They were driven to the forested mountains of central Vietnam, where the newly built and unfinished Xuân Phước reeducation camp of the province of Tuy Hòa, central Vietnam, was located. This was during the war a sparsely inhabited area under Việt Cộng control. The closest civilian houses were a few miles away. In this isolated environment, there were only wardens and inmates. Trụ chuckled at the sight of this camp: this was a far cry from what the warden in Nha Trang had described. The inmate dwellings had straw roofs and walls and were enclosed by a single row of barbed wire. There were four guard towers at the four corners of the camp. Soldiers' housings were located outside the camp. The dwellings had two long rows of stalls, made of woven bamboo. On each row lay 30 straw mats, one for each inmate. Another row of racks was used to hold personal belongings. Three rows of barbed wire, strung the length of the dwelling, one on each side and the third in the middle, were used to hang mosquito netting.

The camp was divided into three sections, A, B, and C. The returnees from *Thương Tín I* had been divided into groups in Nha Trang and sent to different jails for interrogation. They were finally reunited in this camp. Section A was reserved for officers, intelligence personnel, police department. Section B was for non-commissioned officers and C was for soldiers. The daily routine consisted of breakfast then labor, lunch then labor, dinner then self-examination until midnight. Cadres used to snoop behind the door to listen to what was discussed during the self-examination period. There were a few "antennas" who served

8. Repatriates and the Thương Tín I *Odyssey*   127

as spies for the cadres and reported in detail what prisoners had done during the day. Using this system, the cadres soon knew everything that was going on within the group and totally controlled the mind of the inmates. To fight against this system of control, the inmates all wore a mask: they said what the cadres would like to hear and hid their private thoughts. Each person became suspicious of the others.

They tried to adapt and survive as best as they could. The place was dirty. Food was not only horrible, but also lacking: one yam for breakfast, two yams for lunch, and one bowl of rice and a few minnows for supper. Under this regimen, the inmates rapidly lost weight and strength; they felt very weak and exhausted most of the time, especially after a day's work. They were treated like beasts: labor meant taking one's hoe to the field to work all day long and being kept alive with a couple of yams. By the time they came back to the camp after a day of labor, they were too tired to talk or do anything else but just stretch out on the mats. They did not even mind about the smelly sweat that stuck to their clothes and skin.

Six months later, they were allowed to write their first letter home. They were ordered to write that they were healthy and had good food to eat and that life was pleasurable, that everything that was good from the government side, no matter what the reality was. All the letters were read and censored before they were mailed out. And later, each inmate was allowed to receive three kilos of food per month; although this was nothing for the starved inmates, their families barely had enough money to buy them that much food once the breadwinner was jailed. Each inmate could feel that everything had been stolen from him: material life, human rights, and freedom. Except the love of their families.

One year passed by, and there was no news about any release soon. The inmates worked and worked because that was all they had: waiting and hoping. As long as they worked, they could see one or two rays of hope. The arid land had become fertile with rows and rows of yams and cassava. But as the harvest increased, their rations remained the same. Their jailers purposely kept them on a starvation diet to control them better.

Eighteen months passed by. No one had been released, even the lowest soldier. Every day was the same: get in line for breakfast, then labor. Each inmate carried a small bag and a hoe: the bag was stitched together by the inmate himself with pieces of cloth of different colors. In it were two or three yams, a toothbrush and a piece of soap, a towel, and underwear, so that he could take a bath in the river after the day-long labor.

One morning, 120 inmates from the A sub-camp (officers, intelligence and police) were called and trucked to a camp in North Vietnam for more labor. They were told they needed to be protected from the surrounding populace, therefore needed to be sequestered in another area; but they also had to do labor reeducation. The trucks stopped at a camp in Nghệ Tĩnh, deep in the forested hills of North Vietnam about 20 miles from the Laotian border. Surrounded by two sturdy brick walls, the camp consisted of a row of buildings with, on the inside, two rows of stalls, one on each side, to be used as beds. The place was small, smelly, with mildew on the walls. At the end was a bathroom. There was no way to escape from this place. The place really looked like a concentration camp.

Meals were strictly rationed to 100 grams of yams for breakfast, 200 grams each for lunch and supper. They became physically wasted because of the starvation diet. They received one pair of clothing each year, which got worn out after a few days of labor. Their families, which were in poor economic situations, could not send them much. Winter was worse because of the combination of hunger and shivering. It was very cold in the hills without warm clothing and without a decent heating system. They had to work every day without exception, rain or shine, hot or cold, except for Sunday.[28]

It was six years before Trụ got to see his wife and children. He noticed that they too had wasted with time but were still in good health. The visit lasted just one hour despite the long and difficult journey they had taken to get to the camp. Trụ told his wife to take care of the children and advised her not to come to the camp any longer because of the distance and money problem. There was nothing he could do for them right now economically. He was mad at the communists for having created such an oppressive environment. Had he stayed in the U.S., he could have worked and saved a lot of money, which would be useful for his family.

In 1981, inmates from the camps in Nam Hà, six in Nghệ Tĩnh, and three in Tân Kỳ were shipped to southern camps of Z30C (Long Khánh), Z30D (Thuận Hải), and Gia Trung (Gia Lai). The guards were Công An (security police) who were trained in the north. They were wicked and hateful; they only knew how to beat inmates. If they did not like anything about an inmate, they beat him up. One inmate was standing near a fence inside the camp when a guard happened to walk by. Thinking the inmate was trying to communicate with inmates on the other side, he took his chain of keys and beat him on the head, causing severe bleeding. The inmate just wondered what he had done wrong.

Trụ was transferred for a fifth time, this time to Hàm Tân camp, close to Saigon. On 2 February 1988, his name was finally called. After 13 years of incarceration, he was finally released.[29]

8. *Repatriates and the* Thương Tín I *Odyssey*

The story of the repatriates, or the *Thương Tín I* odyssey, is one of the saddest stories of Operation New Life. This is the story of those who wanted to return to their country, thinking that with time they would find freedom and peace within the communist system.

The refugees' stay in Guam at the time was neither completely free nor peaceful, although it was more stable than the unruly life in the communist regime. At least it was anchored in the rules of law, and once released from the camps, the evacuees would find real peace and freedom within the new country. The repatriates, on the other hand, wanted to return home right away hoping to find peace and freedom, only to find neither.

9

Auxiliary Team and Sponsors

When Americans heard about the Vietnamese arriving in Guam, they began writing to local newspaper editors to inquire about the newcomers. But because Guam is a small island far away from the U.S. mainland, mainlanders could not locate it. They placed it all over the world, from the Philippines to Africa. One firm in Texas even put Guam in the British West Indies. They wrote to a staff member of the University of Guam, "University of Guam, Agana, Guam, British West Indies, 96910." The zip code was correct, though.[1]

There are some 44,000 thunderstorms around the world daily. Each storm may produce 800 to 900 bolts of lightning, with each bolt generating 300 million volts. Every second, the Earth is getting whacked about 400 times by lightning. Luckily, storms are rare in Guam, and so are thunder and lightning. Had there been storms and lightning, the evacuees living in the tents, especially those in Tent City, would have been at grave risk for injuries. But typhoons are frequent in Guam.

Medical and Dental Teams

The medical logistics planning for Operation New Life began at 23:30, 4 April 1975.[2] The supply officer of Naval Regional Medical Center, Guam (NRMC), was called to a meeting with the commanding officer, executive officer, director of Clinical Services, environmental health officer, public works officer, and chief of Outpatient Services.

On 10 April 1975, NRMC was alerted. Plans were prepared for opening and supplying at least two additional wards to care for a minimum of 160 additional inpatients. The justification for additional personnel was based on the expansion of bed capacity from 125 to 243 beds for inpatient care and for providing outpatient care at Asan Annex and Orote Point.

The satellite clinic that took shape in Tin City was a Class "A" type dispensary, a regular 30-bed facility with inpatients and run mostly by Vietnamese volunteers (there were many qualified medical doctors and nurses among the refugees).

The first involvement of the Naval Regional Dental Center (NRDC) occurred on 23 April, when personnel of the Branch Dental Facility at the Naval Air Station, Agana, were requested to assist in processing incoming refugees.

Vietnamese dentists were recruited and organized to help identify the most serious problems. The latter were referred to NRDC personnel for care. As their level of expertise was observed, the Vietnamese dentists were utilized as dentists and put to work alongside NRDC dentists.[3]

A dispensary for Orote Point was established in tents on 25 April, utilizing medical personnel from the Mobile Construction Battalion, who were relieved on 29 April by the U.S. Army First Medical Group. Surgical Team 8, consisting of 16 personnel from Oakland, arrived on 25 April as a replacement for NRMC's surgical team, which had deployed to the U.S. Seventh Fleet. The total personnel of the First Medical consisted of 41 officers and 284 enlisted. These units were assigned to Orote Point and provided medical coverage for an estimated camp population of 25,000 refugees.

As the number of refugees increased, NRDC established dental treatment sites at all the major camp sites. During July, Mobile Dental Unit 2 continued to operate full time at the refugee center at Camp Asan.

Dental problems encountered during Operation New Life ran the entire spectrum of dental diseases. Rampant caries were obvious in virtually the entire population of teenagers and young children. The older age group had periodontal diseases.[4]

To support the volume of medical care only $455,351 was expended for medical supplies. The per patient cost, both inpatient and outpatient, was relatively low.[5]

Auxiliary Staff

Round-the-clock efforts by American dependents in the Philippines and on Guam helped keep the lifeline to the U.S. going under Operation New Life. Volunteers worked extra hours and extra shifts to greet ships and planeloads of refugees arriving at these places.

Working in five-hour shifts, 450 American women volunteers offered their help to refugees arriving at Grande Island Camp, which was set up in waters adjacent to the U.S. Naval Base, Subic Bay, Philippines.

On 6 and 7 May 1975, more than 14,000 refugees awaited transportation to other Pacific centers. After Subic Naval Base opened its doors to refugees on 26 April, more than 36,000 were processed through Grande Island directly to the U.S. and 33,000 more routed to Guam.

Volunteers did a variety of jobs—from meeting ships and boats to dispensing soft drinks, disposable diapers, and administrative processing. They passed out items to those whose clothes had been lost or ruined during the flight from Vietnam. More than 2,000 pounds of clothing was donated by the U.S. community at Subic Bay.

The arrival on Guam of more than 120,000 evacuees required significant help from these auxiliary ladies. For the first 60 hours of the evacuation of South Vietnamese refugees to Guam, aircraft arrived at a rate of two per hour. At Andersen Air Force Base and Naval Air Station, Agana, Guam refugees were met by Red Cross volunteers, military wives' clubs, and scores of concerned dependents who came to offer their help. They offered cookies and juice to evacuees. This might seem to be a small task, but it had huge effects on the newcomers. For a tired person who did not know enough English to ask, for children who were hungry and waiting in line for processing, these cookies and cups of juice made all the difference between being argumentative or receptive to questions. When the flow of refugees increased to 6,000 a day, volunteers helped with initial processing, changed diapers, and supervised staging areas.

Secondary camps were organized to house evacuees while the main camps at Asan and Orote Point were being constructed. Each one had its complement of volunteers who arranged entertainment, served food, and helped locate people who had been separated from their families.

Gwen Wyttenbach was one of these lady volunteers. She began meeting ships on 7 May and giving emergency kits to new arrivals. In the compounds, she gave out information and helped bring families together. She even drove one Vietnamese officer from Orote Point to meet his family at Camp Asan. Having just arrived in Guam and still in his uniform, he became aware of his family, who had been transferred to Camp Asan. Later, she sponsored Navy Captain Thông.

The response from volunteers and service organizations was overwhelming. Everyone was ready to volunteer in one way or another. Those who were pregnant or had children helped right in their homes. They made phone calls to line up other volunteers, provided babysitting for other volunteers, or even sewed small duffel bags for the evacuees. Dependent children who were not allowed in the camps organized door-to-door clothing drives in military housing areas.[6]

Without the help of these ladies, the chain of events would have been disrupted at various points, delaying the processing of evacuees. If one single family of evacuees that missed a member could have sent three or four volunteers scrambling to look for that missing person, the effect of three or five families having similar problems would have caused serious delays in the processing effort. These female volunteers usually provided warm comfort and welcoming support to the confused and frightened evacuees, who were lost in the maze of forms and regulations in the new land. Besides, female evacuees, with their language problems, would be more receptive to these auxiliary ladies than to male military personnel. There was the story of an evacuee who was very apprehensive and wanted to have her newly born baby baptized right away by a priest. A male official would not have time to solve the problem. But a lady volunteer went out of her way to call a priest, who baptized the child. When asked why the mother wanted the baby baptized right away, the mother said that she was afraid that her baby would be taken away from her and therefore would miss its baptism.

Nearly 50,000 refugees landed on Guam by 5 May, and 23,000 had been processed and transferred to camps in the continental USA. On 7 May, refugees arrived by ship in masses of 6,000 persons at a time, sometimes in the middle of the night. Volunteers were asked to process 1,000 people hourly and to aid the shipboard evacuees, who needed more help than those who had been airlifted. Again, without the help of these lady volunteers, the tired evacuees would have been stranded at the harbor waiting for immigration clearance.

Sponsors

Admiral Chung Tấn Cang, South Vietnam's new chief of Naval Operations, sat in the office of acting president Dương Văn Minh on 29 April 1975, the day the American embassy closed, to discuss attempted negotiations with the communists. As Admiral Cang learned that the other side did not want to have any contact, he asked Minh,

"What is your solution?"

"I have no special solution," replied Minh.

"Then each one must take care of himself?" asked the admiral.

"That is up to you," Minh answered.

A staff meeting was called. Debate continued for hours until a decision was finally reached. Admiral Cang called his wife and told her to gather the family, pack some clothing, and meet him in his office in one hour. He made the decision to leave Vietnam and seek refuge in the U.S.

He and ten family members later boarded a navy ship—part of the

Kirk-led armada—that headed to Subic Bay, Philippines—where he lost his suitcase and his only change of clothes—then flew on to Guam, where he stayed for 20 days. From there, he was sent to Indiantown Gap Camp, one of the four military bases turned into refugee reception centers by the U.S. government.

Without a sponsor, he could not get out of the camp. Although Americans were generous, in some parts of the U.S. they were nervous about evacuees moving to their neighborhoods. The economy in 1975 was not great and unemployment was high. Others did not want to want to look at reminders of U.S. participation in the war. Sponsorship is a moral, not legal, commitment. The sponsor must provide the bare necessities—food, clothing, shelter—but also must help the evacuees find jobs, enroll their children in schools, cope with cultural adjustments, and help them become self-sufficient. The task may not be as difficult and expensive as it sounds, although it can be time consuming. Just having to drive them to shopping stores and markets the first few months could take a lot of time and effort. Government funds channeled through voluntary agencies like the U.S. Catholic Conference were available.

The military, especially those who had served in Vietnam, felt a personal as well as political commitment to the evacuees. It was in June 1975 that Admiral Cang received a call at Indiantown Gap from Admiral Zumwalt's office in Virginia. He was told that Admiral Zumwalt would like to sponsor him and his family if he did not object.

"Not at all," Admiral Cang replied. "Not at all."

Admiral Zumwalt did not know Admiral Cang, because he had returned to the U.S. before the latter took command of the Vietnamese navy. Admiral Cang, his wife and children, his sister, niece, nephew and a cousin settled in downstairs at the Zumwalt home, with the kitchen being used commonly by the two families.

The tasks were bewildering for the Zumwalts and the refugees: enrolling the children in school, investigating the Safeway supermarket and the Asian store, learning how to drive an American car on U.S. highways, finding a church, and looking for jobs. At that time, there were not many Asian stores in many communities because of the low incidence of Asian people in the U.S. except in large cities like New York, Los Angeles, and San Francisco. The Zumwalts and their children pitched in to help. The teenage daughters took Admiral Cang and his wife on errands and made phone calls for them. Mrs. Zumwalt drove up and down Lee Highway in Falls Church, Virginia, littering every service station, restaurant, and store with job applications. Admiral Zumwalt called friends and wrote letters, trying to help Admiral Cang find work.[7]

9. Auxiliary Team and Sponsors

Commander Tom Brooks also took a family of fourteen people into his home in June 1975. He stated that the U.S. had encouraged the South Vietnamese to stand up and fight the communists. They knew they could count on American help. But when the U.S. pulled the rug from under them, the least he could do was to help a family for a time. On 8 June 1975 there were five people living in Commander Brooks' four-bedroom home in Annandale, Virginia. On 9 June, there were seventeen.

Mr. Nguyễn Như Vỹ escaped with his family and his father, brother, sister and ten-year-old nephew. The size of the group did amaze the Brookses, although there was no way to split that family up. Clare Brooks went to work and put her three sons—ages 2, 4, and 6—into one room, leaving one bedroom for the newcomers plus the large downstairs playroom, which she converted into a dorm. Neighbors and members of the Brookses' church brought furniture and supplies as soon as they learned the family was coming. Clare got fourteen plastic bags of clothing by the time the family arrived. The porch was turned into a dining room.

The hardest thing was communication. Only Mr. Vỹ spoke English; the rest communicated by gestures. Clare enrolled the whole family in a six-week "English as a Second Language" course. The children quickly became playmates, and a game of soccer did not require verbal language.

Then there were jobs to be found. Both Clare and Tom went from store to store, asking the manager if he would hire a Vietnamese person. Mr. Vỹ's brother was hired to work in a drug store in two weeks—a remarkable feat considering that he did not speak English when he came to Virginia. Mr. Vỹ was hired next. Once the head of the national police in Saigon and the former employee of an American company there, he was considered upper class in Vietnam. The job he landed—cashier in a supermarket—might not have been prestigious, but it paid five dollars an hour and double on Sundays. Mr. Vỹ's sister worked as a stock clerk in a drug store.

Between job interviews, there were medical exams, driver's tests. When Mr. Vỹ got his license, Commander Brooks gave him his old car, a '67 Plymouth station wagon. Then there was the search for an apartment. Mr. Vỹ, his wife and six children decided to move into one apartment. After many phone calls, the Brookses finally found them a nice three-bedroom apartment within their price range. The others also moved out later.

When Rear Admiral Crowe became chairman of the Joint Chiefs of Staff, he asked Navy Captain Wyttenbach, then in Guam, to assist with the relocation and care of two Vietnamese families. They were Crowe's counterparts in the Vietnamese navy, who, when they arrived in Guam, asked for his help. Admiral Crowe soon sponsored one Vietnamese Navy Captain with seven dependents and Wyttenbach sponsored the other, Navy Captain Nguyễn Văn Thông.

Thông brought along his bodyguard and two daughters, Hương and Hồng, to Guam. Wyttenbach called his sister in Harrisburg, Pennsylvania, and asked whether she would keep the Vietnamese family during the summer while he was stuck in Guam. When she agreed with the plan, the family was flown to Harrisburg, Pennsylvania. At the end of the summer, when the Wyttenbachs returned to Virginia, they brought Captain Thông to live with them until he was on his feet financially. The bodyguard went off to live with his brother's family. Thông's two daughters continued to live with Wyttenbach's sister. Thông started out as a night clerk at a 7-Eleven store before getting a job at IBM.[8]

Cultural Misunderstanding

When one sponsor gave a young refugee Cheerios and milk for breakfast, she caused the child to throw up in the bathroom. The sponsor later learned that most Vietnamese could not tolerate milk because they lacked the lactase enzyme needed to digest it. And that same good-hearted sponsor fed the refugees three big meals a day, as she had been advised to. But the Vietnamese did not eat that much. She gave them a big dessert, which was too sweet for them. And they liked to wash their hands after dinner but not before. Between language problems and cultural misunderstanding, American generosity missed the mark.

The sponsor, on the other hand, expressed dismay at the refugees' reserve. They seldom thanked her for anything. "There were not very effusive," she said. "There is a little bit of New England in them." The problem stemmed from the fact that the refugees were overwhelmed by their sponsors' generosity. The Americans thought that if one apple was good, three would be better. The refugees did not see it that way, but they did not want to upset their sponsors by refusing to take a gift.

"They gave us everything," the refugee said. "Sometimes they make us very emotional because we don't know how to express to them our thanks."

The problem was compounded by the refugees' reluctance to complain to their sponsors. Their mouth said "yes, yes," but their faces, their eyes showed they were not happy.

There were many unhappy surprises awaiting the refugees in their new life, and some for the sponsors as well.[9]

Refugees vs. Immigrants

Yến Lê Espiritu distinguishes the Vietnamese refugees into two types: objects of rescue (refugees who were in need of help) and immigrants (refugees who successfully incorporated as new Americans).[10] The refugee camps were set up to transform the refugees into future immigrants. However, since the evacuation from Vietnam to the U.S. was permanent because of the loss of South Vietnam, the shortened camp stay (a few weeks to a few months) effectively transformed refugees into voluntary immigrants, although many would not be self-sufficient economically or socially by the time they were discharged from the camps.[11]

Sahara argued that the U.S. humanitarian act of saving and resettling Vietnamese refugees was a political act and a military operation.[12] It was also a symbolic act of defense of U.S. commitment and credibility.[13] Also, the refugees by fleeing communism were perceived as "freedom fighters," those who voted for democracy with their feet.

On the other hand, the acceptance of the refugees enabled the U.S. to represent itself as a moral nation. Aihwa Ong remarks, "The moral imperative to offer refugees shelter has been a hallmark of U.S. policy since 1945—a break from earlier policies, which privileged race, language, and assimilation over concerns about human suffering."[14]

In reality, there were no practical plans about who should be saved and where to resettle them. Therefore, the Americans had evacuated only 65,000 people either by air or by ship, while 65,000 other Vietnamese got out on their own.[15] What was represented as an evacuation turned out to be a "displacement" of people. It was only on 22 April 1975 that the U.S. Justice Department announced a plan for waiving entry restrictions for over 130,000 aliens from Indochina, including 50,000 "high risk" South Vietnamese. Thus, evacuation from Vietnam was a makeshift operation.[16]

10

The Other Camps

The other camps associated with the Operation New Life were Wake Island camp and the CONUS camps.

Wake Island Camp

Wake Island

Wake Island is a coral atoll located in the western Pacific Ocean, 1,500 miles east of Guam and 2,300 miles west of Honolulu. The island is an unorganized, unincorporated territory of the United States that is also claimed by the Marshall Islands. Wake Island is one of the most isolated islands in the world, the nearest island being 600 miles to the southeast.

Wake Island is administered by the United States Air Force under agreement with the Department of the Interior. The center of activity on the atoll is at Wake Island Airfield, which is used as a mid–Pacific refueling stop for military aircraft and as an emergency landing area. Located south of the runway is the Wake Island Launch Center, a missile launch test facility operated by the United States Army Space and Missile Defense Command and the Missile Defense Agency.

Wake consists of three islands, with Wake itself in the center, Wilkes to the west, and Peale to the north. Its land mass is about 2.5 square miles, with 15 miles of coastline. Besides palm trees, it has little vegetation and no topsoil. The island is protected by a coral reef that secures the calmness of the lagoon surrounding the island. The lagoon is generally 6 to 8 feet deep, with its deepest point at 13 feet. Thanks to an easterly trade wind, the highest temperature recorded on Wake was 91 degrees F. The lowest temperature recorded was 64.[1]

In the spring of 1975, the total population of Wake consisted of 251 military, government, and civilian contract personnel whose mission

10. The Other Camps

was to keep the Wake Island Airfield open for emergency purposes. With the imminent fall of Saigon, President Ford ordered the American forces to support Operation New Life, the evacuation of refugees from Vietnam. Subic Bay and Guam were the chosen processing centers outside the States, with Wake Island as an additional center.

In March 1975, the Wake Island commander, Major Bruce Hoon, was contacted by Pacific Air Forces (PACAF) and ordered to get ready to process, screen, and interview evacuees from Vietnam. He requested an additional 60-man security police team to guard a 20-acre water "catchment" basin and to reopen boarded-up buildings and housing; two complete MASH units to set up field hospitals and three fully functional army field kitchens; agents from Naturalization and Immigration Service, and various other personnel. Potable water, food, medical supplies, clothing, and other supplies (20,000 GI mess kits), including a garbage compactor truck from the city of Honolulu, were shipped in.

Before the evacuees began to arrive, the first aircraft in was a cargo 747 with 70,000 pounds of rice. On 26 April 1975, the first C-141 military aircraft carrying evacuees arrived, followed by another C-141 every hour and 45 minutes, each carrying 283 evacuees on board. At the peak of the mission, 8,700 Vietnamese were on Wake. When the airlift ended on 2 August, a total of 15,000 evacuees had been processed through Wake Island.[2]

Refugee Shift to Wake Island

The shift to Wake Island was necessitated by the physical deterioration of the 30-year-old Asan hospital/camp: overflowing plumbing, exposed wiring and hour-long waits outside the dining hall plagued the refugees already there.[3]

While Orote Point Camp in Guam was being built and Camp Asan being fixed, flights to Guam were diverted for a 36-hour period to Wake Island, causing tens of thousands of evacuees to live on Wake Island for a while. Dennis Lowden, who was there as a weatherman, gave us a view of what happened on that island.

With a population of 200 people, plus or minus, without females and children, except for three unmarried females, life on Wake Island was a tropical boredom. No women were permitted on the island unless they had a job, which meant the island contained a lot of morose men. The most common activities were going to outdoor movies and drinking, sailing on the lagoon and drinking, going bowling and drinking, sitting outdoors under the palm trees in the fading light of the evening and drinking. Any event was a cause for drinking because of boredom and because the Air Force did not bring fresh milk, but only wine that cost $5 a gallon in 1975.

Then came 26 April 1975, when the Vietnamese who escaped from their country began arriving in the Philippines. The plan was to screen them at Subic Bay in the Philippines, process them on Guam and fly them to the U.S. Because of the huge exodus of people from Vietnam, Wake suddenly became an overflow center. The boarded-up homes and buildings were opened and mobile units of processing and medical people were flown in to open clinics and welcome the first planeload of Vietnamese arriving on 26 April. Within a week, the 200-person village had grown into an 8,000-person town. Water had to be flown in for the evacuees, as the stored rainwater captured in a catch basin and used by locals would not be enough for the refugees.

The visitors meant two things: women and children. A community without children is warped and lacking in innocence, possibility and optimism. People felt more human around children. From the mid–1930s to the mid–1960s, Wake was an important refueling stop for airlines flying from America to Asia. It supported more than 5,000 people. When it became possible for aircraft to fly long distance, Wake's importance dropped causing the population to drop to about 200.

Dennis Lowden had posted on his website[4] a unique collection of photos of Vietnamese families living on Wake Island or picnicking at the Wake Island beach during this period. Unlike on Guam, where the evacuees were limited to the camps they were assigned to, those on Wake were free to roam around, and this period was a real vacation time for the war-traumatized Vietnamese. The Wake Island camp closed on 2 August 1975, four months after its opening.

Bruce Beardsley served in Vietnam for 2½ years, first in the army (1965–1966) and later, after language training, as a junior FSO (Foreign Service officer) in one of the provinces (1970–1972). When Saigon fell, he was in Afghanistan and received an order to fly to Wake to assist with the evacuation in Vietnam.

Bruce dealt with families who had left Vietnam together but had become separated along the way. He also dealt with another group that wanted to return to Vietnam—typically those who had been ship or aircraft crew members with no choice about departing. There also had been several hundred with relatives in countries other than the United States.

In late April 1975, a Vietnamese general had taken a ranger captain who was his aide de camp on a reconnaissance flight; but instead of flying over the battlefield, without warning the general ordered his chopper out to sea to join the many helicopters landing on vessels of the U.S.

Seventh Fleet. The captain told Bruce his U.S. contacts had assured him that they would see to his family's safe evacuation when the time came. Alas, they had not.

Bruce made inquiries to all the refugee processing camps but received only negative results. The captain decided to return to Vietnam, although he had been advised that his rank and position guaranteed that the new government would not allow him to see his family. He eventually returned to Vietnam and—imprisonment.[5]

The Conus Camps

While Subic Bay, Guam and Wake served as transit screening areas, the CONUS—for Continental U.S—camps were the centers that would eventually process and resettle the refugees. The fact that they were on the mainland made the resettlement process go faster and more easily. They had more manpower and access to a lot more sponsoring organizations. The critical importance of the CONUS camps lay in the fact that if they were unable to accept refugees, they would be bottlenecks causing jams on Guam and Wake.

As the evacuees kept arriving on Guam, it soon became obvious to national authorities that Guam would soon reach its saturation point, as the facilities in the U.S. were not ready to pick up the outgoing flow of refugees. On 28 April, the Joint Chiefs of Staff chose three CONUS camps. These were Camp Pendleton in California, Fort Chaffee in Arkansas, and Eglin Air Force Base in Florida.

Camp Pendleton, California

Camp Pendleton was designated the first reception center to be opened. It had a capacity of 18,000. The camp was located on the West Coast and could accommodate refugees under hard cover (958 tents and 140 Quonset huts).[6] The weather was ideal. Besides being an active Marine Corps installation, it required only a small build-up of support troops; it already had support facilities in place, like hospital, commissary, and dining rooms.

Tidy rows of Quonsets make up Camp Talega, the northernmost part of Camp Pendleton. In April 1975, the first 1,000 Vietnamese refugees from Saigon flew into the El Toro Marine Corps Base nearby. They were then bused to Camp Talega. Nearly 900 Marines and civilians worked six days to set up eight of these mini-cities—which include restrooms, bathing facilities, eating facilities, places to sleep—on the base.

In 1975, the camp was a chaotic hive of Vietnamese refugees living elbow to elbow in military tents. It is credited for reshaping Southern California's refugee population. In the end, it housed a total of 50,418 Southeast Asian refugees, with 18,500 people at its peak. The cost was $17 million for the camp, or $5.04 per refugee per day.

From the camp, people either moved south to San Diego's Linda Vista neighborhood or north to Orange County's Westminster, where Little Saigon is one of the largest concentrations of Vietnamese culture outside of Asia.

Nguyễn, the young chemical engineering student, fled his country with his uncle's family. Camp Pendleton was in full swing when they arrived. He went to college on scholarship and then to the defense industry as an engineer. In 2010, he returned as a supervisor in the base's real estate accounting office. He came back to work and contribute something to the camp.[7]

Some of the first Vietnamese refugees moved into two-bedroom apartments in the City Heights neighborhood of San Diego. Today, people call the neighborhood's main drag "Little Saigon." It's a cultural mash-up where Somali women in headscarves and Burmese women holding parasols stroll past Vietnamese supermarkets and pagoda-style strip malls. Some say the fall of Saigon built the City Heights neighborhood of today.[8]

Fort Chaffee, Arkansas

On the other hand, Fort Chaffee, located in the town of Fort Smith, Arkansas, was a semi-active military installation with sixty-two military and civilian personnel. Eighteen hundred support troops (cooks, clerks, military policemen, and other specialists) were required to staff the installation in order to receive 20,000 refugees. The hospital had to be taken "out of mothballs" and the kitchen area activated. An evaluation of the environmental impact of added sewage into the sanitary disposal system needed to be performed. The problem was a concern because of the threat of pollution of the streams that run through and around Fort Chaffee. This led to an upgrade of the sewage system.

While Camp Pendleton was ready to pick up evacuees but was fast saturated with the inflow of evacuees, Fort Chaffee was not ready to pick up the slack. The World War II two-story barracks had to be reconfigured into family or group living spaces. Washers and dryers had to be installed in many buildings. The company-size messes had to be consolidated into larger messes to meet the demands of the refugees. The problem was serving 66,000 meals a day, roughly during mess hours.

10. The Other Camps

This required a lot of manpower, which the army did not have at that time. Mess operations had to be contracted to a civilian firm, which provided cooks, kitchen helpers, and supervisors. This operational delay caused frustration among some refugees in Guam, who elected to resettle in third countries including France, Canada, and Australia. However, that number was too small to make a dent in the outgoing population in Guam. Eventually Fort Chaffee became the temporary home to 50,000 Indochinese refugees who had sought refugee status.[9]

Nine-year-old Lương was pretty scared when his father, a South Vietnamese marine major, took the whole family on a marine helicopter ride on 29 April 1975 to the South China Sea. They landed on the USS *Hancock* before arriving at Fort Chaffee Camp via a Subic Bay camp and Guam camp. Eventually, they moved to California.

Lương attended the University of California, joined ROTC, and later joined the army. He rose up the ranks and is now major general, commander of the Eighth Army, Japan. He retired from the Army in June 2021.[10]

In the 1980s, when the phone rang at or past midnight in An Ton That's home, he was usually requested to come to Logan Airport to welcome a refugee family who would arrive in a few hours in Boston. As coordinator for resettlement for what was the International Institute of Boston, Mr. An, a former South Vietnamese diplomat, would in the beginning find them coats, crank high the thermostats in their apartments, and get them into classes. Later, he would help with intergenerational conflict, which was serious among Vietnamese. "To build our community, we need both generations working together," he said.

He later became director of the state Department of Public Health's office of refugee and immigrant health and advocated for specialized services to help Boston's Asian, Latino, and Haitian communities.

Mr. An was born in Danang, Vietnam. He studied political science in Paris and joined the Ministry of Foreign Affairs in South Vietnam in 1957, two years after graduating from college. From 1972 to 1975, he was chief of protocol for the president of South Vietnam. He escaped in April 1975 during the fall of Saigon. He arranged for his family to go to Thailand; he contacted a colleague at the American Embassy and was told to go to a certain rooftop, where he was helicoptered out with other ex-officials.

He reconnected with his family in Guam, and they went to Fort Chaffee before resettling in Boston. They first ran a restaurant near Harvard Square. "It was like a sitcom, if you imagine a Vietnamese family running a Greek Pizza and a grinder place at Harvard Square," his son said. Then they converted it into a Vietnamese restaurant. Later, Mr. An worked for the International Institute and the state Department of Public Health's office of refugee and immigrant health.[11]

Eglin AFB Camp

Located in the Florida panhandle near the town of Fort Walton Beach, Elgin AFB Camp was the third facility opened, with a tent city having an initial capacity of 2,500. Camp Pendleton was scheduled to open on 29 April, Fort Chaffee on 2 May and Eglin AFB on 4 May. This schedule opened a new phase of the resettlement process: Operation New Arrivals.[12]

The book *Taste of Ginger* by Susan Jans-Thomas and James Wood is about the reception center at Eglin AFB.[13] It was a tent city that comprised over 500 tents constructed over 4–5 days. There was no fence around the encampment, only a rope that prevented the refugees from wandering off the site.

Volunteers served meals including Minute Rice to the refugees. The refugees asked for real rice and they got it. After a while, they thanked the volunteers and told them they did not know how to cook. The refugees then took over the cooking.[14]

A poll taken by the local radio station revealed that 80 percent of the people of nearby Niceville were opposed to the arrival of Vietnamese refugees to Eglin AFB, although officials had told them that they would not see them. Okaloosa County, like much of the Florida Panhandle, is a rigidly conservative and militaristic region. Unemployment in the panhandle was 12–13 percent and the dread of new competition for jobs was making people nervous.[15]

On 29 April 1975, Tính (Tim) Nguyễn, then twenty-four years old, was waiting at Saigon Tân Sơn Nhứt Airport, trying to catch a plane out of the besieged city. Since the airport and the city had been shelled by the communists early that morning, the runway was closed. Suddenly a C-130A of the South Vietnamese air force was seen taxiing on the closed runway. Tính and other people thought that if they could not catch this plane, they would be stuck forever in Vietnam. They ran as fast as they could and hopped aboard through the open ramp door. The overloaded C-130A, luckily, took off, with a total of four hundred and fifty-two people aboard. An entire subdivision was crammed into an airplane that was designed to carry ninety paratroopers.

The C-130A landed at U–Tapao Royal Thai AFB, and all the passengers were flown the next day to Guam. From Guam, Tính was flown to the relocation base at Eglin AFB. Having lost his shoes during the escape, Tính cut himself two pieces of a two-by-four plank, which he strapped onto his feet. It was then that he met his future wife, a civilian volunteer at the camp, named Cheri. The Nguyễns were married in April 1978 at the Eglin AFB chapel.

A local family sponsored him, and he took English classes and did odd jobs for a living. He went to the University of Alabama, where he earned a bachelor's degree in electrical engineering in 1981. Upon graduation, he applied for a position at the Lockheed-Georgia company but was turned down despite having a 3.7 GPA and working full time at the university medical center. He went to work with Gulfstream Aerospace in Savannah, Georgia. He applied again to Lockheed and was hired to work at the company's Marietta facility in 1983.

Tính got to work for Marietta's SATIN project, or Survivability Augmentation for Transport Installation, which was designed to provide transport planes with a system of defensive equipment to counter infrared and radar-guided threats. That last morning in 1975 in Vietnam, he saw a VNAF AC-119 gunship getting hit by a surface-to-air missile and it crashed right in front of them.

SATIN was a strapped-on kit (a radar warning receiver) that advised the crew of incoming threats. Four dispensers would then launch clouds of chaff, tiny shards of spun aluminum that spoof radar-guided missiles or anti-aircraft artillery, and flares. These particles have higher temperatures than the hotter parts of the aircraft.

In 1990, the air force asked Lockheed and Nguyễn's group to develop a defensive system for the C-5 Galaxy strategic transport. They did it and developed another system for the C-130J. Group A equipment, such as wiring and brackets, is installed in every aircraft on the assembly line. Software to operate the system is built into the mission computer. Group B equipment, the chaff and flare dispensers, is relatively straightforward to install. The system got clearance by the Italian government. The SATIN system is now installed in all transport planes.[16]

Fort Indiantown Gap, Pennsylvania

The refugee situation on Guam and in the CONUS states was further aggravated by the approaching typhoon season, which demanded immediate action. A typhoon is a tropical storm in the northwest Pacific with winds above 64 knots (118 km/h). Options included opening new buildings and erecting more tents, but finally a decision was made to open a fourth U.S. center. Fort Indiantown Gap in Pennsylvania was selected on 14 May for its immediate readiness and location close to a major highway with transportation to major Eastern population centers. And it could house at least 15,000 people.[17]

Located in Lebanon County, Fort Indiantown Gap had served as a refugee center for Eastern Europeans in the past. On 22 May 1975, B.G. Cannon, commander of Task Force New Arrivals at Fort Chaffee, was designated the commander of Fort Indiantown Gap center. The name "Indiantown Gap" derived from the presence of many Native American villages around the installation and in the area. "Gap" results from the separation in the Blue Mountains.[18]

The first plane load of refugees arrived at Harrisburg, Pennsylvania, airport on 28 May 1975—the first of 22,000 refugees to be processed by that facility. They arrived after a 20-hour flight from Guam. Among the people greeting these new arrivals was Mrs. Julia V. Taft, the newly appointed acting director of the Interagency Task Force for Indochina.[19] The governor of Pennsylvania, Milton Shapp, greeted them with a warm welcome: "America has become a home for people of every nation, every belief, every race and every color. It can also be a home for you. After the tragic experience of last year, I hope you will find here in America a place of peace, freedom and opportunity."

A young Vietnamese student who said he had no family was asked why he had left Vietnam. He took the reporter's pen and paper and wrote, "Because we like freedom."[20]

Located at the base of the beautiful Blue Mountains, part of the Appalachian Mountains about 23 miles northeast of Harrisburg, Fort Indiantown Gap is the home of the Pennsylvania National Guard Training Center. A section of the 22-square-mile military base was opened in early June 1975 to house an expected 15,000 Vietnamese until they were resettled in other parts of the country.

However, some of the small towns surrounding the camp were not very welcoming. Civilian officials at the camp were aware of the hostility and did not plan to send the refugees to areas where racial intolerance was high.

On the other hand, the Vietnamese did not seem to realize that once they had entered the U.S., they "could no longer behave like a Vietnamese in a country that was Vietnamese.... For many, this was painful realization.... Many were under the illusion that they would merely pass some time away from home, waiting for the new government [in Vietnam] to fall."[21]

From Guam, we (including the author) flew to the U.S. mainland after stopping for short breaks in Hawaii and Washington state. It was late afternoon when we landed at the Harrisburg, Pennsylvania, airport. We were then transported to Fort Indiantown Gap aboard yellow school buses. Although tired by the long trans–Pacific flight, we were kept awake by the locals who waved in a friendly manner to our passing buses. Did we know them? Certainly not. But this friendly welcome warmed our worried minds and anxious hearts. The final stop was Fort Indiantown Gap, where we were directed to one of the barracks to listen to the rules of the camp and to be assigned a place each in one of the barracks.

It was in Indiantown Gap that Võ Phiến, a professor of literature, wrote a short story called "The Key." A middle-aged man confided that his family had decided to leave their senile father behind when they left Vietnam. He also left money in the elderly person's wardrobe. Whoever could not make the trip could use the money to care for the senior. While getting on his escape boat, he realized that by mistake he had taken the key with him instead of leaving it with the old man. Those left behind thus had no way to open the wardrobe.

The key thus became the regrets the Vietnamese carried with them. Although a key could open new doors, because they could not go back home, the past would irrevocably be locked away. They could no longer reach it except by seeing it in their minds. The story later became so well-known that it was discussed at length by college professors.[22]

The Vietnamese-American poet Linh Dinh, who lived in Philadelphia, had a friend named Giang who visited him from Houston, Texas. Giang, who came to the United States via Fort Indiantown Gap, wanted Linh Dinh to take him to revisit the fort. The two friends during the trip talked about the difference between Americans and Vietnamese.

> There's a Vietnamese saying, "Any two Vietnamese form a political party. Any three, a party and a faction." No puppets or savages, Vietnamese took politics deadly seriously, because it was. In the end, though, they were just pawns of geopolitical schemers and war profiteers, same as the American soldiers who were sent over there.
>
> The US allied itself with Stalin, then fought Communism. It propped up Saddam Hussein, then murdered him. After bombing Hanoi, it now sells weapons to the same regime…. When it comes to geopolitics, there is no ideological consistency. Only war is constant and the flow of refugees.[23]

The shifting U.S. positions, military, economic, or moral, confused the Vietnamese-Americans, who are simpler and tend to stick to one belief and only one. For example, they were anticommunist during the war, and four decades later they still share the same anticommunist stance. Little Saigon remains fervently anticommunist today.[24] The Americans, on the other hand, changed their beliefs frequently. While Washington was against the Vietnamese communists in 1975, President Bill Clinton normalized the relationship between the U.S. and communist Vietnam on 11 July 1995.[25]

11

Follow Up and Untold Stories

We have seen what had happened to the repatriates in Vietnam in general. It would also be nice to follow some of the evacuees who landed on Guam in 1975 and see how they are doing presently. Of course, some have been very successful and others less.

Vietnamese in Guam

The evacuees came and left, and quietness and routine returned to the island. There were no more hurried activities, no more unusually crowded highways, and no more demonstrations or hunger strikes. The people of this island opened their doors and hearts to the 120,000 evacuees, but when the repatriates went on rock-throwing and arson rampages, they said it was enough. The repatriates, however, were only the minority (1 percent). By the time the major disturbances had erupted, the majority had left the island for the mainland camps under the watchful eyes of their sponsors. They were the ones who were grateful to the Guamanians for having opened their hearts to welcome them.

The Nashua Telegraph, a local Guam newspaper, looked at the refugee phenomenon in 1976, one year after they landed on the island. Guam was the first refuge for evacuees from war-torn Vietnam. Of the 120,000 people who arrived in Guam, about 1,000 had stayed there. While some were physically fit, others were exhausted and worn out. The diaspora had been a very stressful ordeal for many, whether young or old. Vietnamese families did go together, usually in groups of two or three generations, with the young ones caring for the old ones. The common denominator they were looking for was safety, something they did not have in their native country.

They stayed on Guam because of the nice warm climate, which was similar to that of Vietnam, because the people are gentle and warm, and because Guam was only six hours away by air from Vietnam. Other

11. Follow Up and Untold Stories

people had business offers. Pan American World Airways hired ten people, with a total of forty dependents. The lowest-paid Pan Am worker was paid $5.70 per hour. One success story was Đinh Văn Minh, once a cargo sales agent in Saigon. He started at the bottom to become a lead agent, the highest rung before moving to management level. He had moved out of government housing to an apartment with his brother and his wife. They paid no rent and utilities and received a small salary for taking care of this twenty-unit apartment complex.

Other evacuees worked as service station attendants, electricians, store clerks, auto mechanics. Fishermen and farmers were doing well. A few businesspeople opened a nightclub, a roadside snack bar, and a landscaping business.

Camp Asan was a navy hospital for wounded soldiers evacuated from the fighting in Vietnam. It then housed the evacuees, but after April 1976 it remained silent and rusty. Since no one used the buildings, they again fell into disrepair. All electrical wiring and plumbing fixtures were removed. Luckily or unluckily, Supertyphoon Pamela came in May 1976, destroying all the Asan buildings and causing $500 million in damage to the island. The Asan buildings were subsequently removed. In 1978, the property was acquired by the National Park Service and turned into the War in the Pacific National Historical Park.

The evacuees were indeed lucky to arrive on Guam in 1975 instead of 1976. Had they come in 1976, many would have been severely injured or even killed by typhoon Pamela. All the tents would have been blown away and there would have been no place for them to stay.

Orote Point, the site of the sprawling and huge Tent City, has returned to its wilderness state and once again is reclaimed by thick tropical vegetation. The only signs of the camp are the holes made by the stakes drilled on the asphalt.[1]

Hoàng Trường, a South Vietnamese soldier, came to Guam in 1975 as part of the second wave of evacuees, probably on board of one of the Vietnamese navy ships. He left behind a pregnant wife and six children. Instead of fighting to return to Vietnam, or moving to the continental U.S., or causing problems, he quietly settled on Guam and mingled with the locals. He was within the age group of the repatriates; he left his family in Vietnam, and he was a former soldier like them. Instead of being enraged about the situation and becoming violent, he settled down and first worked as a lowly gardener for Triple J. Enterprises' Asan apartments, then became their building maintenance worker.

It was only a year later that he was able to contact his wife Út by mail to tell her he was alive on Guam. Having not heard from him for a year, Út thought he had died during the war, fighting the enemy. She told him that life was tough for his family living in Vietnam under the communist regime. They struggled hard for food every day and did not know in the morning whether they would have dinner or lunch. They could work hard all day and still go hungry at night. Sometimes they could not afford clothes and had to wear rags. Út survived by cooking and selling her food, sometimes having her children carry her baskets. With Trường staying on Guam, she had no one to help her support the family, as all her children were minors.

In the meantime, Trường continued to work and save money. He built two houses for his family without getting into debt. He did it with part-time labor, and by getting his friends to help. He got help from Catholic Services in New York, and a local attorney filled out the necessary paperwork for his family. Their reunion in Guam in 1986, eleven long years later, was made possible with the help of Triple J Enterprises' owner, president and CEO, Robert Jones. Trường's lowly salary did not allow him to bring his family of eight people to Guam. He did not have money to move the paperwork faster. When the family arrived on Guam, it needed many things, and donations came in from the local community.

Trường's daughter mentioned that her father had made the right decision in leaving Vietnam and giving the family a chance for a new life. She mentioned that her father prayed every day, thanking the Lord that his family was reunited. Trường died in 2001. Bob Jones helped the family start its businesses after Truong died. The family, which struggled to feed and clothe itself after the war, now owns and operates a restaurant and an automobile air-conditioning shop on Guam.[2]

Vietnamese in America

Thiên Hương Thị Nguyễn, age 7, arrived in Guam in 1975 with her sister and father, Navy Captain Nguyễn Văn Thông. They had witnessed war in their native country of Vietnam. On Guam, they were sponsored by Captain Wyttenbach, who sent the two young girls to his sister, Mrs. John Buckley, in Pennsylvania. In 1987, the 19-year-old girl became an American citizen at a ceremony in York County Common Pleas Court. Four days later, she graduated from Mount Zion Elementary School, Lewisberry, taught by her guardian foster mother, Mrs. Buckley.[3]

Joseph Phạm, the last passenger of the disabled navy ship *Lam Giang*, arrived at Subic Bay aboard the *Kirk*. His pregnant wife was evaluated at the Subic Bay Naval Hospital and found to be stable. The Phạms were shipped to Guam aboard one the MSC ships. On 18 May, she delivered a boy at Guam's Naval Regional Medical Center. They remained at Camp Asan until mid–June, when they boarded a flight to Camp Pendleton, California. They were sponsored by the Murphys in Fort Worth, Texas. In 1976, they relocated to Seattle, Washington, where he presently works as a court reporter.

Đàm Thúy Nguyễn escaped from Saigon along with her nephew aboard a navy ship before transitioning to one of the MSC ships. On arrival at Subic Bay Base, they were shipped to Guam, where they stood in line for meals in the dust and sun. She and her nephew decided to get one meal so that they could use the other plate to shield the food from the dust. They received one scoop of wet rice and some fishy fish, which they doused with Tabasco sauce to make it red and spicy. They went up to a hill near a tree, where they shared the meal.

After three weeks, they were transferred to Fort Indiantown Gap, Pennsylvania, where they found real beds, showers, ample food, and some mobility. They were sponsored by some people in Fort Worth, Texas, where she found a job teaching GED students and sold Avon products in the evenings and on weekends. Two years later, she found teaching work in Michigan before being offered a YMCA position as director of refugee services for metropolitan Washington, D.C.

In 1989, Đàm Nguyễn was honored as one of *Washingtonian* magazine's "Washingtonians of the Year." She proudly declared, "Vietnam and America. I love them both. I was born in Vietnam and reborn in this country.... Now this is my land and I will die here."

Đàm Nguyễn has since married retired Army Major General Victor Hugo, Jr. Her nephew became a chemist, got married and has two children.[4]

Lieutenant Thanh Phạm, the former commanding officer of escort patrol boat *Vạn Kiếp II* (HQ-14), brought his ship alongside a pier at Grande Island in Subic Bay. He and his family arrived at Guam, transported aboard an MSC ship, on 13 May 1975. They were transferred to Camp Indiantown Gap and were sponsored by people in Wilkes-Barre, Pennsylvania. They moved to an apartment Catholic Charities rented for them. They were joined by Phạm's parents, his wife's parents, and her brother's family. They all lived in the apartment for more than a year before moving to a bigger place. He worked as a cabinetmaker while attending Wilkes College. He graduated in 1980 with a degree in electrical engineering and worked as a field engineer for a Long Island company specializing in navigational systems. After working as a software designer for a large company in Annapolis, Maryland, he retired in 2006. But he began working again as a software designer for a health care management firm in Annapolis.[5]

Ba Nguyễn was the C-47 Chinook pilot who tried to land on the *Kirk* deck in 1975. Almost out of gas, he realized he could not land the huge Chinook on the small *Kirk* deck. Passengers had to either jump down or be thrown into the arms of the GIs below. Once the passengers were out of the helicopter, the co-pilot jumped to the deck. The pilot then steered the craft from the *Kirk*'s bow, leaned the helicopter to the left and jumped out the right-handed side into the water.

As soon as the blades hit the water, they exploded into pieces, some big, some small. It sounded like a giant train wreck. The pilot soon emerged from the water, to the excitement of the *Kirk* sailors, who dove into the water to try to save him. The pilot was brought to the ship. For that heroic feat of airmanship more than three decades earlier, the *Kirk* crew pinned an Air Medal on the pilot's sports coat in a summer reunion of the *Kirk* crew outside Washington, D.C.

Ba and his wife lived in Seattle, Washington, where both worked for the aerospace giant Boeing.

Mina, 2-year-old daughter of Ba, was thrown from the Chinook to the arms of GIs 18 feet below on the deck. Three decades later, she is now a pediatric neuropsychology doctor.[6]

We have seen Tony Lâm (born in 1936) working as camp manager for three long months in 1975. He then moved to the U.S., where life was hard for the new immigrant; but he survived and even thrived. In 1992, he became the first Vietnamese American elected to public office in the U.S. and became a three-term councilman of the city of Westminster, California.

He was a respected community leader, secretary of the Vietnamese Lions Club in Westminster, and the first vice-president of the Vietnamese Chamber of Commerce in Orange Country, California. He retired in 2002 at the age of seventy-five. He also owned a public relations firm and was a part owner of a Vietnamese restaurant in the city of Westminster.[7]

Lâm was appointed by Janet Nguyen, then Orange County Supervisor, now a former California state senator, to the county planning commission from 2007 to 2011 and the airport commission from 2011 to April 2014.[8]

Lê Bá Kòng visited the United States in 1963 by invitation of the U.S. State Department. His visit was related to his work as principal of an English school. He was fluent in Vietnamese, English, Cantonese, and French.

By chance he got acquainted with the William Goodwin family in Galesburg, Illinois, which he and his wife visited a few years later as members of the Vietnamese Jaycees Club. They stayed at the Goodwin home during their visit.

11. Follow Up and Untold Stories   153

On 22 April 1975, before the fall of Saigon, he contacted the Goodwins to enquire whether they would sponsor him, his wife, his 17-year-old son and his mother to the United States.

The Goodwins mailed an application to the proper authorities in Washington, D.C., agreeing to sponsor the Lê family. In the meantime, the Lê family escaped to the U.S. and were processed on Guam, from where the Goodwins sponsored them to Galesburg. Dr. Lê Bá Kòng is well-known for his many Vietnamese-English and English-Vietnamese dictionaries.[9]

Minh Quang Nguyễn escaped with his family of eleven on one of the cargo ships on the Saigon River. The ship was steered by South Vietnamese soldiers toward Singapore until a U.S. ship rerouted them and guided them toward the Philippines. From there, they were shipped to Guam. They signed up for Camp Pendleton, California, but were told to wait for another month. Unwilling to wait that long, they opted for Camp Indiantown Gap. Nguyễn is now a senior professor of accounting and computer and information systems at Harrisburg Community College in Pennsylvania.[10]

Nho Trọng Nguyễn, now 77, the eldest of eight children and the son of a farmer, was the first in his poor family to go to college; he went on a scholarship for forestry engineering. After graduating, he enlisted in the South Vietnamese army and took leave to run for congress several years later.

Eight years later, the communists approached Saigon. His family had already evacuated, and he got a call from U.S. officials to go to an emergency location for evacuation, but no U.S. personnel showed up. He went to the U.S. Embassy, climbed over the wall and told the guards he was an elected official. He was flown to a U.S. carrier, then to Guam, where he scanned lists of evacuees and spotted his daughter's name—his family had made it to California.

Nho Trọng Nguyễn joined his family at camp Pendleton. He worked as a handyman's helper before eventually becoming a judge in California. His three children became lawyers and a doctor.[11]

Magdalena (aka Madalenna) Lai came to the U.S. in 1975 via Guam. She was 34, penniless and the sole provider for four children, all younger than ten, while her husband, an ARVN officer, was detained in reeducation camp in Vietnam for almost a decade.

She put herself through school, starting beauty shops in El Monte and then in Pomona before opening a cosmetology school in Pomona. She raised her children by herself and saw the life she cultivated in the U.S. as a gift from the people and country that adopted her.

She was so grateful to get a second life in the U.S. that she decided to build a float to express her thanks to America. Once her idea was accepted, she sold her house to raise the $100,000 required for the project. Her dream was finally realized when her float, carrying a boat braving the seas, decorated with flowers and adorned with a "Thank You America and the world" sign, made it to the 2002 Tournament of Roses in Pasadena, California.[12]

In 2005, after thirty years of living in the United States among the overseas Vietnamese, the renowned and prolific singer and composer Phạm Duy returned to Vietnam to live his last years under the communist regime he was so fearful of. He was as capricious and polarizing as he was talented. In the 1940s, he joined the communists and participated in their insurrection against the French in North Vietnam. Six years later, he moved south after becoming disenchanted with their censorship. His "reactionary music" was banned in communist-controlled areas during and after the war. After 1975, he moved to the U.S. and continued his minstrel's life.

He faced criticism when he returned to live in Vietnam, forgetting that he had left Saigon while the heroic South Vietnamese soldiers were still fighting to defend his freedom, giving him and thousands of other people enough time to flee. Now that the danger has passed, his thinking about the past has changed. When interviewed by the BBC in December 2012, Duy was asked about the "refugee songs" and "infamy songs" he had written in the refugee camp in 1975. He told the interviewer he did not want to talk about it: "These songs were composed when I was [in a] panic; please don't bring it up. I forgot about it already."[13]

Americans

Richard Wyttenbach-Santos graduated from the U.S. Naval Academy. He served two naval combat tours as a weapons officer in Vietnam in 1966 and 1968. In graduate school, he earned two master's degrees and a PhD. He had another combat tour to Vietnamese waters in 1972. In 1974, he became the first legal resident of Guam to command a warship, having to change his residency to become the first "special assistant" for Guam Matters. In 1975, he became the coordinator for Operation New Life. He sponsored Navy Captain Nguyễn Văn Thông and his two children. He divorced his wife and married Bernice Santos Miller in 1989. They remained in Guam. His ex-wife, Gwen Wyttenbach, lives in Fairfax, Virginia. He retired in August 1991, as a captain in an admiral's position.

Ricardo Bordallo was the governor of Guam from 1976 to 1980 and

11. Follow Up and Untold Stories

1984 to 1988. In 1987, he was convicted of bribery and extortion in connection with favors he performed in office for campaign contributions. His court appeals were partially successful. He appealed to the Supreme Court, but it refused to hear his case. In December 1989, he was resentenced to serve four years on the remaining convictions.

On 31 January 1990, as he was about to report to a minimum-security facility in California, he drove to the Paseo Loop, where the bronze statue of Indian Chief Quipuha, the first indigenous chief who converted to Christianity, is located. With his back to the rear of the statue, he placed around himself handwritten placards and draped himself with a flag of Guam. One of the four placards around him says, "I have only one life to give to my island." He then killed himself with a .38 caliber pistol. He was pronounced dead at the U.S. Naval Hospital.[14]

Mrs. Madeleine Bordallo, as the First Lady of Guam, promoted the indigenous Chamorro culture. She served as a Guamanian senator in the Democratic Party between her husband's two terms as governor. In 1994, she became lieutenant governor. During her tenure she championed island beautification as a way to promote Guam's tourism. In 2003, she became Guam's representative in the U.S. Congress.[15]

Richard L. Armitage, the "brains of a successful rescue,"[16] had a busy post–Vietnam career that is beyond the scope of this book. He was a Republican politician who was appointed the 13th United States deputy secretary at the State Department, serving from 2001 to 2005 under President George W. Bush.

The *Kirk*, a destroyer escort deployed to the U.S. Navy Seventh Fleet during the late 1960s and early 1970s, has a story of her own, which endures because of its "powerful human component and what it says about caring and compassion." Commissioned in September 1972, she was decommissioned in August 1993 when she was transferred to Taiwan as *Fen Yang*.

Point Udall is named for former Arizona congressman Morris "Mo" Udall. It was the site of Orote Field airbase during World War II. The point was called "Orote Point" until it was renamed "Point Udall" in May 1987.[17] It was built by Japan during its occupation of the island from 10 December 1941 to 21 July 1944. Beginning in May 1944 and continuing during the second Battle of Guam, the airfield was attacked from the air. American troops established their beachhead on either side of the Orote Peninsula on July 21 to seize the airfield and the deep-water harbor nearby. The airfield was recaptured by July 30.

Another Point Udall, in the Virgin Islands, is the easternmost point in the United States and was named for Mo Udall's brother Stewart. In a 1987 statement regarding H.R. 2434, Denny Smith and Guam's nonvoting congressional delegate Ben Blaz said, "If our legislation is approved, America's day would begin and end at a Point Udall." When Mo Udall died in 1998, President Bill Clinton issued a statement saying in part, "It is fitting that the easternmost point of the United States, in the Virgin Islands, and the westernmost point, in Guam, are both named 'Udall Point.' The Sun will never set on the legacy of Mo Udall."

Operation New Life Costs

Listed below are the itemized costs of Operation New Life, an operation that has helped save 120,000 Vietnamese evacuees.

A total of 129,792 Indochinese (Vietnamese, Laotians, Cambodians, and Chinese) were relocated to the U.S., 6,632 to third countries, and 1,546 back to Vietnam. There were 822 births and 77 deaths.[18]

Table 11-1. Operations New Life/New Arrivals: Department of Defense Obligations

Refugee Evacuation and Onward Movement	
Pacific Command (steaming cost for 43 warships in South China Sea)	$7,277,000
Military Sealift Command (plus $5.7 M in Post-war Reconstruction Funds)	8,754,000
Military Airlift Command (flights on government-owned or chartered aircraft)	84,600,000
Refugee Camps/Staging Areas and Reception Centers	
Establishment (erection of temporary and conversion of preexisting facilities)	$12,923,000
Maintenance (including processing, food, supplies, services, equipment, et al.)	104,177,000
Phase Out (facility closure and rehabilitation exclusive of costs for Ft Chaffee)	1,375,000
Medical Care (refugee inpatient and outpatient treatment at military installations)	4,300,000
Total Costs (Army, Navy, Marine Corps and Air Force)	$223,006,000

SOURCE: *Report to the Congress by the Comptroller General, "Operation New Life," 1 June 1976, pp. 33–35.*

Thus ended Operation New Life, a complicated, chaotic operation that turned out to be one of the most successful U.S. military operations during the last five decades thanks to thousands of volunteers and military personnel who through their hard work, determination, and courage were able to process the more than 130,000 Vietnamese evacuees and deliver them to CONUS camps. This was no small feat, because the operation was totally unprecedented and unplanned.

Role of the CONUS Camps

Despite being saved by the warm welcome of the Guamanians and American sponsors, in May 1975 the Vietnamese arrived in the U.S. at a time of severe unemployment and economic recession. The 1973–1975 recession was a period of economic stagnation in much of the Western World during the 1970s, leading to high unemployment and high inflation.

The main cause of the recession was the 1973 oil crisis, during which members of the Organization of the Petroleum Exporting Countries (OPEC) proclaimed an oil embargo targeted at nations perceived as supporting Israel during the Yom Kippur War.[19] By the end of the embargo in March 1974,[20] the price of oil had risen 300 percent, from $3 per barrel to nearly $12 globally. The U.S. Bureau of Labor Statistics estimates that 2.3 million jobs were lost during the recession.[21] In May 1975, the unemployment rate reached its height, for the cycle, of 9 percent.[22]

A 1975 Gallup poll asking whether the recently evacuated South Vietnamese should be permitted to settle in the United States indicated that 52 percent of the national sample opposed resettlement of the refugees here and 36 percent favored allowing the Vietnamese to rebuild their lives in the United States.[23] In U.S. mainland camps the evacuees were immediately educated in preparation for life in America, then kicked out into the American society and told to build their future.

If Vietnamese actions, especially in leaving their country, had their roots in Vietnamese history and society, Vietnamese actions in U.S. camps, especially the resettlement to low-income and rural areas, while still controlled by the Americans, was dependent on the long-term thinking and ingenuity of the Vietnamese.

The transition from a Vietnamese world to an American one was rapid and dizzying. The Vietnamese realized that their reaction to such a change would ultimately affect their future and societal standing in America.

The role of the camps, according to the Interagency Task Force (IATF), was to resettle the immigrants by scattering them throughout the country. This would speed up absorption into American society[24] and prevent exacerbation of widespread nativism and racism at a time of high national unemployment and limited social services.[25] The impact of this policy was challenged by one refugee: "The worst thing they have done to us since we came here was to put us in different places all over the country. We depend on each other.... We have been through so much together."[26] Reyes explained that Vietnamese efforts to adapt to U.S. society or be integrated into it could "not be mandated." They tend to hold on to old ways against the day of their return.

Twelve government agencies were tasked to do the work, with the assistance of nine resettlement agencies. The government would only give a $500-per-person resettlement grant, although the Lutheran Immigration and Refugee Service (LIRS) argued that adequate resettling would cost about $5,601 per family of four.[27]

In the camps, the Vietnamese had no control over their future. They were even forced to accept jobs at below minimum wage (less than $2.39 per hour in 1976) in rural areas in order to get out of the camps. The work they found was often temporary and tended to offer little or no possibility of advancement.[28]

That was how an air force colonel became a newspaper delivery person and night watchman. A medical doctor turned into a limousine driver; another doctor became a dish washer. A bank manager in Vietnam took the job of a janitor at a U.S. bank. An ARVN chief of staff worked as a waiter, while an ARVN colonel was a garbage collector.[29] They went to work, but as they could not make ends meet with their below-minimum wages, they were forced either to rely on subsidies from their sponsors or to go on welfare.

After 15 December 1975, realizing they were in dead-end jobs, many made the decision to move out of the cold northern states and isolation from other Vietnamese to southern warmer states and into large communities of Vietnamese. They resisted the U.S. government's forced integration in the American lower classes because they knew it would be a dead end; they silently revolted by regrouping in urban centers and going into welfare after exhausting the resources of sponsors and volunteer agencies. This was one of the ways they could have a say about U.S. resettlement: either by working as low-wage earners in America or becoming Americans.[30]

12

The Two Vietnams

As I stand on the southern bank of the Potomac River from the Virginia side and look toward Washington, D.C., I imagine myself standing 45 years ago on the bank of the Saigon River while looking back at my beloved downtown Saigon.

When 30 April 1975 came, northern communist tanks broke through the gates of Independence Palace and took over the country. The first wave of 120,000 Vietnamese fled the country to look for freedom somewhere else.[1] The consequences—psychological, social, political, economic and moral—were often tragic and painful.

To fully understand these consequences and their impacts on the South Vietnamese, one has to discuss the loss of South Vietnam, the Little Saigons, the two Vietnams, and a new way of being Vietnamese.

Loss

With the fall of Saigon, the world as the South Vietnamese knew it ended abruptly. There were many dramatic changes.

1. *Punishment(s)*. Trương Như Tảng[2] acknowledged, "In the first year of liberation, some three hundred thousand people were arrested."[3] Overall, more than a million government officials and military personnel were hauled to reeducation camps where they were starved, assaulted, punished, and forced to do hard labor.[4] This was a wholesale enslavement of the country. Prisoners were treated harshly without any rights: "We were less than animals and not really humans."[5] Even the communist Bùi Tín[6] wondered, after visiting various reeducation camps in the South as well as the North, "Why pursue a policy of such harshness towards hundreds of thousands of people?"[7]

2. *Suppression of basic freedoms*.[8] One could not even visit

one's friends a few miles away without the approval of government officials. Basic freedoms were abolished and replaced by communist rules—those of the invaders. "In the eyes of our communist leaders, an enemy 'puppet,' whether alive or dead, was always a puppet—a second class citizen who had no citizen's rights at all."[9] In March 2007, Father Nguyễn Văn Lý, who has fought for human rights in Vietnam for decades, was muzzled in the courtroom after yelling anti-communist slogans.[10] This was a far cry from the so-called liberation of Vietnam.

3. *Impoverishment.* Private property, bank accounts, houses and businesses were confiscated and turned over to communist officials. The latter "fought over houses, cars, prostitutes, and bribes. [Communist] soldiers and officials ... were suddenly confronted with what seemed to them an almost fairy tale richness, theirs for the taking."[11]

4. *Escape and readjustment.* Unable to tolerate an illegitimate and cruel regime, more than 2 million people braved the seas, storms and pirates to look for freedom elsewhere.[12] This was an exodus by sea and land of epic proportion in modern times. This was also the loudest rejection of communism and communist regimes in the world.

5. *Nightmares.* They have been the constant followers of many Vietnamese for the past four-and-a-half decades, especially for those who went through reeducation camps. The inhumane treatment[13] of the prisoners by sadistic jailers—"they did not [always] kill you outright in the camp by shooting you. Instead they slowly tortured and terrified you"[14]—left an indelible and painful mark on many. And today, a scratching at the door will still wake up a former camp inmate and leave them sweating all over.[15]

San Juan wrote about a refugee who had relocated to the U.S.:

> It is hard to say that the war was over...
> The past like a nightmare endlessly haunts...
> It is like a dream he cannot forget...
> The past that [he] enjoyed in Vietnam is meaningless in the United States...
> [His] dream torment and has no satisfactory resolution in the present.[16]

Memories have been a prominent feature in the lives of those who had escaped from Vietnam—the overseas South Vietnamese. This led to community-building and place-making.

Their wounds, like all wounds, tend to bleed and heal and cyclically bleed again: "Periodically, these festering wounds bleed again ... [resulting] in vigorous protests.... What the Vietnamese-American community wants to do with these protests is to remind themselves, and other Americans too, not to forget the old South Vietnam that they know and love."[17]

In life, there are three types of loss. First, there is casual loss—loss of money, wallet, keys...—that can be replaced.

The second type of loss is that of a relationship. One day, he or she leaves us: that person who has been so dear to us in many ways is no longer around. We become heartbroken. And until we recover, we feel that something in us is missing. We are no longer whole. Our mind wanders, making it difficult for us to concentrate or work.

The third type is the loss of a country: the biggest of all losses. "There is no greater loss than that of losing one's country," claimed Phan Bội Châu, one of the greatest Vietnamese non-communist revolutionaries, in 1906.[18] What he meant was that losing independence to the French was akin to losing one's country, although it was still there.

But in 1975, the South Vietnamese lost it completely: belongings, properties, land, families, country, and independence. The 1975 loss was complete: it was a tragedy, and they had no chance of regaining their country, properties, or belongings back. They did not live during that period: they just "floated" or survived as best as they could between the past and the future before slowly reacclimatizing to the present. They then had the sense of belonging to two worlds—Vietnam and Vietnamese-America—and to neither, and of responsibility for the communities to which they are not always sure they belong.[19] They had lost the old Vietnam but had not become Vietnamese-American yet.

But "to be Vietnamese means to endure."[20] They had endured the 21-year war: the war that was brought to them by the North Vietnamese; the war with all its drawbacks. And they endured pain, tribulations, defeat, isolation, and discrimination to survive and to see another tomorrow.

And when they set foot on the American shore, they felt that "history is already against us. Vietnam goes on without us. America goes on without acknowledging us."[21] And they had to learn to tune out from their lives sorrow, pain, weakness, and misery. But what they had left was "dignity, an ironic sense of hope, and believe it or not, a sense of humor."[22] For "perhaps only a loser knows real freedom. Forced outside of history away from home and hearth he can choose to remake himself."[23] And they will remake themselves to be better and to deserve the trust America had given to them.

The Little Saigons

With time, the Vietnamese refugees became Vietnamese-Americans, people who walked around with hyphens between their names. They were no longer Vietnamese, but were not yet, or might never be, Americans. They were in limbo between the two worlds, one that had rejected them and one they had not become familiar with.

This is not a new phenomenon, as the sociologist Georg Simmel discussed in the 1900s. About the immigrant, he wrote, "The stranger intends to stay, although he cannot ever become native." Born of Jewish parents in Berlin, Germany—his father later became a Roman Catholic and his mother a Lutheran—he never felt accepted by the German academia, despite his talents. He was turned down for many vacant chairmanship positions before being elevated to full professor without chair in 1901.[24] He, therefore, knew what it meant to be a stranger in a new land.

Along the same vein, a successful Vietnamese businesswoman, despite having married an American military lawyer and having children with him, declared, "As for me and the Vietnamese of my generation, there will always be memories of another time and place, another life. I will forever remain an immigrant here. And even when I am happiest, I will remember my beloved Vietnam and the fate of my people. I am the child of war, I am a Vietnamese."[25]

The Vietnamese-Americans, therefore, have to define themselves and their identity before being able to sell it to the American public. They have to submerge themselves in or feel confident about their nature culture before feeling comfortable within American culture.

"Vietnam for the community is an 'era, an epoch, and of course the war, but not a people or a nation. Vietnamese-Americans put forth their own social memories as a way to assert their presence in this country.'"[26] In order to preserve their identity, their wholesomeness, to validate themselves, and to some degree to boost up or restore their pride, they congregated in ethnic enclaves that are called "Little Saigons," where they could express their Vietnamese-ness within the boundaries of American society.

This may apply to the older generation—the Saigon government officials and military personnel who wielded power in the past, were sent to reeducation camps for a long time and lost everything including their ranks, properties, belongings, and prestige. However, this may not apply to those who came here later to make a new life or to second-generation Vietnamese-Americans.

The latter, born and raised in the U.S., feel fairly at ease within

American society. At home, however, they can feel pressure from their parents, who force them to follow Vietnamese traditions and remain Vietnamese instead of Vietnamese-Americans. Those who do not want to disrespect their parents, therefore, can be torn apart by the different, sometimes contradictory, Vietnamese and American traditions.

The Vietnam War was a war of conquest—an invasion of superior northern military forces against the southern Republic of Vietnam. By April 1975, Hanoi had sent all of its military divisions—minus one left to protect North Vietnam—racing down National Route One toward Saigon. The arrival of northern communist tanks through the gates of Independence Palace in Saigon was a flagrant violation of the 1972 Paris Accords, one of a long series of violations of human rights against the South Vietnamese. Hanoi had finally thrown down its mask and proved to the world that it had waged a war of conquest against South Vietnam.

When the South Vietnamese Trương Như Tảng, a National Liberation Front (NLF) official and minister of justice of the Provisional Revolutionary Government (PRG), returned from the jungle to Saigon on the bandwagon of the northern communists, his mother told him, "My son. You have abandoned everything ... to follow the communists. They will never return to you a particle of the things you have left. You will see. They will betray you, and you will suffer your entire life."[27]

On 15 May 1975, in Saigon, Tảng witnessed on the review stand with northern communists a parade in celebration of the conquest. One organization after another paraded in front of the officials, followed by representatives of all the northern military units. At last came a few unkempt NLF troops under the Hanoi's flag. Befuddled, Tảng turned to General Văn Tiến Dũng and enquired about NLF divisions one, three, five, seven, and nine. Dũng told him, "The Army has been reunified."[28] Tảng then realized that the PRG was only subordinate to the Hanoi government and all orders then came from Hanoi. Realizing that he had been betrayed by Hanoi, Tảng retired from the PRG and managed to escape from Vietnam as a boat refugee like all the southerners in 1976.

Hanoi committed a crime against humanity by invading South Vietnam, waging a 21-year war, killing millions of people, incarcerating hundreds of thousands of people and shoving millions of others to the seas. As a reaction, it caused tens of thousands of angry overseas Vietnamese to become more vocal and anti-communist than before. Hanoi's war was not a war of liberation like the communists pretended: it was a pure and simple war of conquest. The communists just wanted to take over South Vietnam because of its riches and because in the 1970s South Vietnam was more advanced economically, socially, and intellectually than North Vietnam.[29]

Tuan Hoang argues, "Diasporic anticommunism in the last forty years [in the U.S.] is not a new phenomenon, but the latest manifestation of Vietnamese anticommunism."[30] Opposition to communism rose out of the competition among different political parties, communist and non-communist, during the 1930s and early 1940s. Many non-communist parties (Đại Việt, Việt Nam Quốc Dân Đảng or VNQDĐ or Vietnamese Nationalist Party) later opposed socialist internationalism. Much of the anticommunist ideology was shaped by fighting among the Vietnamese, especially ICP-directed violence against non-communist groups.[31]

The situation took a sharp turn after the August Revolution and yet another turn after the Geneva Accords of 1954. Then anticommunism became an ideological mainstay of the government of South Vietnam. State-sponsored anticommunism was part of the nation-building competition between Saigon and Hanoi.[32]

Anticommunism became the rallying point against the new communist rulers and the Vietnamese-Americans' renewed identity after the fall of Saigon. The old divide between expatriates and current Vietnamese rulers, capitalism versus communism, became more visible than in the past, as the Vietnamese-Americans affirmed their identity. The shock of the national loss and the suffering of incarceration in reeducation camps provided a one-two punch that strengthened diasporic anticommunism and the determination to oppose the Vietnamese communist party at all costs.[33]

The Two Vietnams

The Two Vietnams was the title of a book published by Bernard Fall in 1963 in which he compared the two Vietnamese states—northern communist and southern democratic[34]—following the partition of the country in 1954. What people did not realize was the country has been psychologically, socially, geographically, and politically divided into two or more entities on various occasions since its formation some two thousand years ago.

According to mythology, the Vietnamese are the offspring of King Lạc Long Quân (dragon king) and the fairy Âu Cơ. The latter gave birth to a sac containing one hundred eggs that developed into one hundred children. The idyllic dragon-fairy union, however, did not last long, because one day Lạc Long Quân asked for a divorce. The couple split up and Âu Cơ took fifty children to the mountains and Lạc Long Quân guided the remaining fifty children to the seaside.[35] It is worth mentioning that this probably the first recorded divorce in any country in the world. The legend is engrained in the Vietnamese psyche. Descendants of the highlanders (Thượng or Mường) and lowlanders (Kinh) presently account for 15 and 85 percent of Vietnam's population. The ancient division between Thượng and Kinh gave way to a northern-southern rivalry by the end of the 16th century. Either by design or fate, the Vietnamese originally divided into two different entities. That design eventually became a curse for the Vietnamese people.

From 1600 to 1802, for more than 200 years, Vietnam was geographically and politically divided into two states: *đàng ngoài* (outsider or north) and *đàng trong* (insider or south), the boundaries of which roughly corresponded to the 1960s North and South Vietnam. The north was ruled by the Lê King with the support of the Trịnh lords, while the south was ruled by the Nguyễn lords. Without diplomatic and commercial connection between the two states during these two centuries, northerners and southerners evolved apart. The short period of reunification (1802–1859) could not erase the two-century cultural and economic differences between north and south.

When the French moved in and controlled Vietnam (1859–1940), they separated central Vietnam from the south and attached it to the north to reshape the country according to administrative realms of the time. Since the Vietnamese king ruled from Huế, central Vietnam, the French could not leave it connected to the south without destroying the unity of his kingdom.

Cochinchina (south), which was first occupied by the French in 1859, became a French colony that was ruled from Paris. The bloc consisting of Annam (center) and Tonkin (north) in 1884 became a protectorate that was administered by a Nguyễn king, but again controlled by the French. Cochinchinese subjects, as a result, enjoyed rare political perks unknown to those living in Annam and Tonkin. They could become French citizens and had the right to own a newspaper (freedom of press).

During the Vietnam War (1954–1975), Vietnam was again divided into two regions as described earlier by Bernard Fall: a communist North Vietnam and a western-style, democratic-leaning South Vietnam.

Therefore, throughout the almost 400-year history from 1600 to 1975, north and south evolved separately for more than 300 years, or 80 percent of the time.[36] That separation has left deep marks on both sides of the country, marks that manifested major cultural, social, economic, and political differences that will not be erased by a short reunification period amid lingering suspicions between northerners and southerners.

The history of the fall of Saigon is that of a country divided by two ideologies, totalitarian communism against democratic capitalism:[37]

One party state against democracy,
Repression, enslavement against freedom
Red flag against yellow flag.[38]

The history of the fall of Saigon is that of the "Little Saigons," of Vietnamese America, of Vietnamese who walk around with hyphenated labels like Vietnamese-American and Vietnamese-French. It is the history of injustice against justice. And as long as there is injustice, corruption, a one party-state and communism in Vietnam, there will always be two Vietnams.

Table 12-1. Vietnam's Names Through the Years
(names are in **bold** characters)

	North	South
1600–1802	**Đàng ngoài**	**Đàng trong**
(under)	(Lê-Trịnh Dynasty)	(Nguyễn Dynasty)
1802–1859		
(under Nguyễn rule)	**Đại Việt**	**Đại Việt**
1859–1954		
(under French rule)	**Annam Tonkin**	**Cochinchina**
1954–1975	**North Vietnam**	**South Vietnam**
	Communist	Nationalist
Democracy		
1975–present	**Socialist Vietnam**	**Little Saigons**
Dictatorship	Democracy	

A New Way of Being Vietnamese[39]

How does one define the South Vietnamese, their war, and their patriotism? Is there such a thing as southern patriotism? During the war, Westerners raised questions about South Vietnamese nationalism, which was thought to be nonexistent or at best soft, based on the simple fact that they did not fight as hard as they should have to protect their identity and country. To link battle losses to a lack of mental vigor or even patriotism is to make a superficial and erroneous assumption about the Vietnamese, or worse, shows little knowledge of the lengthy and convoluted Vietnamese history.

12. The Two Vietnams

The Vietnamese have a long history of fighting against outsiders and insiders, from 939 CE until today, to preserve their freedom. They fought wars but also built a new nation out of nothing, because South Vietnam did not exist prior to 1600 CE. The land they called South Vietnam once belonged to the Chams and Khmers, Hinduized cultures that once flourished on the Indochinese peninsula.[40] And the year 1600 marked the date when the Vietnamese—mature enough as a nation— began splitting into two countries, north and south, that would rise and compete against each other through till today. This is not to deny its ancient and rich roots in its legendary history some 2–4 millennia ago.

Vietnam is a country built by wars so much that wars are in the blood of the Vietnamese. They live in wars, with wars, and by wars. It seems like no Vietnamese generation has been immune to wars. If there was no major warfare, there was some type of revolt or uprising somewhere to be dealt with.

During the last four centuries (1600–2000), Vietnam was embroiled in four major wars that lasted a total of 105 years. The first internecine Vietnam war (1627–1675) pitted the north (*đàng ngoài*) against the south (*đàng trong*). Without external help, the war dragged on for 48 years until neither side could afford to fight and both finally settled for a truce that kept *đàng ngoài* and *đàng trong* separated and divided for almost 200 years (1627–1800). The second Vietnamese war (1773–1800), which lasted for almost three decades, began as a civil war in the south, pitting the Tây Sơn against the Nguyễn before involving the northern Lê-Trịnh.[41]

It became an Asian war as the Siamese (Thai) and Chinese jumped in to fight on one side or another; it ended with a definitive victory of the southern Nguyễn over the Tây Sơn and the Lê-Trịnh. Then came the third (1945–1954) and fourth (1954–1975) Vietnam wars between the communists and the French, then communists against the South Vietnamese and Americans. All these wars destroyed properties, harvests, countryside, and economies, leaving people destitute. Not acknowledging these Vietnam wars would lead to major historical errors.

Without wars, Vietnam would not have been enslaved by foreigners or insiders. Without wars, it would not have been a free country. Defeat and humiliation are followed by victories and triumphs. And the link between these events is war and death. Safer commented that the fabric of Vietnam is "soaked in humiliation and triumph and the blood of millions."[42]

Wars, however, are destructive, and people usually lose when they get involved in them, winners included. Carnage and destruction ravage each countryside. If wars enslave people, they also destroy society, justice, and properties, impoverish everyone, and tear families apart, especially the way Hồ, Giáp, and Lê Duẩn prosecuted the war. Safer wrote that Giáp was "utterly brainwashed by ambition. Sending so many young men to die is never a matter of moral hesitation.... Brave men are the tools for carving one's initials in the pantheon."[43]

Wars are a tragedy, especially in Vietnam, where they are so common. This has to do with Vietnam being a nation or coalition of polarized people. The last civil war between communist North and nationalist South Vietnam represents a fight over the *nature* of the Vietnamese society. They fought over whether the country should become a Western democratic society or a totalitarian communist country. The fact that the South Vietnamese lost does not mean that their cause—freedom and independence from the communists—was wrong. It simply means that they were outmaneuvered.[44] Their cause will stand and be picked up by other people for democracy to prevail.

Four decades after the fall of Saigon, Americans still talk about "the unending debate"[45] and the "war that never ends."[46] They argue about the orthodox, revisionist, and anti-revisionist theories and wonder why the ghost of the Vietnam War is still around fifty years later. First, they simply forget that it was a three-way war—North and South Vietnamese and Americans, or a five-way war if we include the Soviets and Chinese—not two-way as some authors have written in the past. Take one party out of the equation and the war does not make sense. Second, the Americans just packed their bags in 1973 and decided, "Mission accomplished and we are going home," while the war was still raging on. Third, it was not a usual type of war, because its end was negotiated on the backs of the South Vietnamese. It was a war that ended unjustly, suddenly, and in such an incoherent manner that it left many South Vietnamese at a loss for words. It was that injustice that has caused the war to be debated again and again. What if the Americans had remained until the end? We will never know the answer because it did not happen that way.

The war ended as a violent and bloody military conquest of South Vietnam by the communists. While the South Vietnamese could not withstand the communist invasion, they still continue to fight today for the freedom and human rights of the Vietnamese people living under the communist regime.

In sum, the South Vietnamese have been at the forefront of Vietnamese culture and civilization. It was their forebears who promoted the *nam tiến* (southern advance) that vastly expanded the nation from north to south while carving under Lord Nguyễn Hoàng and his successors a frontier region named "South Vietnam." They were in Nha Trang

(1653), Saigon (1698), and Hà Tiên (1780). Without them, there would be no South Vietnam.

A southern lord, Nguyễn Ánh (King Gia Long), reunified the northern and southern parts of the country in 1800, doubling its original size and renaming it Đại Việt. Southerners fought against the communists from 1954 to 1975 and paid dearly as a result. They not only lost their country and identities but were also sent to reeducation camps, only to escape later from communist enslavement as refugees.

From 1975 onward, those who could escape abroad (3 million people) built diasporic communities worldwide that stand in opposition to the Hanoi communist regime. Today, 45 years after the fall of Saigon, they stand under the yellow flag, which is better known overseas than the red communist flag. No other exiled community has been able to fly its flag overseas as proudly as the South Vietnamese. Second, the Vietnamese are rather insular people. Despite having a long coastline, there have never ventured very far from their shores. But in 1975, they spearheaded a massive sea escape from Vietnam that transformed 3 million insular people into modern seafarers. This was the largest diaspora in world history of a people in search of freedom and away from Marxism-Leninism. They settled worldwide in Australia, Europe, Asia, Africa, and America.

It is time to acknowledge the existence of two Vietnams: a communist Vietnam well as a democratic Vietnam, as there are two Koreas and two Chinas. It was the pioneering spirit of the South Vietnamese that brought them to South Vietnam in the seventeenth and eighteenth centuries, where they flourished into an independent *đàng trong*. Through sheer military power, they reunited Vietnam and fought in the late 1970s to preserve its independence from communist attack and oppression. By escaping overseas following the fall of Saigon, they reaffirmed their rights and freedom to live in a country free of communism.

The fighting spirit and the pioneering zeal of the South Vietnamese characterize their new way of being Vietnamese. What define the South Vietnamese are the *nam tiến* and diaspora. By leaving the north in 1600 CE they founded South Vietnam, and through the diaspora, by abandoning Saigon to the invading communists in 1975, they found true freedom elsewhere in the world.

Abbreviations

ARVN—Armed Forces Republic of South Vietnam
AW—Air Wing
CB—Construction Battalion (Seabees)
CINCPAC—Commander in Chief, Pacific
CINCPACREP GUAM/TTPI—Representative in Guam and the Trust Territory of the Pacific Islands
CIO—Central Intelligence Office
CES—Civil engineer squadron
CNO—Chief of naval operations
CO—Commanding officer
COMNAV-MAR—Commander, Naval Forces Marianas
CONUS—Continental U.S.
DAO—Defense attaché office
DE—Destroyer escort
HO—Humanitarian operation
IATF—Interagency task force
LAMPS—Light Airborne Multipurpose System
LCC—Amphibious command ship
LKA—Amphibious cargo ship
LPD—Landing platform/dock
LSD—Landing ship dock
LSM—Landing ship, medium
LST—Landing ship, tank
MAP—Military assistance program
MSC—Military Sealift Command

NAS—Naval air station
NVA—North Vietnamese Army
OPTAR—Operations target
PCF—Patrol craft, fast
TCN—Third country citizens
ULV—Ultra low volume
UNHCR—United Nations High Commissioner for Refugees
USAID—United States Agency for International Development
USNS—U.S. Navy ship
VNAF—Vietnamese Air Force
VNN—Vietnamese Navy (South)
WAC—Women's Army Corps
XO—Executive officer

Appendix I: Chronology of Important Events (1975)

3 April—Arrival of the first orphans in Baby Lift at the Presidio in San Francisco, California.

18 April—Interagency task force (IATF) was established to coordinate activities related to the processing and resettlement of Indochinese refugees.

22 April—Establishment of refugee centers in Guam: Operation New Life begins.

23 April—First evacuees arrive on Guam.

26 April—Wake Island refugee center opens.

28 April—Guam and Wake Island are saturated with refugees.

29 April—First refugees arrive in Camp Pendleton, California. Operation New Arrivals begins in CONUS. U.S. Embassy, Saigon, closes; Operation Frequent Wind evacuates remaining U.S. citizens, selected Vietnamese and third country nationals.

2 May—First refugees arrive at Fort Chaffee, Arkansas.

4 May—First refugees arrive at Eglin Air Force Base, Florida.

13 May—The 100,000th Indochinese evacuee arrives on Guam.

14 May—Refugee population on Guam peaks at 50,430.

24 May—President signs the Indochina Migration and Refugee Assistance Act of 1975 (PL 94–23), appropriating $405 million for the Indochinese refugee evacuation and resettlement program administered by IATF.

27 May—Mrs. Julia Vadala Taft, deputy assistant secretary of Health, Education, and Welfare is appointed acting director of the Interagency Task Force for Indochina.

Appendix I: Chronology of Important Events (1975)

28 May—First group of refugees arrives at Fort Indiantown Gap, Pennsylvania.

14 June—DA directs increases in center capacities—25,000 at Fort Chaffee and 17,000 at Fort Indiantown Gap—to reduce refugee population on Guam.

17 June—Peaceful demonstrations conducted on Guam by Vietnamese asking for repatriation; they protest decision to transfer them to Wake Island.

24 June—Refugee population reaches its peak at Fort Chaffee: 25,055. Vietnamese repatriates from Fort Chaffee moved to Camp Pendleton to consolidate all CONUS repatriates.

26 June—Refugee population at Fort Indiantown Gap reaches its peak: 16,809. Eglin Air Force Base refugee population peaks at 5,997.

5 July—All CONUS repatriates are airlifted to Guam for consolidation and control purposes at Camp Asan.

21 July—Mrs. Julia V. Taft is designated director of the Interagency Task Force for Indochina as operational responsibility is shifted from the State Department to the Department of Health, Education and Welfare.

30 July—IATF announces the decision to keep Fort Indiantown Gap open until 1 December 1975 and to keep Fort Chaffee open for an indefinite period.

10 August—President Ford visits Fort Chaffee reception center.

31 August—Hundreds of repatriates conducted a violent demonstration on Guam during which they burn two buildings and injure four U.S. Marshals.

3 September—Repatriates set fire to a third building on Guam.

7 September—Repatriates oust their radical leaders and elect a group of moderates who promise a policy of nonviolence.

15 September—Eglin Air Force Base closes as a reception center after processing over 10,000 refugees in 20 weeks.

29 September—Repatriates on Guam become restive once again.

30 September—Repatriates are allowed to return to Vietnam on *Thương Tín 1*.

16 October—With 1,546 repatriates, the *Thương Tín 1*, after refitting and provisioning, sets off for Vietnam from Guam.

Appendix I: Chronology of Important Events (1975)

25 October—The *Thương Tín 1* is reported to have reached Vietnam.

31 October—Camp Pendleton closes as a refugee reception center after processing over 50,000 refugees

1 November—Military support of Operation New Life on Guam terminates.

15 December—Fort Indiantown Gap closes as a reception center after processing over 22,000 refugees.

30 December—Fort Chaffee closes after processing over 55,000 refugees.

30 December—IATF suspends its activities and is dissolved.[1]

Appendix II: Motion

To the Government & the People of the United States of America

We, the undersigned intellectuals who have been evacuated to Guam, recognize the great efforts of the American Government, the Governor and the people of Guam in securing our safety.

However, most of the highly qualified professionals are still stranded in Vietnam. We therefore urgently entreat the Government and the People of America to continue the effort in bringing them back to Freedom. We, who have been more fortunate in being brought here before, are ready to share our place and the little we have in order to save as many of our fellow-countrymen as possible with us.

Guam, April 28th, 1975
List of 55 names and signatures:

Le-Quoc-Hanh, M.D., Nguyên Lôc, M.D., Tu Thi My, M.D., Do Ngoc Thu, M.D., Phan Thi Kim Doanh, M.D., Ho Thi Loan, M.D., Lê-Hoang-Dziêu, M.D., Nguyen Tran Chuyen, Nguyen Van Thieu, M.D., Trinh Dinh Thien, Economist, Nguyễn Lê Hiếu, M.D., Nguyễn Quốc Ân, Phạm Duy Cẩn or Phạm Duy, Nguyễn-Bich Hue, Administrator General, Le Xuan Khoa, Director VAA, Mrs. Pham Thi Mong Thu, Docteur ès Sciences, Nguyen Ngoc Ky, M.D., Mrs. Ha Thi Phan, Pharmacist, Mrs. Nguyen Tuyet Bich, Pharmacist, Mr. Le Trung Lap, Professor, Mr. Nguyen Van Dinh, Professor, Tran Tien Huyen, M.D., Tran Tien Sum, M.D., Dao Duc Hoanh, M.D., Le Van Diem, M.D., Nguyen The Anh, Doctor of History, Dư Thi Mỹ Lang, Dentist; Trịnh Đình Hiếu, Dentist; Nguyen Tien Dung, M.D., Trịnh Ngoc Toan, Civil Engineer, Đỗ Phan Hanh, Doctor of History, Tô Thị Diễn, M.A., Vu-Huu-Bao, M.D., Pham Thi Luu Phuong, M.D., Nguyen Thanh Tri, M.D., Vinh Huyen, Past Chairman of Vietnamese American Association, Nguyen Van Vinh, M.D., Tran Quoc Trinh, Marine Surveyor and Sea Master, Pham Cao Duong, Doctor of History, Nghiêm-Xuân-Tuân, M.D., Nguyen Phuc Buu Tap, M.S., Le Thi Mong Lan, Pharmacist, Pham Ky, LTC retired,

Chau Thanh Thuy, Ph.D., Univ. of North Carolina, Pham Doan Duong, Engineer, Phan thi Tuyet Nhung, Pharmacist, Phạm thị Lạc Nhân, Professor, Duong Minh Chau, M.D., Nguyen Van Trương, Pilot, Tu Uyen, M.D., Bui Khac Nghiep, Pharmacist, Duong Quang Hien, Pharmacist, Nguyen-Huu-Nguon, Nguyễn Hải Bình, Ph.D., Nguyen Van Thanh, M.D.

Appendix III: By the Numbers

Refugee Arrivals

1. Andersen Air Force Base 39,141
2. Naval Air Station Agana 31,610
3. By ship 40,999

Refugee Transport

Aircraft 443
Ships 21

Refugee Departures

1. Andersen AFB 109,553
2. Naval Air Station Agana 1,756
3. Guam community 455
4. Deaths 25

Quick Glance

1. 4 miles of chain linked fence erected
2. 180 street and floodlights installed at Asan Annex and Orote Tent City
3. 280 power poles installed
4. 1,300 acres of land cleared and graded
5. 2,500 feet of coral-based roads constructed
6. 2,500 tons of rice from Chieh Chuan
7. 3,664 tents erected
8. 14,109 U.S. military and DOD civilians participated
9. 5,241 tons of material and food issued within the first 10 days
10. 80,000 gallons of detergent
11. 92,000 toilet paper rolls

12. 327,000 plastic bags
13. 3,900,000 paper towels
14. 9,500,000 paper plates
15. 19,000,000 paper cups
16. 17,500,000 sets of plastic flatware[1]

Chapter Notes

Acknowledgments
1. SACEI (Saigon Arts, Culture, and Education Institute) is a non-profit organization (www.Sacei07.org) that promotes Vietnamese-American culture.

Introduction
1. Joe Murphy, "Pipe Dreams," *Pacific Daily News*, 3 June 1975.
2. Numbers range from 120,000 to 135,000 Asian evacuees. More than 6,000 were relocated to other countries including France, Canada, and Australia. There were also more than 8,000 Cambodians and Laotians within this group. Once these people are subtracted, there remain roughly 120,000 Vietnamese involved in Operation New Life.
3. Mary Cargill, *Voices of Vietnamese Boat People*; Sucheng Chan, *Vietnamese American 1.5 Generation*; Chat V. Dang et al., *Vietnamese Flowers of 1975*; James Freeman and Nguyen Dinh Huu, *Voices from the Camps*; Bruce Grant, *The Boat People*; Jade Huynh, *South Wind Changing*; Courtland Robinson, *Terms of Refuge*; John TenHula, *Voices from Southeast Asia*; Nghia M. Vo, *Vietnamese Boat People*.
4. James Freeman, *Hearts of Sorrow*; Robert McKelvey, *A Gift of Barbed Wire*; Edward Metzner et al., *Reeducation in Postwar Vietnam*; Nghia M. Vo, *The Bamboo Gulag*; Tran Tri Vu, *Lost Years*; Lu Van Thanh, *Inviting Call of Wandering Souls*.
5. Nhi Thi Lieu, *American Dream in Vietnamese*; Nghia M. Vo, *The Viet Kieu in America*; Thi Bui, *The Best We Could Do*.
6. Operations and Readiness Office; Armstrong, *The Island Ark*.

Chapter 1
1. Willbanks, *Abandoning Vietnam*, p. 185.
2. *Ibid.*, p. 184. President Diệm was given the same message that had been sent to President Thiệu.
3. Davidson, *Vietnam at War*, p. 746.
4. *Ibid.*, pp. 747–748.
5. Tom Glenn, "Bitter Memories: The Fall of Saigon (Part 1)," *Baltimore Post Examiner*, August 2013, http://baltimorepostexaminer.com/bitter-memories-the-fall-of-saigon-part-1/2013/08/18.
6. Snepp, *Decent Interval*, pp. 177–179.
7. A river in Belarus.
8. *The Wordsworth Pocket Encyclopedia*, Hertfordshire, 1993, p. 17.
9. Snepp, pp. 192–194.
10. *Ibid.*, p. 256.
11. Dawson, *55 Days*, pp. 266–67.
12. Veith, *Black April*, pp. 436–454.
13. Dawson, pp. 283–285.
14. Tom Glen, "Bitter Memories: The Fall of Saigon (Part 2)," http://baltimorepostexaminer.com/bitter-memories-fall-saigon-part-2/2013/08/25.
15. *Ibid.*
16. Lehman, "Last Message," in Engelmann, p. 38.
17. Dawson, pp. 318–319.
18. Stuart Herrington, "Khong Ai Se Bi Bo Lai: Dung Lo," in Engelmann, pp. 95–96.
19. Although the North Vietnamese were the invaders, the South Vietnamese have always talked about reconciliation. However, there is no thought of reconciliation in the mind of the invading communists, since they continue to this day to control a one-party state and have

prohibited any free democratic or republican party to compete in any election during the last four and a half decades.
20. Snepp, pp. 454–455.
21. Herrington, "Khong Ai Se Bi Bo Lai: Dung Lo," in Engelmann, pp. 93–106.
22. Glenn, "Bitter Memories: The Fall of Saigon (Part Two) https://baltimorepostexaminer.com/bitter-memories-fall-saigon-part-2/2013/08/25.
23. Xuan Vinh Pham, "Our Journey to Freedom," http://www.oneviet.com/archives/2006/08/.
24. Jim Kean, "There Has to Be a Better Way," in Engelmann, pp. 127–128; Dougan and Fulghum, *Fall of the South*, pp. 160–164.
25. Kean, p. 129.
26. Dougan and Fulghum, pp. 167–169.
27. Kean, pp. 131–132.
28. *Ibid.*, pp. 134–136.
29. Cong Luan Nguyen, *Nationalist in the Vietnam Wars*, p. 460.
30. Le Thi Anh, "The New Vietnam," *National Review,* 29 April 1977.

Chapter 2

1. Herman, pp. 55–58.
2. Kiem and Kane, *Counterpart*, pp. 196–197.
3. *Ibid.*, pp. 210–212.
4. Herman, pp. 66–72.
5. Nguyen Quoc Dinh, "Oh, Man, Get Out of My Boat," in Engelmann, pp. 249–252.
6. Tran Minh Loi, "They Could Not Move So They Could Not Shoot Us," in Engelmann, pp. 263–264.
7. Nguyen Tai Ngoc, "Visiting Old Refugee Camp Fort Indiantown Gap, Pennsylvania, April 2013," http://saigonocean.com/trangNguyenTaiNgoc/NguyenTaiNgoc/van120.htm.
8. Nguyen Ngoc Bich, "Absolutely Hell," in Engelmann, pp. 264–265.
9. Ngọc Lũy Phạm, *Trường Xuân's Last Voyage*, p. 1.
10. *Ibid.*, p. 10.
11. *Ibid.*, pp. 16–18.
12. Uong Minh, "How I Escaped Vietnam," *New York Times*, 12 December 2015, http://www.nytimes.com/2015/12/20/travel/saigon-vietnam.html?hpw&rref=travel&action=click&pgtype=Homepage&module=well-region&region=bottom-well&WT.nav=bottom-well&_r=0.

Chapter 3

1. "Operation Frequent Wind: April 29–30, 1975," http://www.navalhistory.org/2010/04/29/operation-frequent-wind-april-29-30-1975; Herman, p. 25.
2. Nguyen Phuc Thieu, "Stand Back, Boys. The War Is Over," in Engelmann, pp. 246–247.
3. John Degler, "To Hell with What You Said. We're Coming In Right Now," in Engelmann, pp. 168–171.
4. Herrington, "Khong Ai Se Bi Bo Lai: Dung Lo," in Engelmann, pp. 98–103.
5. Wolf Lehman, "This Is the Last Message from Embassy Saigon," in Engelmann, pp. 33–45.
6. Thomas Polgar, "We Were a Defeated Army," in Engelmann, p. 62.
7. *Ibid.*, pp. 60–74.
8. Fox Butterfield, "Turn Out the Light," in Englemann, p. 177.
9. *Ibid.*, pp. 178–179.
10. Keyes Beech, "Christ Almighty, How Can They Do This?" in Engelmann, p. 186.
11. Bruce Branson, "A Planned Program of Terrorism," in Engelmann, p. 216.
12. Herman, pp. 30–43.
13. *Ibid.*, p. 1.
14. *Ibid.*, pp. 78–92.
15. *Ibid.*, pp. 108–113.
16. Vo, *Viet Kieu*, pp. 55–57.
17. *Ibid.*, pp. 58–59.
18. Dougan and Fulghum, pp. 162–163.
19. Harold J. Murphy, "We Were Their Saviors," in Engelmann, pp. 107–112.
20. Dunham and Quinlan, *U.S. Marines in Vietnam*, p. 219.
21. *Ibid.*, p. 221.

Chapter 4

1. "The Doctrine of Discovery, 1493," Gilder Lehrman Institute of American History, https://www.gilderlehrman.org/history-by-era/imperial-rivalries/resources/doctrine-discovery-1493. Pope Alexander VI, through a papal bull, gave the king and queen of Spain all the lands west and south of a pole-to-pole line 100 leagues west and south of the islands of the Azores or the Cape Verde islands.
2. Rogers, *Destiny's Landfall*, p. 6.

3. *Ibid.*, pp. 7–8.
4. *Ibid.*, p. 14.
5. *Ibid.*, pp. 47–48.
6. *Ibid.*, p. 57.
7. Cited by Rogers, *Destiny's Landfall*, p. 63.
8. Rogers, p. 71.
9. *Ibid.*, p. 73.
10. *Ibid.*, p. 84.
11. *Ibid.*, p. 79.
12. *Ibid.*, p. 105.
13. *Ibid.*, pp. 106–107.
14. *Ibid.*, p. 127.
15. *Ibid.*, pp. 158–161.
16. *Ibid.*, pp. 193–200.
17. "Asan Beach Unit," National Park Service, http://www.nps.gov/wapa/planyourvisit/asan-beach-unit.htm.
18. Rogers, pp. 250–252.
19. Operations and Readiness Office, pp. 3–5.
20. Mackie, *Operation New Life*, p. 13. Kissinger's letter has been excerpted by Mackie.
21. *Ibid.*, p. 15.
22. *Ibid.*, p. 16.
23. Operations and Readiness Office, pp. 8–9.
24. A Seabee is a member of the United States Construction Battalion (CB). The word "Seabee" comes from initials "CB."
25. Armstrong, *The Island Ark*, p. 6.
26. Malcolm, "Refugee Airlift to Guam Resumes." *New York Times,* 28 April 1975.
27. Armstrong, p. 14.
28. Alderton.
29. Armstrong, pp. 20–22.
30. *Ibid.*, p. 50.
31. *Ibid.*, p. 58.
32. *Ibid.*, p. 54.
33. Operations and Readiness Office, p. 12.
34. *Ibid.*, pp. 5–6.
35. Armstrong, p. 26; Operations and Readiness Office, p. 14.
36. Armstrong, pp. 34–36; Operations and Readiness Office, p. 15.
37. http://www.guampdn.com/guampublishing/special-sections/operation_newlife05/05_map.htm.
38. Armstrong, p. 62.

Chapter 5

1. Pham Thi Kim Lien et al., "Surveillance of Dengue and Chikungunya in Dong Thap Vietnam," *Asian Pacific Journal of Tropical Medicine* 9 (1) (January 2016): 39–43, https://www.sciencedirect.com/science/article/pii/S1995764515002291. Vietnam has hyperendemicity, with all four serotypes being present all year long throughout the country but affecting mostly the southern part since 1960.
2. This mosquito is also the carrier of another virus, Zika. Zika causes birth defects resulting in microcephaly, or a small-sized head. While the disease seems to be benign in Africa and Asia, it recently caused a rash of microcephaly in children in South America.
3. Malathion is a pesticide that is widely used in agriculture, residential landscaping, public recreation areas, and in public health pest control programs, such as mosquito eradication programs. Environmental Protection Agency, https://www.epa.gov/pesticides#malathion.
4. Mackie, pp. 54–59.
5. R. Shaw, "Preventive Medicine in the Vietnamese Refugee Camps on Guam," *Military Medicine* 142 (1977): 19–28. According to Mackie, the CDC announced that there were 24 cases of malaria by 18 May 1975. Mackie, p. 54.
6. *Ibid.*, pp. 23–24.
7. *Ibid.*, p. 30.
8. *Ibid.*, p. 33.
9. Alderton.
10. For gold transactions in Vietnam, one tael is a measure that is equivalent to 37.5 grams.
11. Sablant Gault, "Gold Taels Allowed in States—Sometimes." *Sunday News*, 11 April 1982.
12. Joseph C. Murphy, "Four Old Ladies in Black Pajamas," *The Sunday News*, 1 June 1975.

Chapter 6

1. Armstrong, p. 9.
2. *Ibid.*, p. 11.
3. Andrew Malcolm, "On Guam, a Jungle Is Becoming a Vast Refugee City Overnight," *New York Times,* 27 April 1975, https://www.nytimes.com/1975/04/27/archives/on-guam-a-jungle-is-becoming-a-vast-refugee-city-overnight.html.
4. Peter Tran Long, https://petertranlong.wordpress.com/2012/03/23/refugees/.

5. A diet of 1,400 calories a day (the average of 1,200 and 1,600) was probably marginal for these healthy young individuals who, although they were not working, were very active in the camps.
6. Susan Guffey, "Flights of Refugees Shifted from Guam," *Washington Post*, 27 April 1975.
7. *Ibid.*, p. 15.
8. Dan Knickrehm, "The 43rd and Operation New Life." Pope Airforce Base, June 4, 2010.
9. Joe Murphy.
10. Guffey, "Flights of Refugees."
11. Tai Ngoc Nguyen.
12. Josephine Mallo, "His Art, Himself Are All He Has," *Pacific Daily News*, 4 August 1975.
13. Lipman, p. 1–31.

Chapter 7

1. Military Sealift Command is the leading provider of ocean transportation for the navy and the rest of the Department of Defense.
2. Susan Guffey, "Asan Loses Leader," *Pacific Daily News*, 26 July 1975.
3. Le Khac Ly, "Only I Am Left to Tell You the Story," in Englemann, pp. 232–233.
4. Author's copy, on file.
5. Watts, pp. 42–43.
6. *Ibid.*, pp. 54–56, 62–64, 68–69.
7. Andrew Malcolm, "48,000 Refugees Jammed on Guam," *New York Times*, 10 May 1975, https://www.nytimes.com/1975/05/10/archives/48000-refugees-jammed-on-guam-3-new-ships-make-influx-largest-since.html.
8. Paul M. Arnow, John C. Hierholzer, James Higbee, and Dudley Harris, "Acute Hemorrhagic Conjunctivitis: A Mixed Virus Outbreak Among Vietnamese Refugees on Guam," *American Journal of Epidemiology* 105 (1) (1977): 68–74.
9. Mackie, p. 33.
10. Gail Paradise Kelly, "Coping with America: Refugees from Vietnam, Cambodia, and Laos in the 1970s and 1980s," *Annals of the American Academy of Political and Social Science* 487 (September 1986): 138–149.
11. Operations and Readiness Office, p. iii.
12. Kelly, *From Vietnam to America*, p. 49.

13. *Ibid.*, p. 54.
14. Doris Flores Brooks, "Guam and the Vietnamese Refugees," *Washington Post*, 13 June 1975 (Letter).
15. Mackie, pp. 16–17.
16. Joseph C. Murphy, "Four Old Ladies in Black Pajamas," *The Sunday News*, 1 June 1975.
17. Arlene Lum, "Refugees Face Racial Hostility, *Pacific Daily News*, 15 June 1975.
18. William Stevens, "Klan Inflames Gulf Fishing Fight Between Whites and Vietnamese," *New York Times*, 25 April 1981, http://www.nytimes.com/1981/04/25/us/klan-inflames-gulf-fishing-fight-between-whites-and-vietnamese.html?pagewanted=all.

Chapter 8

1. Although the PRG was controlled by the Democratic Republic of Vietnam, the two institutions, PRG and Democratic Republic of Vietnam, only merged into a single entity in the 1976 country reunification.
2. Operations and Readiness Office, p. ii.
3. *Ibid.*, p. iii.
4. Lipman, p. 14.
5. *Ibid.*, p. 15.
6. Operations and Readiness Office, p. iv.
7. Tru, *Viet Nam Thuong Tin*, p. 299.
8. *Ibid.*, p. 16.
9. *Ibid.*, p. 402.
10. *Ibid.*, pp. 70–71.
11. *Ibid.*, pp. 88–91.
12. *Ibid.*, pp. 95–100.
13. Lipman, p. 18.
14. Tru, pp. 104–109.
15. "80 Refugees Want Repatriation Now," *Pacific Daily News (PDN)*, 24 April 1975.
16. Tru, pp. 116–124.
17. *Ibid.*, pp. 128–133.
18. *Ibid.*, pp. 146–156.
19. *Ibid.*, pp. 171–174.
20. *Ibid.*, pp. 176–179.
21. *Ibid.*, pp. 184–189.
22. Lipman, p. 22.
23. Tru, pp. 200–208.
24. *Ibid.*, pp. 210–226.
25. *Ibid.*, pp. 279–294.
26. *Ibid.*, pp. 332–336.
27. *Ibid.*, pp. 340–373.

28. *Ibid.*, pp. 377–392.
29. *Ibid.*, pp. 400–419.

Chapter 9

1. Joe Murphy, "Pipe Dreams," *Pacific Daily News*, 3 June 1975.
2. Operations and Readiness Office, p. 61.
3. *Ibid.*, p. 64.
4. *Ibid.*, p. 65.
5. *Ibid.*, p. 66.
6. Patricia Brennan, "Refugees Depend upon Dependents," *Wifeline*, Summer 1975, pp. 3–5.
7. Ann Taubeneck, "Vietnamese in America: Stories of Military Sponsors," *Ladycom*, December 1975: 4–7, 56–59.
8. Alderton.
9. David Gelman, "Refugees 'Know One Thing—To Accept.'" *Pacific Daily News*, 30 July 1975.
10. Yến Lê Espiritu, "Toward a Critical Refugee Study," *Journal of Vietnamese Studies* 1 (1–2) (2006): 425.
11. Rutledge, pp. 15–34; Kelly, *From Vietnam to America*, p. 62.
12. Sahara, p. 34.
13. Kolko, p. 535.
14. Ong, p. 80.
15. Robinson, p. 18.
16. Snepp, p. 411.

Chapter 10

1. "Wake Island," https://en.wikipedia.org/wiki/Wake_Island.
2. Bruce Hoon, "A Wake Island Story." http://c141heaven.info/dotcom/tall_tales/a_wake_island_story.php.
3. Susan Guffey, "Flights of Refugees Shifted from Guam," *Washington Post*, 27 April 1975.
4. Dennis Lowden, "Wake Island 1975," https://www.wakeisland1975.com/.
5. Bruce Beardsley, "Vietnam: Endings and Beginnings," https://www.afsa.org/vietnam-endings-and-beginnings.
6. A Quonset hut is a lightweight, prefabricated structure of corrugated galvanized steel having a semi-cylindrical cross-section. The name comes from the site of their first manufacture at Quonset Point at the Davisvillle Navy Construction Battalion Center in Davisville, Rhode Island.
7. Jeanette Steele, "1975 Vietnamese Camp Relived at Pendleton," *San Diego Union Tribune*, 8 April 2010, https://www.sandiegouniontribune.com/sdut-1975-vietnamese-camp-relived-pendleton-2010apr08-htmlstory.html.
8. Megan Burks, "How the Fall of Saigon Turned San Diego into a City for Refugees," NPR, 1 May 2015, https://www.npr.org/2015/05/01/403093395/how-the-fall-of-saigon-turned-san-diego-into-a-home-for-refugees.
9. "40 Years Ago, Arkansas Military Base Became Refugee Camp," NPR, https://www.ualrpublicradio.org/post/40-years-ago-arkansas-military-base-became-refugee-camp.
10. Tom Bowman, "The Frightened Vietnamese Kid Who Became a U.S. Army General," NPR, April 30, 2015, https://www.npr.org/sections/parallels/2015/04/30/403082804/the-frightened-vietnamese-kid-who-became-a-u-s-army-general.
11. Bryan Marquart, "An Ton That, 85, Former Diplomat Who Aided Refugees in Boston," *The Globe*, 28 October 2017, https://www.bostonglobe.com/metro/obituaries/2017/10/28/tonthat-former-diplomat-who-aided-refugees-boston/48gnV7F4rPQb427tpD4FLK/story.html.
12. Operations and Readiness Office, pp. 40–41.
13. Danielle Freeman, "Taste of Ginger: The 1975 Vietnamese Refugee Reception Center at Eglin Air Force Base," WUWF, 19 February 2016, https://www.wuwf.org/post/taste-ginger-1975-vietnamese-refugee-reception-center-eglin-air-force-base#stream/0.
14. "From Vietnam Escape to Air Force Success," http://niceville.com/from-vietnam-escape-to-air-force-success/.
15. James T. Wooten, "The Vietnamese Are Coming, and the Town of Niceville, FL, Does Not Like It," *New York Times*, 1 May 1975, https://www.nytimes.com/1975/05/01/archives/the-vietnamese-are-coming-and-the-town-of-niceville-fla-doesnt-like.html.
16. Jeff Rhodes, "Tim Nguyen: A Life with *Flare*," *Code One Magazine*, 21 August 2014, https://www.codeonemagazine.com/c130_article.html?item_id=145.

17. Operations and Readiness Office, p. 43.
18. "Fort Indiantown History," https://www.ftig.ng.mil/History/.
19. Arlene Lum, "Refugees Face Racial Hostility, *Pacific Daily News*, 15 June 1975.
20. Deb Kiner, "Fort Indiantown Gap After the Fall of Saigon in 1975," https://www.pennlive.com/life/2017/04/fort_indiantown_gap_after_the.html.
21. Kelly, *From Vietnam to America*, p. 3.
22. Renny Christopher, "Vietnamese Exile Writers," http://www2.iath.virginia.edu/sixties/HTML_docs/Texts/Reviews/Christopher_VN_exile.html.
23. "Postcard from the End of America: Fort Indiantown Gap, PA," Countercurrents.org, 24 August 2016, https://countercurrents.org/2016/08/postcard-from-the-end-of-america-fort-indiantown-gap-pa/.
24. Don Terry, "Passions of Vietnam War Are Revived in Little Saigon," *New York Times*, 11 February 1999, https://www.nytimes.com/1999/02/11/us/passions-of-vietnam-war-are-revived-in-little-saigon.html.
25. "Old Enemies Become Friends: U.S. and Vietnam," Brookings Institute, 1 November 2006, https://www.brookings.edu/opinions/old-enemies-become-friends-u-s-and-vietnam/.

Chapter 11

1. "Guam: The First Refuge for Vietnamese Refugees," *Nashua Telegraph* (Agana, Guam), 29 April 1976, http://news.google.com/newspapers?nid=2209&dat=19760429&id=JJ8rAAAAIBAJ&sjid=S_wFAAAAIBAJ&pg=7091,5457815.
2. Masako Watanabe, "Left Behind: Truong Family Reunited 11 Years Later," *Guam Pacific Daily News*, May 2003, http://www.guampdn.com/guampublishing/special-sections/operation_newlife05/03_truong (accessed 26 April 2011).
3. Dean Wise, "A Long Way from a Foxhole," *York Daily Record* (York, PA), 5 June 1987.
4. Herman, *The Lucky Few*, pp. 118–119.
5. Ibid., pp. 121–122.
6. "Mina Nguyen's Incredible Escape from Saigon," ABC News Videos, 28 September 2014, http://news.yahoo.com/video/mina-nguyens-incredible-escape-saigon-163723654.html.
7. "Tony Lam," Wikipedia, https://en.wikipedia.org/wiki/Tony_Lam.
8. Thi Vo, "Little Saigon Political Pioneer at Center of Money Laundering Investigation," Voice of OC, 22 October 2014, http://voiceofoc.org/2014/10/little-saigon-political-pioneer-at-center-of-money-laundering-investigation/.
9. Tom Wilson, "Vietnamese Refugees Escape to United States," *The Register-Mail*, 26 April 2015, http://www.galesburg.com/20150426/NEWS/150429793 (accessed 27 January 2016).
10. Debbie Truong, "40 Years Later, Former Vietnamese Refugees Reflect on Road to Resettlement That Led Through Fort Indiantown Gap," http://www.pennlive.com/midstate/index.ssf/2015/04/40_years_later_former_vietname_1.html (accessed 27 January 2016).
11. "Fall of Saigon 1975: Vietnam Refugees Fled by Helicopter 40 Years Ago Today," AP, April 30, 2015, http://www.al.com/news/index.ssf/2015/04/fall_of_saigon_1975_vietnam_re.html (accessed 27 January 2016).
12. Vo, *Viet Kieu in America*, p. 189; Mimi Thi Nguyen, *Gift of Freedom*, pp. 1–2.
13. Pham Duy, "Toi ve day vi toi yeu nuoc," BBC, 29 December 2012, https://www.bbc.com/vietnamese/vietnam/2012/12/121219_phong_van_pham_duy_phan_2.
14. Rogers, *Destiny's Landfall*, pp. 288–289.
15. "Ex-Guam Governor Killed on Eve of Jailing for Corruption," *New York Times*, 1 February 1990, http://www.nytimes.com/1990/02/01/us/ex-guam-governor-kills-himself-on-eve-of-jailing-for-corruption.html.
16. Herman, *The Lucky Few*, p. 123.
17. In 1987, H.R. 2434.
18. Social Security Administration, "Report to the Congress of the HEW Refugee Task Force," 15 March 1976, https://eric.ed.gov/?id=ED166318.
19. Charles Smith, *Palestine and Arab-Israeli Conflict: A History with Documents*" (New York: Bedford/St Martin's, 1976), p. 329.

20. "Oil Embargo, 1973–1974," U.S. Department of State, Office of the Historian, https://history.state.gov/milestones/1969-1976/oil-embargo.
21. Michael A Urquhart and Marillyn A. Hewson, "Unemployment Continued to Rise in 1982 as Recession Deepened," https://stats.bls.gov/opub/mlr/1983/02/art1full.pdf.
22. U.S. Bureau of Labor Statistics, "Labor Force Statistics from the Current Population Survey," https://www.bls.gov/cps/.
23. Richard Schaefer and Sandra Schaefer, "Reluctant Welcome: U.S. Responses to the South Vietnamese Refugees," *Journal of Ethnic and Migration Studies* 4 (1975): 366–370.
24. Kelly, *From Vietnam*, p. 62.
25. Ibid., p. 64.
26. Quoted in Adelaida Reyes, *Songs of the Caged, Songs of the Free: Music and the Vietnamese Refugee Experience* (Philadelphia: Temple University Press, 1999), p. 73.
27. Kelly, *From Vietnam to America*, pp. 67, 112.
28. Ibid., pp. 143, 175.
29. Ibid., p. 179.
30. Ibid., p. 186.

Chapter 12

1. Thompson, p. 29.
2. Trương Như Tảng was the minister of justice of the Provisional Revolutionary Government of the Republic of South Vietnam. Disillusioned by the Socialist Republic of Vietnam, he escaped by boat from Vietnam in 1978, two-and-a-half years after the fall of Saigon, to live in exile in France.
3. Truong Nhu Tang, *A Viet Cong Memoir* (New York: Vintage, 1985), p. 282. This included Tảng's two brothers, who previously worked for the government of South Vietnam.
4. Vo, *Bamboo Gulag*, pp. 117–132, 151–156; James M. Freeman, pp. 244–247; McKelvey, pp. 41–43.
5. McKelvey, p. 155.
6. Bui Tin was a People's Army of Vietnam colonel. In 1990 he defected to the West and became a dissident.
7. Tin, *Following Ho Chi Minh*, p. 90.

8. Cargill, pp. 10–12; McKelvey, pp. 197–199.
9. Tin, p. 95.
10. "Dissident Vietnamese Priest Nguyễn Văn Lý Recovering After Heart Attack," Licas News, 4 March 2020, https://www.licas.news/2020/03/04/dissident-vietnamese-priest-nguyen-van-ly-recovering-after-heart-attack/.
11. Tang, *Viet Cong Memoir*, p. 289.
12. Vo, *Vietnamese Boat People*, pp. 115–129.
13. "Inhumane" was the word used by Bui Tin to characterize the communist leadership: "lack of moral values, the inhumanity and blindness of a communist leadership which had become arrogant and lost touch with the people" (Tin, p. 95).
14. McKelvey, p. 187.
15. Ibid., p. 67.
16. Aguilar-San Juan, *Little Saigons*, p. 68.
17. Viet Thanh Nguyen (2003) in Aguilar-San Juan, p. 84.
18. After failing to mobilize the gentry to get rid of the French, Phan Boi Chau (1867–1940) decided that modernizing the country would achieve the same goal. He, therefore, promoted the Dong Du (Eastern Travel) Movement to send students study abroad, especially in Japan. The movement died down when the French forced Japan to deport Phan Boi Chau in 1909. He then organized open rebellions against the French. Caught in 1925, he was sentenced to life in prison but received a commuted sentence to serve life under house arrest.
19. Aguilar-San Juan, p. 86.
20. Khoi Luu, "Family Ties," in Tran, Lam, and Nguyen, *Once Upon a Dream*, p. 93.
21. Andrew Lam, "Love, Money, Prison, Sin, Revenge," in Tran, Lam, and Nguyen, p. 85.
22. Luu, in Tran, Lam, and Nguyen, p. 93.
23. Lam, in Tran, Lam, and Nguyen, p. 88.
24. "Georg Simmel," Wikipedia, https://en.wikipedia.org/wiki/Georg_Simmel (accessed 3 November 2020).
25. Nguyen, Thi Thu Lam, p. 206.
26. Aguilar-San Juan, p. 88.
27. Tang, p. 260. What his mother had

predicted became a reality a year later (1976) when Tang realized that the North Vietnamese ran South Vietnam like a fiefdom. "Communist officials fought over houses, cars, prostitutes, and bribes." Tang, a communist, escaped from Vietnam as a boat person and landed in France as a refugee (pp. 289, 304–309).

28. Tang, p. 265.
29. Nguyen, Cong Luan, pp. 511–12; Bui Long, *Returns of War*, pp. 178–181.
30. Tuan Hoang, "From Reeducation Camps to Little Saigons: Historicizing Vietnamese Diasporic Anticommunism," *Journal of Vietnamese Studies* 11 (2) (2016): 48.
31. *Ibid.*, p. 54.
32. *Ibid.*, pp. 49, 57.
33. *Ibid.*, p. 67.
34. The Americans or the world can laugh about South Vietnam's democracy, but it was more democratic than the communist north.
35. David Leeming, *Oxford Illustrated Companion to World Mythology* (New York: Tess, 2005), p. 310.
36. Nghia M. Vo, "Vietnam and the Vietnamese," in Vo, Dang, and Ho, *Men of Vietnam*, pp. 7–22.
37. Nghia M. Vo, "Confucianism and Communism," in Vo, Dang, and Ho, pp. 111–122.
38. Nghia M. Vo, "The Duality of the Vietnamese Mind," in Vo, N.M., *Sorrows of War*, pp. 111–122.
39. Nghia M. Vo, "A New Way of Being Vietnamese," *Vietnam Veterans for Factual History* 1 (3): 4–6.
40. The Chams and Khmers lived in present-day Central and South Vietnam, respectively.
41. Kiernan, *Vietnam*, pp. 221–223.
42. Morley Safer, *Flashbacks* (New York: St. Martin's, 1990), p. 20.
43. *Ibid.*, p. 19.
44. Bernard Fall, *Last Reflections on the War* (Mechanicsburg, PA: Stackpole, 2000), p. 220. Fall wrote, "When a country is being subverted, it is not outfought; it is being outadministered."
45. Gary R. Hess, "The Unending Debate," *Diplomatic History*, Spring 1994.
46. David L. Anderson, *The War That Never Ends* (Lexington: Kentucky University Press, 2007).

Appendix I

1. Operations and Readiness Office, pp. 24–29.

Appendix III

1. David V. Crisostomo, "Guam Hosts Refugees in 1975," *Pacific Daily News*, 18 July 2005.

Bibliography

Aguilar-San Juan, Karin. *Little Saigons: Staying Vietnamese in America*. Minneapolis: University of Minnesota Press, 2009.

Alderton, Judith. "Operation New Life." *Pacific Daily News*, 14 October 1990.

Armstrong, Anne. *The Island Ark: Operation New Life on Guam*. Marianas Naval Officers Wives Club, June 1975.

Arnett, Peter. *Saigon Has Fallen*. New York: Rosetta, 2018.

Berg, Tom, Roxanna Kopetman, and Chris Hare. "How They Became Us." *OC Register*, 1 May 2015.

Bui, Long. *Returns of War: South Vietnam and the Price of Refugee Memory*. New York: New York University Press, 2018.

Bui, Thi. *The Best We Could Do*. New York: Abrams Comic Arts, 2017.

Campi, Alicia. "From Refugees to Americans: Thirty Years of Vietnamese Immigration." American Immigration Council Fact Sheet, June 1, 2005.

Cargill, Mary. *Voices of Vietnamese Boat People*. Jefferson, NC: McFarland, 2015.

Chan, Sucheng. *The Vietnamese American 1.5 Generation*. Philadelphia: Temple University Press, 2006.

Dang, Chat V., Hien V. Ho, Nghia M. Vo, and Anne R. Capdeville. *The Vietnamese Flowers of 1975*. Charleston, SC: Book Surge, 2009.

Davey, Monica. "In Kansas Proposed Monument to a Wartime Friendship Tests the Bond." *New York Times*, 2 August 2009.

Davidson, Phillip. *Vietnam at War: The History 1946–1975*. Novato, CA: Presidio, 1988.

Dawson, Alan. *55 Days: The Fall of South Vietnam*. Englewood Cliffs, NJ: Prentice-Hall, 1977.

Do, Anh. "Vietnamese Immigrants Mark Black April Anniversary." *LA Times*, 25 April 2015.

Dougan, Clark, and David Fulghum. *The Fall of the South*. Boston: Boston Publishing, 1986.

Dunham, George R., and David A. Quinlan. *U.S. Marines in Vietnam: The Bitter End, 1973–1975*. Washington, D.C., 1990. https://ehistory.osu.edu/books/end.

Dýõng, Hiếu Nghĩa. *Hồi Ký Dang Dở* (Unfinished Memoirs). http://chinhnghiavietnamconghoa.com/hoi-ky-dang-do-duong-hieu-nghia/.

Engelmann, Larry. *Tears Before the Rain: An Oral History of the Fall of South Vietnam*. New York: Oxford University Press, 1990.

Freeman, James, and Nguyen Dinh Huu. *Voices from the Camps*. Seattle: University of Washington Press, 2003.

Freeman, James M. *Hearts of Sorrow: Vietnamese-American Lives*. Stanford: Stanford University Press. 1989.

Grant, Bruce. *The Boat People: An Age Investigation*. New York: Penguin, 1979.

Ha, Nathan. *Business and Politics in Little Saigon, CA*. Thesis, Rice University, May 2002.

Haines, David W. *Refugees as Immigrants: Cambodians, Laotians, and Vietnamese*. Totowa, NJ: Rowman and Littlefield, 1989.

Hare, Chris. "Little Saigon's Vietnam War Memorial Gets Something to Better Connect to Its History: Computers." *Orange County Register*, 5 April 2016.

Hein, Jeremy. *From Vietnam, Laos, and

Cambodia: A Refugee Experience in the United States. New York: Twayne, 1995.
Herman, Jan K. *The Lucky Few: The Fall of Saigon and the Rescue Mission of the USS Kirk.* Annapolis: Naval Institute Press, 2013.
Huynh, Jade. *South Wind Changing.* Minneapolis: Graywolf, 1994.
Kelly, Gail Paradise. *From Vietnam to America: A Chronicle of the Vietnamese Immigration to the United States.* Boulder, CO: Westview, 1977.
Kiem, Do, and Julie Kane. *Counterpart: A South Vietnamese Naval Officer's War.* Annapolis: Naval Institute Press, 1998.
Kiernan, Ben. *Vietnam: A History from Earliest Times to the Present.* New York: Oxford University Press, 2017.
Kolko, Gabriel. *Anatomy of a War: Vietnam, the United States, and the Modern Historical Experience.* New York: Pantheon, 1985.
Lam, Andrew. "Banh Mi: The Rise of the Vietnamese Sandwich." *HuffPost,* 14 July 2015.
Le, Hung. "Vietnam Is the Ninth Highest Receiver of Remittances." *Vietnam Express International,* 30 January 2019. https://e.vnexpress.net/news/business/economy/vietnam-is-ninth-highest-receiver-of-remittances-3876047.html.
LeTran, Vivian. "Vietnam War Memorial Gives Alliance Its Due." *Los Angeles Times,* 21 September 2002.
Lieu, Nhi Thi. *The American Dream in Vietnamese.* Minneapolis: University of Minnesota Press, 2011.
Lipman, Jana. "'Give Us a Ship': The Vietnamese Repatriate Movement." *American Quarterly* 64 (1): 1–31.
Mackie, Richard. *Operation New Life: The Untold Story.* Concord, CA: Solution, 1998.
McKelvey, Robert. *A Gift of Barbed Wire.* Seattle: University of Washington, 2002.
Metzner, Edward, Huynh Van Chinh, Tran Van Phuc, and Le Nguyen Binh. *Reeducation in Postwar Vietnam: Personal Postscripts to Peace.* College Station: Texas A&M University Press, 2001.
Nguyen, Cong Luan. *Nationalist in the Vietnam Wars: Memoirs of a Victim Turned Soldier.* Bloomington: Indiana University Press, 2012.
Nguyen, Mimi T. *The Gift of Freedom: War, Debt, and Other Refugee Passages.* Durham, NC: Duke University Press, 2012.
Nguyen, Thi Thu Lam. *Fallen Leaves.* New Haven, CT: Yale Southeast Asia Studies, 1989.
Ong, Aihwa. *Buddha Is Hiding.* Berkeley: University of California Press, 2003.
Operations and Readiness Office. "Department of the Army After Action Report: Operation New Life/New Arrivals. US Support to the Indochinese Refugee Program, 1 April 1975–1 June 1976." Washington, DC: Office of the Deputy Chief of Staff for Operations and Plans, 1977. https://cgsc.contentdm.oclc.org/digital/collection/p4013coll11/id/1278.
Phạm, Ngọc Lũy. *Trýờng Xuân's Last Voyage.* Translated by Võ Đại Thiện and Đàm Trung Phần. N.p.: 2009.
Pope, John. "Developer Scraps Plan for Bridge in Little Saigon." *Los Angeles Times,* 3 July 1996.
Reyes, Adelaida. *Songs of the Caged, Songs of the Free: Music and the Vietnamese Refugee Experience.* Philadelphia: Temple University Press, 1999.
Robinson, Courtland. *Terms of Refuge.* London: Zed, 1998.
Rogers, Robert F. *Destiny's Landfall: A History of Guam.* Honolulu: University of Hawaii Press, 1995.
Rutledge, Paul. *Vietnamese Experience in America.* Bloomington: Indiana University Press, 2000.
Sahara, Ayako. *Operation New Life/Arrivals: U.S. National Project to Forget the Vietnam War.* M.A. Thesis, Ethnic Studies, University of California, San Diego, 2009.
Skager, Shawn. "Let's Build a Monument, a Place to Heal." *Auburn Register,* 10 July 2013.
Snepp, Frank. *Decent Interval: An Insider's Account of Saigon's Indecent End Told by CIA's Chief Strategy Analyst in Vietnam.* New York: Random House, 1977.
Tang, Truong Nhu. *A Viet Cong Memoir.* San Diego: Harcourt, Brace Jovanovich, 1985.
Tenhula, John. *Voices from Southeast Asia: The Refugee Experience in the United States.* London: Holmes and Meier, 1991.

Thanh, Lu Van. *The Inviting Call of Wandering Souls*. Jefferson, NC: McFarland, 1997.
Thao, Vi. "Late Vietnam's PM Letter Gives No Legal Basis for China's Island Claim." *Thanh Nien News* (Ho Chi Minh City), 2 June 2014.
Thompson, Larry C. *Refugee Workers in the Indochina Exodus, 1975–1982*. Jefferson, NC: McFarland, 2010.
Thuy, Vo Dang, Linda Trinh Vo, and Tram Le. *Vietnamese in Orange County*. West Columbia, SC: Arcadia, 2015.
Tin, Bui. *Following Ho Chi Minh*. Honolulu: University of Hawaii Press, 1995.
Tran, De, Andrew Lam, and Hai Dai Nguyen. *Once Upon a Dream...: The Vietnamese-American Experience*. Kansas City: Andrews and McNeel, 1995.
Tran, Mai, and Bonnie Harris. "11th Hour Bush Visit to Little Saigon Today Sends Host Hustling." *LA Times*, 13 September 2000. https://www.latimes.com/archives/la-xpm-2000-sep-13-me-20288-story.html.
Tru, Tran Dinh. *Viet Nam Thuong Tin: Con Tau Dinh Menh*. Houston: Thien Nga, 1994.
Turner, Robert F. *Vietnamese Communism: Its Origins and Development*. Stanford: Hoover Institution Press, 1975.
Veith, George J. *Black April: The Fall of South Vietnam, 1973–1975*. New York: Encounter, 2012.
Vo, N.M. *The Sorrows of War and Peace*. Denver: Outskirts, 2008.
Vo, N.M., C.V. Dang, and H.V. Ho. *The Men of Vietnam*. Denver: Outskirts, 2009.
Vo, Nghia M. *The Bamboo Gulag: Political Imprisonment in Communist Vietnam*. Jefferson, NC: McFarland, 2004.
_____. *Four Decades of Medical Training, Research, and Practice (1975–2015)*. Scotts Valley, CA: Create Space, 2015.
_____. *The Viet Kieu in America: Personal Accounts of Postwar Immigrants from Vietnam*. Jefferson, NC: McFarland, 2009.
_____. *The Vietnamese Boat People: 1954 and 1975–1992*. Jefferson, NC: McFarland, 2006.
Vu, Nguy, and Richard Sindt. *Risking Death to Find Freedom: Thirty Escape Stories by Vietnamese Boat People*. Westminster, CA: NV, 2005.
Vu, Tran Tri. *Lost Years: My 1,632 Days in Vietnamese Reeducation Camps*. Berkeley: University of California, 1988.
Watts, Ralph S. *Saigon: The Final Days*. Boise, ID: Pacific, 1990.
Whale, Robert. "Solemn Service at Auburn's Vietnam War Memorial Groundbreaking." *Kent Reporter*, 15 March 2018.
Willbanks, James. *Abandoning Vietnam: How America Left and South Vietnam Lost Its War*. Lawrence: University of Kansas, 2004.
Wise, Lindsey. "Veteran Chronicles Vietnam War Memorials." *Houston Chronicle*, 10 November 2011.
Wright, Jeff. "Vietnam War Leaves Deep Legacy in the U.S., Experts Say." *The Guardian Register*, 30 April 2000.
Zake, Ieva. *Anti-communist Minorities in the U.S.: Political Activism of Ethnic Refugees*. New York: Palgrave, 2009.
Zhou, Min, and Carl Bankston. *Growing Up American: How Vietnamese Children Adapt to Life in the United States*. New York: Russel, Sage, 1998.

Index

Agana 66
Alexander VI 50
American Challenger 29, 43–46, 49
An Tôn Thất 143
Andersen AFB 61, 66, 69, 76, 88, 179
Annam 165, 166
Anticommunism 164
Apra Harbor 55, 61
Armitage, Richard 3, 23, 24, 26, 41, 155
Asan Camp 3, 4, 80, 85–87, 90–94, 97, 116, 117
Âu Cơ 164

B-52 bomber 1, 70, 88
Baby Lift 62, 173
Bạch Đằng 24
Ban Mê Thuột 8–9
Bordallo, Paul 58, 60, 62, 66, 154, 155
Brooks, Tom 135
Bùi Tín 159, 187, 191
Butterfield, Fox 39–40

Cam Ranh 9, 28, 124
Cambodian 71, 107
Cao Văn Viên 9, 17, 97
Cessna 37–38
Cham 167
Chamorro 51–58, 155
Chinook 41, 152
Chu Tử 29, 100
Chung Tấn Cang 24, 26, 133
Clara Maersk 30–31, 34
Clinton, Bill 147, 156
Cochinchina 165–66
Côn Sơn 26, 28
Công An 125, 128
Cộng Hòa 22
conjunctivitis 42, 47, 68, 101
Contender 3, 37, 48–49
CONUS 2, 74, 112, 138, 141, 145, 157, 171, 174

convoy 9
Coogan, Robert 36

Đà Nẵng 10–11
Đại Việt 164, 166, 169
đàng ngoài 165–167
đàng trong 165–167, 169
Đào Đức 64
Dầu Giây 12–13
dengue 72–73
Đinh Quốc Hưng 33
Đinh Văn Minh 139
Đỗ, Kiêm 3, 23–24, 26
Dương Văn Minh 33, 44, 64, 111, 133

Eglin AFB 4, 141, 144
Ellis Island 95
Elvis Phuong 31
Endure 161

Flores, Felixberto 87
Ford, Pres. Gerald 2, 11, 12
Fort Chaffee 4, 80, 97, 116, 141–144, 174
Fort Indiantown Gap 4, 90, 108, 134, 145, 147, 151153, 174
Freedom 2, 24, 46, 52, 64, 73, 81, 93, 101, 125, 127,129, 137, 146, 154, 159, 161, 165–67
Frequent Wind 2–3, 18, 20, 37, 66, 173

Galveston 108
Glenn, Tom 13–14, 18
Goodwin, William 152

Herrington, Stuart 21, 39
Hồ Chí Minh 39, 112, 118
Hoàng Cơ Minh 114
Hoàng Trường 149
Hoon, Bruce 139, 185
Hua, Tony 64
Huey 18–19, 41

impoverishment 160
Interagency Task Force 2, 157, 171, 173–4

Khánh Hội 31
Khmer 13
Kinh 165
Ku Klux Klan 108

Lạc Long Quân 164
Lai, Magdalena 153
Lâm, Tony 4, 91, 152
Lâm Giang 27–28, 150
Laotian 71, 128
Lê Bá Kòng 152–153
Lê Đức Thọ 39–40
Lê Khắc Lý 97, 184
Lê Minh Đảo 12–13
Lê Minh Tân 115–116,118–119, 124
Lê Quốc Hanh 93, 177
Linh Dinh 147
Loma Linda 97, 99
Long Khánh 128
Lowden, Dennis 139, 140, 185

Magellan, Ferdinand 50–51
Marcos, Ferdinand 42–43, 62
Martin, Graham 3, 8, 48, 20–22
McCain, Eugene 86, 90
Military Sealift Command 12, 34, 35–37, 49, 100
Minter, Charles 62–63, 65
Morrison, Steve 62, 65
Murphy, Harold 48

Nam Căng 25, 114
Nam Hà 128
Nam tiến 168
Napoleon 8
New Life 58, 62, 66, 71, 73–75, 77, 79, 81, 83–84, 86, 88. 89, 100, 110, 129–131, 136, 138–39, 154, 156
Nghệ Tĩnh 128
Ngô Quang Trưởng 9
Nguyễn, Đàm Thúy 151
Nguyễn, Minh Quang 153
Nguyễn, Nho Trọng 153
Nguyễn, Tính (Tim) 144–145
Nguyễn Ánh 169
Nguyễn Cao Kỳ 32, 80, 90
Nguyễn Công Luận 22, 182, 188
Nguyễn Hoàng 168
Nguyễn Hữu Hải 119
Nguyễn Lê Hiếu 93, 177
Nguyễn Ngọc Bích 29. 182
Nguyễn Như Vỹ 135
Nguyễn Phúc Thiệu 37

Nguyễn Quốc Định 28
Nguyễn Tài Ngọc 92, 182
Nguyễn Thanh Phước 91
Nguyễn Văn Lý 160
Nguyễn Văn Mộc 4, 93, 94
Nguyễn Văn Nghé 33
Nguyễn Văn Thiệu 7–11, 37
Nguyễn Văn Thông 136, 150, 154
Như Văn Úy 116, 138
Nixon, Pres. Richard 7
Nước mắm 43

Orote Point 60–61, 63, 65–67, 74, 82–87, 92, 114–15, 130–32, 139, 155

Pacific Ocean 1, 50–51, 63, 138
Paris Accords 7, 21, 24, 163
Pendleton 4, 99, 141–142
Phạm, Joseph 150
Phạm, Thanh 151
Phạm Duy 154
Phạm Duy Tất. 9
Phạm Ngọc Lũy 30–31
Phạm Văn Đồng 39
Phan Bồi Châu 161
Philippines 1–3, 26, 29, 34, 43, 46–51, 54–56, 59, 67, 76, 92, 100, 114, 130, 140, 153
Phú Quốc 25, 28, 32, 43–45
Point Udall 155–56

Quảng Trị 9–11
Qui Nhơn 28

Rạch Giá 43
Repatriate 112, 115, 120, 124
Rừng Sát 28

Safer, Morley 167–68
Saigon, Little 159, 162, 166
San Francisco 1, 113, 134
San Juan 160
San Vitores 52, 53, 55
Seabee 66
Simmel, Georg 162
Snepp, Frank 22
South Vietnamese 1–5, 7–8, 11, 13–19, 22, 28, 31, 35, 37, 41, 43, 48, 58, 80, 90–91, 99–100, 104–5, 111,132, 135, 143–44, 149, 153–54, 159–63
Stranger 162
Subic Base 3, 29, 34, 42, 43, 48, 61, 64, 92, 96, 100, 131–32, 140, 141
Summers, Harry 38–39

Tael 79–80
Taft, Julia 146, 173–74

Tân Kỳ 128
Tân Sơn Nhứt 16–18, 37, 111
Tân Nam Việt 32
Task Force 73 36
Task Force 76 3, 35, 37, 39, 41, 43, 45, 47, 49
Task Force 77 36
Tây Sơn 167
Tent City 3, 64, 66–68, 82–84, 87
Tin City 61, 65–67, 88, 99
Tonkin 165–66
Tordesillas 50–51
Trần, Long 83
Trần Đình Trụ 4, 112–14, 117–18, 121–26, 128
Trần Đình Trường 31–32
Trần Hưng Đạo 24
Trần Minh Lợi 29
Trần Nhật Duật 26, 28
Trần Phú 24
Trần Văn Hương 13, 15, 16
Transcolorado 99–100
Trương Như Tảng 163, 187
Trường Xuân 3, 23, 25, 31–34
Tuấn Hoàng 164
Two Vietnams 164–66

Văn Tiến Dũng 12, 163
Vasco da Gama 50
Việt Cộng 126
Việt Nam Quốc Dân Đảng 164
Việt Nam Thương Tín I 90, 97
Việt Xuân Lương 143
Vietnamese Navy 27–29, 33, 34, 42, 43, 48, 94, 96, 100, 134, 135, 149
Vinh Phạm 27
Võ Phiến 147
Vong Hong Ni 28
Vũ Văn Mẫu 16–17
Vũng Tàu 16, 25, 27–29, 33, 35, 46, 48, 100, 125

Wake Island 29, 61, 69, 76, 87, 89, 112, 120, 138–40
White Christmas 12, 18
Whitmire, Donald 36, 41
wounds 22, 86, 160, 161
Wyttenbach, Gwen 132, 154
Wyttenbach, Captain 61–63, 65, 77–80, 135–36, 150, 154

Xuân Lộc 3, 59, 12–13

Zumwalt, Elmo 134

www.ingramcontent.com/pod-product-compliance
Ingram Content Group UK Ltd.
Pitfield, Milton Keynes, MK11 3LW, UK
UKHW021846140426
5217IPUK00022B/1611